Flt ... 'Frenchie' ... ... in 1976 to a French mother and Scottish father. Brought up near Paris, he came to England in 1995. In August 2000, he was commissioned into the Royal Air Force and selected for rotary wing training, qualifying as a Chinook pilot and joining A Flight, 18 Squadron. He has amassed over 2,000 hours flying the Chinook and has undertaken operational tours to Iraq and Afghanistan, where he was commended for gallantry. In 2008, he was awarded the Distinguished Flying Cross – the air equivalent of the Military Cross and one of the highest awards for bravery – for two actions less than a week apart.

SWEATING THE METAL

FLYING UNDER FIRE. A CHINOOK PILOT'S BLISTERING ACCOUNT OF LIFE, DEATH AND DUST IN AFGHANISTAN

FLT LT ALEX 'FRENCHIE' DUNCAN DFC

with Antony Loveless

HODDER

First published in Great Britain in 2011 by Hodder & Stoughton
An Hachette UK company

First published in paperback in 2012

1

A CIP catalogue record for this title is available from the British Library

ISBN 978 1 444 70800 4

Typeset in Bembo by Hewer Text UK Ltd, Edinburgh

Printed and bound by Clays Ltd, St Ives plc

Hodder & Stoughton policy is to use papers that are natural, renewable and recyclable products and made from wood grown in sustainable forests. The logging and manufacturing processes are expected to conform to the environmental regulations of the country of origin.

Hodder & Stoughton Ltd
338 Euston Road
London NW1 3BH

www.hodder.co.uk

To my wife Alison, and my boys Guy and Max

Destiny chose me to fly the sky, since conception in the womb,
While nurtured by my mother's breast, I had a duty to assume.
For I have flown past heaven's door, to places you've not seen,
Constantly lived my boyhood dreams, in the places I have been.
I've flown the depths of darkness, by the light from stars alone,
I am utterly spellbound by that world, the world I call my own.

Taken from 'The Fighter Pilot' by Bazza

ACKNOWLEDGEMENTS

First and foremost, I'd like to express my deepest and most heart-felt thanks to my lovely wife Alison, my boys Guy and Max, and to my parents, for their unflinching love and support through some extremely testing times in my career as a military pilot.

Thanks are due to James at Watson, Little and to my publisher, Rupert Lancaster, for seeing the potential in this book from the very beginning. They both shared my belief that the work of the Chinook Force should be brought to a wider audience. Also to Kate Miles and all at Hodder and Stoughton who worked for so long to bring the book to life. I can't thank you enough for your support, enthusiasm and sheer hard work. Thanks to Tara Gladden for polishing the manuscript – you really did a sterling job.

I'm indebted to the Ministry of Defence and its staff, in particular Squadron Leader Stuart Balfour, for allowing this story to be told and for supporting and facilitating Antony Loveless and those who worked to make it happen. Thanks Stuart, for shepherding the manuscript through to publication and for your advocacy in ensuring that what I wrote saw it through to the end.

Although the events that I describe in this book are as they appeared to me, they also represent the words and memories of countless others. To all of you, both named and anonymous, who gave up your time and your memories, thank you.

Huge thanks are due to all of my friends and colleagues in the Chinook Force at RAF Odiham, in particular the crewmen who work so tirelessly and give so much to make each sortie a success. I salute your commitment. The great unsung heroes of the Chinook

Force are the technicians and engineers who keep us flying – thank you all. And a special thank you to JP, a brilliant leader, tactician and friend.

Special thanks to my friends and family who have backed and encouraged me throughout.

The final word must go to all those men and women of the British Armed Forces who fight so hard under such punishing and inhospitable conditions, while living in spartan, basic accommodation. Thank you all. You are a credit to yourselves, to your uniform and to the nation, and I feel proud to work alongside you. And to those who never made it back – you will never be forgotten.

PICTURE ACKNOWLEDGEMENTS

Author's collection: 8, 10 above, 11 below, 16. Sgt Freedy G. Cantu: 10 below. © Crown Copyright: 2 below, 3 below/Att. CSgt Baz Shaw, 9 above/Att. Cpl Barry Lloyd RLC, 9 centre/Att. Cpl Jon Bevan, 9 below/Att. Cpl Ashley Keates RAF, 11 above/Att. PO Sean Clee, 12/ Att. Sgt Rupert Frere RLC, 13/Att. Cpl Barry Lloyd, 15 above, 15 below/Att. SAC Andrew Morris. © Getty Images/photo Marco Di Lauro: 7. © Antony Loveless: 1, 3 above, 4, 5, 6, 14 below. Sgt Jesse Stence: 14 above. © UK MoD Crown Copyright 2011: 2 above. © UK MoD Crown Copyright 2010: 3 centre.

CONTENTS

PROLOGUE

I check my watch; we've been sitting 'turning and burning' – rotors spinning, burning fuel – on the pan at Camp Bastion, for fifty minutes now.

Early afternoon – Helmand Province in May – and the outside air temperature display on the instrument panel says it's 50°C. The Chinook's windscreen takes the full glare, turning the cockpit into a greenhouse where the ambient temperature is nudging 65°C. Hot doesn't even come close; there's no frame of reference for this.

A bead of sweat trickles from underneath my helmet and into my eye. I've had enough; I radio control . . .

'Bastion Ops, Black Cat Two Two. Where's the armourer?' I ask.

'Black Cat Two Two, Bastion Ops. Should be with you now.'

I twist and look over my left shoulder and see him walking up the ramp; I motion for him to sit on the jump seat. Bob Ruffles, my No.2 crewman, assists the armourer and plugs his helmet into the comms.

'Okay, this is what we've got,' I tell him. 'We landed at Gereshk to refuel with our formation leader an hour ago, and his cab had a massive fuel leak. It's completely soaked his Defensive Aids Suite, so his flares are now bathed in it. We'll fly you to Gereshk so you can replace them. We'll be back for you after our next sortie – about forty-five minutes.'

I look past him to the full load of passengers in the back. We've been briefed that they're VIPs. They were supposed to be our wingman's next load, but his cab isn't going anywhere with fuel-soaked flares; it's the armourer's mission to replace those. Ours is to get the VIPs to Musa Qala.

I don't know who they are except they're very well dressed, so they look a bit out of place. Their questioning glares and furrowed brows tell me they're an unhappy group of suits. I guess I'd be pissed off too if I'd waited in the heat for over an hour before boarding.

Time to get moving. Ordinarily, we'd be going nowhere without an Apache watching our backs, but we've been flying all morning and our escort – an Apache with the call sign Ugly Five Zero – is already at Musa Qala waiting for us.

'Bastion Tower, Black Cat Two Two ready for departure.'

'Black Cat Two Two, cleared for take-off and cross as required. Visibility 5km, wind two-five-zero at ten knots.'

'Pre take-offs good, ready to lift,' says Alex, my co-pilot, from the left seat.

'Clear above and behind.' This from Neil 'Coops' Cooper, my No.1 crewman at the ramp. Bob mans the port-side Minigun as we lift.

'Take-off, Black Cat Two Two.'

I pull pitch and lift into the afternoon sky. It's a short hop to Gereshk, just east of Camp Bastion, and we're in the air no more than five minutes before I land us and drop off the armourer. Thirty seconds on the ground, no more. Coops gives the all clear and I lift us once again into the crystal-clear azure sky and turn due north for Musa Qala.

Ten more minutes and we're about six miles from the target. I radio ahead to the Apache: 'Ugly Five Zero, Black Cat Two Two. Inbound. Next location in five.'

'Black Cat Two Two, Ugly Five Zero, visual. Be aware, enemy forces moving weapons along your route. Hold; we're checking it out.'

This could indicate that something major is afoot. The Taliban often ditch their weapons, cache them and melt back into the civilian population. Once they do that, they know that our moral and ethical code prevents us from returning fire. The upside, though, is that if they want to launch an attack, they need to move the weapons into place. The Apache crew are using their reconnaissance pod to investigate.

We don't have long to wait.

'Black Cat Two Two, Ugly Five Zero. Enemy forces moving weapons to the south-west – suggest you try alternative routing. Guys, the ICOM chatter has got ten times worse. They're up to something.'

If Taliban radio traffic has increased markedly, something is brewing. I feel the hairs on the back of my neck stand up.

I click the PTT button on the end of the cyclic to confirm I've received the message.

I decide to fly a feint into FOB Edinburgh. It's a couple of miles away from Musa Qala but it's on higher ground so if the Taliban are laying in wait for us, they'll see us landing there and assume its our intended destination. I brief the crew. 'I'll just do a low-level orbit over Edinburgh and use terrain masking so they won't see us at Musa Qala.'

Our biggest threat comes from rocket-propelled grenades (RPGs), but if we're fast and low we're that much harder to hit. Normally we fly an approach 50ft on the light and 45 on the noise; that means that if I go below 50ft, a warning light will come on and at 45ft a noise will sound. As the non-handling pilot, Alex has the noise and I have the light.

I brief Alex. 'Okay, I want you to put us four miles north of Edinburgh. There's a deep valley (or "wadi") there, and I want to be flying low through it at max speed on the approach. Bug the RadAlt down to 10ft; I'm gonna put the light on at 20 and we're going to go in as fast and as low as we dare.'

It's called a CAD, or Concealed Approach and Departure; when less experienced guys train in the UK they do it with speed and height commensurate with safety. The received wisdom is that speed is life, altitude is life insurance; no one has ever collided with the sky. But whoever said that was clearly unfamiliar with Helmand Province. As captain, I'm responsible for the safety of the aircraft and everyone on it. And for me, here and now, that means going low and fast.

'Bob, get on the starboard Minigun. Standard Rules of Engagement; you have my authority to engage without reference to me if we come under fire. Clear?'

'Clear as, Frenchie.'

I want him on the right because, looking at the topography of the area, that's where we'd most likely take fire from. He can scan his arcs, I've got the front and right, and Alex and Coops have the left. We're as well prepared as we can be, even if it does feel like we're flying into the lion's den.

Alex gets us into the perfect position and I drop down low into the wadi as I fly us towards FOB Edinburgh at 160 knots. Trees are rushing past the cockpit windows on either side but I'm totally focused on the job at hand so they barely register. We're so low, I'm climbing to avoid tall blades of grass as we scream along the wadi and I'm working the collective up and down like a whore's knickers, throwing the aircraft around. Anyone trying to get a bead on us is going to have a fucking hard time.

It's about twenty seconds later when I see the Toyota Hilux with a man standing in the back. It's alongside the wadi in our 1 o'clock position and about half a mile ahead. It's redolent of one of the Technicals – the flat-bed pick-up trucks with a machine-gun or recoilless rifle in the back that caused so much mayhem in *Black Hawk Down*. They're popular with the Taliban, too. Suddenly, alarm bells are ringing in my head. They're so loud, I'm sure the others can hear.

'Threat right,' I shout as both Alex and I look at the guy in the truck.

My response is automatic. I act even before the thought has formed and throw the cyclic hard left to jink the cab away from danger. Except the threat isn't to the right; the truck is nothing to do with the Taliban.

The threat lies unseen on our left, on the far bank of the wadi. A team has been brought in specifically to take us out and they have a view of the whole vista below them, including us.

I've flown us right into the jaws of a trap that's been laid specially for one particular VIP that we're carrying.

PROLOGUE

BANG, BANG, BANG, BANG, BANG!

The Defensive Aids Suite comes alive and fires off flares to draw the threat away from us; too late though. Everything happens in a nanosecond but perception distortion has me tight in its grip, so it seems like an age.

I feel the airframe shudder violently as we simultaneously lurch upwards and to the right. I know what's happened even as Coops shouts over the comms: 'We've been hit, we've been hit!'

There's no time for Bob to react on the gun. The aircraft has just done the polar opposite of what I've asked of it. And for any pilot, that's the worst thing imaginable – loss of control.

'RPG!' shouts Coops. 'We've lost a huge piece of the blade!'

The Master Caution goes off and I'm thrust into a world of *son et lumière*. Warning lights are flashing, and the RadAlt alarm is sounding through my helmet speakers – we've got system failures. We've got sixteen VIPs in the back. And we're still in the kill zone.

We're going down.

PART ONE
BEGINNINGS

1

ACCROCHES-TOI À TON RÊVE

I always wanted to fly. I was six when my uncle gave me a book called *Les Ailes d'or L'Aéronavale US* (Golden Wings of the US Navy). Full of high-quality photos of F-14s, it awakened within me an interest in flying which then demanded attention like a recalcitrant child. Once I'd opened my mind to the concept of flight, I dreamed of being a fast jet pilot and began an enduring love affair with aviation that remains with me still.

My father is British. He's an accountant, and my mum (who's French) is an English teacher. They met when my dad was reading French at Oxford and, as part of his degree, went to France for a year to work as the assistant to an English teacher – that teacher was my mum. I was born in Belgium in 1976, where my father was working at the time, but moved to Paris when I was one.

Paris dominates my memories of growing up, so the city had quite an impact on my sense of identity. We lived in a spacious apartment near the Seine in a suburb to the south-west of the city. We spoke English and French at home, so I passed the exam for a bilingual secondary school and eventually graduated with my Baccalaureate. England, though, was also a huge influence on me; my paternal grandparents lived in Sevenoaks and I adored it there. I travelled there regularly from a young age and when I was older I'd spend summers there to improve my English so I had a pretty good grounding in British culture.

We travelled a fair bit when I was younger and I looked forward to the flights almost more than I did the actual destinations. I was always asking my dad to draw aircraft or make paper airplanes for me; I wasn't so much concerned with how a plane was kept in the sky, it was the graciousness of it – there was a certain magic about the fact that it flew.

I don't think the French Air Force ever figured in my thoughts, even from when I first dreamed of flying; it was always the RAF. When I learned about World War II, I always imagined I was in the cockpit of a Spitfire. So when it came to choosing a university, it had to be one in England. I read Aerospace Engineering at Manchester and after graduating in July 1999 (alongside my degree, I also acquired the nickname 'Frenchie') I was accepted into the Royal Air Force as a direct-entry pilot.

The RAF's motto is '*Per Ardua Ad Astra*', which, roughly translated, means 'Through Adversity to the Stars'. A very loose translation might be, 'It's a rocky road that leads to the stars,' and having travelled that arduous, winding and infinitely long road to gaining my wings, it's a maxim that really means something to me.

I was well aware of what the process involved when I did my initial assessment with the RAF, but somehow, by the time I presented myself at RAF Cranwell (the RAF's equivalent of Sandhurst) on August 6th 2000 to begin my six months of officer training, it's like I'd forgotten. I knew on an abstract level that you don't just join the RAF and start flying on day two, but there was still a part of me that expected to be given the keys and told to go ahead and fly!

The process of turning civilians into functioning, capable military officers is an exact science, tried, tested and honed over generations, but basically it boils down to breaking and then remaking you. The process irons out all the flaws, the bad habits, the laziness, lack of fitness and absence of discipline that are hallmarks of civilian life, and replaces them with military bearing, an ability to march, work as part of a team and lead by example. It was February 2001 when I passed out as Flying Office Alex Duncan but, because there were no slots immediately available at the Elementary Flying Training School (EFTS), I didn't start my basic flying training until May.

The four-month course is broadly similar to the course that civilian pilots do to obtain a Private Pilot's Licence, except it's much more comprehensive and the pace of learning is accelerated. You can be flying in formation, hanging off the wing of another aircraft, with around fifteen hours flying under your belt, a time when many PPLs have only just soloed. The training is exceptionally good and despite not being a naturally gifted pilot, I aced all of my final exams and left EFTS with sixty-five hours, experience in my logbook.

Despite now being able to fly a light aircraft in cloud, alone, and perform aerobatics and low-level flying, you're still of no use to the RAF. EFTS is all about identifying your strengths so you can be streamed to one of three arenas that the brass thinks you're most suited to, depending on where they have the greatest need at that particular time – fast jets, multi-engine or rotary. Fast jets was my first choice, followed by multis and finally, rotary, which is what I got. I'd sailed through all my exams and handling tests, and I was informed I'd achieved the grade, but there was a problem affecting the Tucano T1, the aircraft on which the RAF teaches basic fast jet flying. It created a huge backlog of pilots, so they looked at my performance and decided I had the aptitude to be a good helicopter pilot.

I was so gutted at first that I even considered leaving the RAF, but ultimately I accepted the decision because I realised it was about what the Air Force needed, not what I wanted. Whatever I flew, be it fast jets or helicopters, I'd love the job because I would still be flying. Maybe a different kind of flying to what I'd dreamed of, but still flying nonetheless.

Because I thought I'd be streamed fast jet, I'd already arranged a holding post with the fast jet test squadron at Boscombe Down. I couldn't change it, so there was nothing else to do but change my perspective. If I couldn't be a fast jet pilot in the RAF, at least I'd be able to live the life for a few months and get it out of my system.

So that's what I did. After a period of leave, I arrived at Boscombe

Down in November 2001 for four months. I had the time of my life and can look back on having flown the Jaguar, the Hawk and the Alpha Jet. Although the time I spent in them wasn't loggable because I hadn't earned my wings then, it didn't matter. Firstly, I made loads of memories. Secondly, when you're talking to mates outside of the RAF, one of the first things they ask you is, 'Have you flown a fast jet?' At least now I can say, 'Yes.'

RAF Shawbury in Shropshire is home to the Defence Helicopter Flying School and the Central Flying School (Helicopter) Squadron; it's where you come if you want to fly helicopters for the Army, Navy or RAF. So in March 2002 I arrived ready to learn everything I needed to know about rotary-winged aircraft – or helicopters, as they're more widely known.

At this stage, I really didn't know a great deal about them, but when I looked at the RAF's fleet of helicopters I set my sights on the Chinook from the off. There was something different about it. That said, I still felt apprehensive. To me, helicopters were the devil's machines. I know how fixed-wing aircraft stay aloft but I regarded helicopters as little more than six million separate pieces flying in an unstable formation. So far as I was concerned then, it was aerodynamically impossible for a helicopter to fly, so the only conclusion that I could draw was that they're so fucking ugly that the earth repels them. I wasn't sure I could deal with that.

The course began with a month of ground school where we learned the principles of flight and looked at vector diagrams that apparently proved that helicopters can, in fact, fly. I'm sure that anybody with a first in Engineering or Pure Maths could quickly prove otherwise, but the school did a pretty good job of convincing us, so I parked my scepticism and concentrated on the finer points of helicopter meteorology. As ground school progressed, we learned the various checks in a procedural trainer, which is a cardboard mock-up of the cockpit. The needles on the dials move and the sim makes all the relevant noises, but it's just to get you used to where everything is. Eventually, we actually started walk-arounds so we were up close and personal with this mythical flying beast.

It was a single-engine Eurocopter Squirrel HT1 – the ideal platform in which to learn the rudiments of helicopter flying, according to the RAF. The engine is tiny – about 2ft long by 11 inches high – but it's worth about a million pounds, so there's clearly more to it than simple pistons. It must be all the pixie dust that they put in there to keep the thing aloft.

Everything about the Squirrel is small and light – you can lift the tail with a finger because it's plastic, thin and very, very light. The blades are no more than five inches wide, yet they spin at 225rpm and somehow keep you airborne. One thing you don't want is to see the engineers working on the tail rotor before you fly, because if you do, you'll see the transmission tube that runs the length of the boom to keep the tail rotor spinning, which is no more than finger-thickness and spins at 1,000rpm. It really is best not to think about it too hard.

My first actual flight in it is a familiarisation one with an instructor, and it's the only free ride on the course. There were three of us riding along for that. The instructor walked out to the line, helmet on, dark visor down. Standing there before me and my two fellow students he assumed almost mythical status, for he can fly this thing.

So, picture this . . . we get in – I'm in the back and I just can't compute how we're going to get airborne with four adults inside. The instructor runs through his checks and starts the aircraft, his hand whizzing around the cockpit. He reaches to his left and pulls on a lever that looks just like the handbrake in my car and suddenly we're in the air. We go straight up, taxi in between some other helicopters, fly gently over the grass on the airfield, turn through 180° to make sure there is nothing behind, and off we go. Down goes the nose and we are flying. I'm dumbstruck because it feels just how I'd imagine a flying carpet would feel.

For someone schooled in flying fixed-wing aircraft, it meant a whole new frame of reference and an entirely new way of thinking; if anything goes wrong, for example, you don't have to find a runway, you can just slow down, find a field, and hover. And you could just hover there for hours, beating gravity. Once I'd accepted the concept, I realised that it opened up entirely new horizons in flying. I must confess that all my previous misgivings melted away as we flew, and I actually began to think, 'Hey, this is pretty cool.' I couldn't believe I'd actually considered leaving the RAF. This tiny glimpse of rotary-winged flight showed me there was nothing to regret; it was going to be good – real good!

My instructor was John Garnons Williams (John GW to us), and he was awesome. He was an old boy, a retired Wing Commander – very well educated, a very, very good pilot and an absolute gentleman to boot. It was a privilege to know him and I was deeply saddened to hear that he died in a training accident in January 2007.

I felt reasonably confident about my first lesson. I mean, how difficult could it be? I'd just finished a month of ground school so I was more than familiar with the functionality of the flight controls. And I knew all the theory: basically, the controls in a helicopter affect the rotors – rotating blades on top of the fuselage, and a tail rotor at the end of the boom. The three blades on the roof are essentially rotating wings – rotary wings – and form a disc. It's the disc that flies; the rest of the helicopter simply follows along.

Unlike commercial and private fixed-wing aircraft, where the co-pilot or student traditionally occupies the right-hand seat, it's role-dependent in a helicopter. The right seat is generally for handling sorties, the left for navigation sorties. So to the left of my seat was the 'handbrake'; that's the collective and it controls altitude. Raise it and it affects all four rotor blades at the same time – 'collectively'. It increases their pitch angle, causing the disc – and the helicopter – to rise. Lower it and the effects are reversed; the pitch angle is reduced and the helicopter descends. On some helicopters, there's a twist-grip throttle on the end of the collective and it's much the same as the throttle on a motorbike – twist to go faster. Things are simplified on the Squirrel, so there's no conventional 'twist' throttle per se. Instead, the throttle has three more or less permanent positions: flight, ground idle and off.

So the collective controls altitude and the throttle controls rotor speed, which is known as 'NR'. Rising vertically from the floor between the pilot's legs is the cyclic control stick; moving it in any direction causes the disc to increase pitch on one half of its cycle while feathering on the other half. The cyclic change of pitch means that the disc tilts and moves in the same direction as the stick. Simple enough so far, right?

There's one more major control and that's the pedals, which work on the tail rotor. The reason that most helicopters have a tail rotor at the end of the boom is to counteract the huge forces generated by the main rotors as they move clockwise. Without the tail rotor, those forces would rotate the fuselage in the opposite direction, an effect known as torque. The tail rotor pushes the tail sideways against the torque so the amount of push – and the direction of the nose – is controlled via the foot pedals. The left one pushes the tail against the torque, so the nose moves to the left. Pushing the right one has the opposite effect.

Like I said, I knew how to fly and I knew the principles of flying a helicopter, so how difficult could it be?

John GW took us up to hover height at 5ft. 'Okay Frenchie, see that tree at our 12 o'clock?'

'The small one on the nose? I see it.'

'Okay, I want you to keep us pointed at that tree. I'll handle the rest of the controls. Got it?'

I thought about the thousands of vibrating, spinning and turning components that comprised the aircraft, each one seemingly with its own mind, powering this wild beast, this unbroken horse somehow tamed and made benign by John's input. In his hands, the helicopter sat solidly at 5ft, rigidly pointed towards the tree about fifty yards off the nose, moving neither forwards nor backwards, neither left nor right. Minus the visual cues, we could have been motionless on the tarmac.

'You have control,' he said.

I pushed gently against the left pedal. And for a second or so, all seemed well. Nothing changed. Then the tree was at my 10 o'clock. I pushed against the right pedal . . . and I watched as the tree moved past the nose to my 3 o'clock, like a roll of film scrolling across my field of vision.

'You see the tree I'm talking about?' John asked. I clicked the push-to-talk button on the cyclic and confirmed I did. 'Well, if you could try to keep us pointed towards it, that would be good,' he said, like a kindly uncle.

I focused. And gradually, the tail's movements became less extreme. The arcs narrowed. And the tree stayed, for the most part, between our 11 o'clock and our 1 o'clock. For some of the time, I actually managed to keep it at our 12 o'clock. It was all about anticipating the response of the pedals and pressing them accordingly.

'Much better,' said John. When he thought I'd got control of the pedals, he gave me the collective.

'Okay, you've got the collective. Look at 12 o'clock, keep the height.' And for a while, I did. Then we started to rise and fall like we were a yo-yo controlled by some giant unseen hand.

'Anticipate, anticipate,' I told myself. I reduced my input on the collective – small, tiny movements. We settled.

'Well done, Frenchie. Very good,' he told me, giving my ego a nice boost. I could do this. And then he said, 'Right, I'll give you the cyclic, and I'd like you to keep us in the same position on the ground.'

I did that pretty well and I was thinking to myself, 'This isn't too bad.'

'Okay. That was pretty good. Do you think you're up to trying all of the controls at once?' he asked. Buoyed by my success so far, I told him I'd give it a go. 'Okay, you have control,' John said.

'I have control,' I confirmed.

And I did. At least I did for a few seconds – although, as I realised later, that was mainly because he'd trimmed the aircraft for me and it flattered to deceive. Then the wind increased and I overcorrected for it. Keeping us level and static was like herding cats. If I pushed the cyclic forward, the nose went down and the aircraft descended and started to accelerate. I brought the nose up to slow down and pulled on the collective to climb and I doubled my height. When I finally managed to check the acceleration, I slowed us down so much that we were going backwards. Move the cyclic left and the aircraft slides left; right cyclic and the aircraft slides right, just like a fixed-wing aircraft, but you have to put a bit of pedal on to adjust the balance. It's like patting your head and rubbing your stomach at the same time, while also playing keepy-uppy with a football.

'I have control of the aircraft,' said John, trying not to sound too nervous, although I'm sure inside he was a paragon of fear. But then, that's the instructors' lot. John, bless him, never seemed fazed by anything we did, and his voice – its timbre, tone, manner – never deviated. He was never flustered.

A few days later, I'd finally mastered the hover and we were out doing some ground cushion work – hovering but manoeuvring, not staying in the same position.

'Right, when I give you control, Frenchie, I want you to look at this white line that's at 3 o'clock. Whilst pointing the aircraft at the trees straight ahead of us, gently manoeuvre the aircraft left along the line.'

And because everything had been coming together for me, and I could hold the hover and generally control things, I thought *piece of piss*. Obviously, the minute I took over the controls the manoeuvre was like a dog's breakfast. I tried, but I just couldn't get it right.

'I have control,' says John. 'I was expecting a bit better than that. We'll try again tomorrow.'

As he flew us back to the pan at Shawbury, I felt an enormous sense of disappointment because I thought I'd cracked it. John made you want to do well. He never criticised or put you down and every comment was constructive. Even when you felt he was disappointed in you, he never said it explicitly. Always it was the soft voice, the kindly manner. It was as if your dad was teaching you something but you didn't get it, and you'd disappointed him. He was like everyone's dad.

Another week, though, and I'd put everything behind me. Although I was nowhere near John's standard, he was delighted with my progress. I was holding it all together, and my basic handling was good. And I was enjoying myself. With fixed wing there are rules; but helicopters don't obey any rules whatsoever which, I suppose, makes them quite quirky. There's an element of me that liked that.

There wasn't a real eureka moment for me when all the various elements of flying and controlling a helicopter came together. The way we learned means it happens slowly, so you don't necessarily notice it. I think the first time I knew that I'd cracked it was after about fourteen hours of instruction. It was a Friday, May 17th, and it had been a routine sortie. When we landed, John said, 'Okay Frenchie, I'm going to step out and I want you to take-off from here, go around, then come back and pick me up.' Fourteen hours and I was left in total command of an aircraft costing one and a half million pounds. I loved it!

After the solo, things moved pretty quickly and I started to learn much more advanced handling. Things like utilising a phenomenon called 'cushion creep', which allows you to take off when the aircraft is too heavy and you don't have enough power to lift straight up. I learned how to do quick stops when the aircraft is carrying too much speed to land – you adopt a nose-up attitude flare and perform a series of rapid, tight turns to scrub it off. Very quickly it seemed, I'd amassed more than thirty-seven hours on the aircraft and the end of the course was just around the corner. I passed the basic handling test with flying colours, which meant I had all the necessary skills to fly the aircraft, could handle emergencies and knew advanced handling techniques, but I was still a long way from getting my wings. I wasn't a pilot yet.

2

THROUGH ADVERSITY TO THE STARS

You travel a long road as a prospective RAF pilot before getting your wings. I was still a long way from the Holy Grail after the best part of two years' flying training. It was like running for an oasis in the desert. The closer I got, the further away it seemed.

I was full of optimism when I arrived at 705 Squadron at RAF Shawbury (more an administrative move than a physical one). It was here that the basic skills I'd learned so far were consolidated and developed into more applied techniques. The syllabus included instrument flying, basic night flying, low-level and formation flying and, finally, mountain flying.

Instrument Flying (IF) is all about trusting your instruments, not what your sense of balance or your senses or anything else is telling you. It's drummed into you from the off. You fly with covers on the windscreen and the cowling so you can't see out; you have no visual references at all. IF is all based on scanning your instruments.

The main instrument, which sits right in front of you, is the AI, or Attitude Indicator. It displays your position against the horizon, so you can see immediately if the aircraft is rolling, yawing, climbing or descending – it shows you nose up, nose down, angle of bank, left or right, and it has a little suspended ball that tells you whether the aircraft is in balance or not. It's the only instrument with back-ups. There are four on the aircraft: two main ones and two smaller standbys.

Underneath the AI is the HSI or Horizontal Situation Indicator – basically a compass, except it's rather more complex. It's overlaid with other instruments to indicate the direction of navigation beacons. It enables us to fly an approach to an airfield in cloud or in the dark and that's why it's called a Horizontal Situation Indicator and not a compass – it gives you an awareness of where the aircraft is in space.

The Altimeter tells you your height and there are two; a Radar Altimeter or 'RadAlt' which gives the height of the aircraft as it passes above the ground, and a barometric one which uses pressure to work out the height above mean sea level, or above the ground when you're at higher altitudes.

The VSI or Vertical Speed Indicator shows how fast you're climbing or descending. Finally, we rely on the ASI or Air Speed Indicator to tell us how fast the aircraft is flying through the air.

Instrument Flying is an absolutely alien sensation because you have no references and your inner ear is blind, deaf and dumb to reason, so when confronted with the instruments it acts like Kim Jong-il in the face of international condemnation. I never had a trust issue with the instruments. I did, however, suffer from 'the leans', which is a bizarre phenomenon. With the leans, your ear doesn't believe it when the instruments say you're flying straight and level, so your body tilts to a 45° angle. I soon got over that, but it wasn't the best of starts.

The real issue for me was scanning the instruments and maintaining control because I was a bit rough with the aircraft. Initially, I wasn't a talented pilot; I had to work at it. I didn't have finesse, so I was quite 'agricultural'. That's a description of my flying used by many instructors in debriefing. 'Frenchie passed, albeit being a bit agricultural with the aircraft.' But as we say, a kill's a kill, and I completed the course successfully.

You might think that having concluded advanced flying training at 705 Squadron the RAF would now recognise me as a pilot – but no. Having learned to fly the Squirrel – a 'basic' four-seater helicopter – the next rung up the ladder was something more complex: the Griffin HT1, a military version of the Bell Textron 412EP. It's twin-engined, has a cruising speed of 120 knots (138mph) and an endurance of three hours, so it's an altogether different beast and massively more capable than what we'd been used to. As well as being multi-engined, the Griffin is also multi-crewed, meaning that we'd be introduced to the concept of Crew Resource Management (CRM) – basically, learning to work as part of a crew.

Over the next thirty-four weeks, we acquired a whole range of new skills such as underslung-load carrying, flying using night-vision goggles, procedural instrument flying, formation flying, low-flying navigation and an introduction to tactical employment, which included flying operations from confined areas. It even encompassed a short Search and Rescue (SAR) procedures course, which included elements of mountain flying and maritime rescue winching.

I remember when I first approached the Griffin, thinking: 'This is the Daddy!' It made the Squirrel look like a tadpole in comparison. The cockpit felt massive, with lots more instruments, levers and switches, but what really stood out was the collective. In the Squirrel, it's literally the shape and thickness of your average hand-brake lever in a car. In the Griffin, it's huge, with a vast array of buttons. At first I'd no idea what they all did, but it looked dead cool to me. After my familiarisation flight, I was walking around with a huge grin on my face, born of knowing that I'd just flown a 'proper' aircraft. With its looks and profile redolent of the classic Huey, I felt just liked I'd flown in Vietnam.

One of the biggest learning curves for me was flying on night-vision goggles (NVGs). We went back to Henlow for a course on the physiological aspects of this, but what really surprised me was just how quickly you lost your sense of depth perception. You're immersed in a bizarre, eerie world on NVG; everything has an ethereal green hue. It takes some getting used to. I was night flying with my instructor – a brilliant guy called Tony McGregor, who had an astonishing fifteen thousand flying hours under his belt – and after I had completed an approach to the hover, he said, 'Frenchie, do you think we could hold a hover just over the one spot?' Because of the way NVGs limit your depth perception, I'd been gradually edging ever closer to some trees.

The thing that stands out most for me on the Griffin occurred while I was at RAF Valley doing the SAR element of the course. You start doing some dry-winching over what's called the golf course at RAF valley – picking up oil drums from the ground. When you've got that, you move on to picking them up from water. And then, when the crewman believes that you're capable of pulling him out of the water, you winch him down into it, he releases, and then you fly a short circuit and winch him up again. To complete that element of the course, you winch the crewman on to a boat.

I was flying with my instructor and was into a hover slightly off the stern of a P2000 Royal Navy training vessel. I was pretty tense because I had the crewman at the end of a wire suspended beneath the aircraft and I was squeezing the cyclic so hard I was worried I'd pop all the buttons off the end!

It's a really difficult manoeuvre. You're flying into wind, the boat is rolling and listing on the waves somewhere beneath you, and you've got a man on what is effectively a very long pendulum swinging underneath the aircraft. Everything seemed fine; I had a good visual on the boat, and I thought the crewman had landed on. The intercom had gone quiet and I remember looking down and there was the crewman sprawled face-down on the zodiac at the back of the boat. He wasn't moving. My heart sank, my stomach flipped and I thought, 'Shit, I've killed him!'

I was in the hover above the boat but the intercom was dead quiet. I was sat there thinking, 'Well they must be able to see it too, but what the fuck do I say? How do I explain this one? I haven't got my wings and I've killed a crewman.' I looked over at my instructor and his mouth was open but his stomach was heaving. He hadn't got the mike keyed though, so it took me a second or two to realise he was belly laughing. The fuckers had planned this all along! They all had a good laugh at my expense.

It felt like everything finally came together for me at 60 Sqn; the instruction seemed better somehow, but I think it was also that we were treated like adults. We'd left the basic training behind, we'd evolved, and it felt like we were recognised for that. I only failed one sortie in the whole thirty-four weeks and that was due to no more than me having an off day – I couldn't have found my own arse that day! I re-did it the following morning and got a very good pass, and then took the nav test, technical exercises and the final flying test all in my stride. I landed at the end of the three-hour final handling sortie that marked the end of the course, and my instructor looked at me and said, 'Congratulations mate. You've got your wings.'

Getting your wings in the RAF is a huge event, but somehow it can feel like a bit of an anticlimax. Bear in mind that I'd started at RAF Cranwell in August 2000 and it was now May 2003; it felt like I'd been working for most of my adult life to get to this point. Given all that had happened, the ups and downs, I'm not sure I could quite believe that I'd done it. Finally, after everything, I was a pilot.

Graduation is a big affair, with a formal lunch and a party later in the evening, but on that morning you also find out what you'll be flying. For me, the news was the best I could have hoped for – Chinooks! My best mate Philip and his wife came over from France, as did Mum and Dad, and everyone dressed up to the nines for the ceremony.

We're all stood to attention in our number one uniforms and then when your name is called, you march up to the front, halt smartly, and the reviewing officer – a General of at least two-star rank – pins your wings to your chest and shakes your hand. It's immense, actually, and when it happens you feel the enormity of the achievement wash over you. There were my parents looking at me with pride, my mate Philip smiling, and suddenly the realisation hit me. Everything I'd done, the lifelong desire to fly, the hard work, the disappointment . . . it all led to this point, the culmination and realisation of a dream. Finally, I could call myself a pilot.

Next stop: RAF Odiham and the Operational Conversion Flight (OCF), where I'd learn to fly the Chinook and become combat ready. First though, there was two months' leave to look forward to . . .

3

THE BEAUTY OF THE BEAST

RAF Odiham, near Basingstoke in the leafy Hampshire country-side, is home to the Royal Air Force's three Chinook Squadrons: 7, 18 (B) and 27 Squadron. As well as being an operational unit, 18 (B) Squadron is also the training flight where pilots and crewmen learn to operate the Chinook.

There's been an airfield at Odiham since 1925, but it became RAF Odiham on October 18th 1937 when it was officially opened by Field Marshal (then General) Erhard Milch, Chief of Staff of Hitler's Luftwaffe. Apparently, Milch was so impressed with what he saw that he is reputed to have told Hitler, 'When we conquer England, Odiham will be my Air Headquarters,' and ordered his pilots not to bomb it. Whether or not this story is true, the fact remains that RAF Odiham wasn't bombed during the war.

I drove through the gates of RAF Odiham to join the OCF in July 2003, and it's been my home base ever since. This was a new world for me, a new start, and I wanted to set off on the right foot because until you're combat ready, you can still lose your wings. Although they'd been tailored on to my uniform, metaphorically speaking, they were Velcroed on.

The OCF was all about operating the aircraft as opposed to simply 'flying' it, and there's a crucial difference between the two terms. The fact that I could fly was a given now, so the OCF took things to another level entirely. It's where you learn how to really get the best out of the Chinook. Take the Squirrel: all it can do is move people. The Chinook, on the other hand, is a tool: with it you can influence combat, resupply troops and bases, evacuate wounded soldiers, move them for assaults, move heavy loads . . . there's just so much it can do.

When I first walked out to the aircraft, I was a well of excitement; I don't think I'd felt anything similar since I was six and it was the run-up to Christmas. I simply had to get into that aircraft. I couldn't wait to start it up and fly it. Outside I was the cool professional, an officer of the RAF and a competent pilot. That's what the world saw. Inside, though, a ten-year-old kid was dancing for Harry, England and St George.

I looked up to the rotor head and it was about twenty feet above me . . . twenty feet! On the Griffin, it was three feet. It took four minutes just to walk around the bloody thing. And I was thinking, 'This is a war machine; a real man's aircraft.' It looked like pure muscle and power. And it had this funny paradoxical charm – it was ugly but still beautiful. Its ugliness somehow highlighted and enhanced its beauty. It's a beast, yet it's so very graceful when airborne. I'll never forget my first flight at the controls and the smell on walking into the cockpit, an evocative mixture of oil, hydraulic fluid and sweat. It's strangely compelling and somehow brilliant. Every Chinook smells the same.

Your frame of reference is all based on increments; from the single engine of the Squirrel to the twin engines and complexity of the Griffin. This, though, rewrote the rule book and threw the old one out. It was Arsenal or Manchester United against a Sunday League pub team: the Chinook was in another division. Take off in the Squirrel and you're using 95% or more of available torque. In the Chinook, I couldn't believe that by only moving my arm by three inches I was lifting sixteen tonnes of metal and only using 50% of the available power. It had more of everything: six blades, six fuel tanks, five gearboxes, two rotor heads and two engines. It was ridiculous, and it hinted at capabilities that I had only dreamed of.

It's huge – 99ft from end to end. It's not a contemporary aircraft; it was designed and built by Boeing in 1962, so it saw service throughout the Vietnam War. Despite this, because there's nothing more up-to-date out there to compare it with, it doesn't look dated. The real beauty is its available, usable space inside the cabin, and it's this that is the *raison d'être* behind the aircraft's design. The rear is dominated by a massive hydraulic ramp, which means fast loading or unloading of whatever is in the cabin – vehicles, freight or troops (up to fifty-five of them). A tail rotor would not only hinder loading and unloading, but it would divert power from the engines and make the aircraft more difficult to manoeuvre. As it is, 100% of the power is available for lift.

Everything I'd flown up until this point had a tail rotor, but not this. Instead, it had two discs driven by two engines combined in one huge mother of a transmission. It's called combining transmission. It splits the 3,750 horses generated by each of the two Textron Lycoming T55-L712F turbine jet engines via sync shafts to the forward and aft heads. If one engine fails, the other can drive both rotors. In each head, there's a gear that transfers the rotation from the longitudinal plane into the vertical plane.

There are three blades on each rotor, each one 3ft wide and 30ft long. At rest, they bow groundwards and there's an air of tranquillity about them. When turning though, they spin at 225rpm – almost four times a second – and make no mistake: stray too close during the last stages of a shutdown and they'll take your head off. The really stunning thing is that the blades on each disc intermesh – one blade will go then the other, then the other. They're on the same level and they're synchronised via a series of linked shafts that render it mechanically impossible for the blades to hit each other. It's absolutely amazing when you think about it. The two discs rotate in opposite directions so the torque is cancelled out, which is why there's no tail rotor. It also means you don't use the pedals to counter the side-to-side movement (or 'yaw'); they're really only used in the hover – they turn the fuselage around a central axis.

The Chinook is massively flexible, so there are lots of options for control. The aircraft is fitted with three hooks – one with hydraulic release and two with electrical release – so the possibilities for picking up underslung loads are tripled: there are so many permutations. It has a maximum permitted take-off weight of over twenty-four tonnes, so it can carry a pretty hefty payload – including another Chinook.

You look at it and you'd imagine it handles like a Bedford truck, but it's more like one of those crazy monster trucks that they use for the Paris–Dakar rally. It's an exceptionally easy aircraft to fly – you almost think what you want it to do and it responds, so you only need the subtlest of touches on the control surfaces. Its incredible manoeuvrability and responsiveness belie its size, so you'd never think you have 60ft of cabin behind you; it feels like it stops right behind your arse. Its acceleration is phenomenal for a helicopter. It cruises at around 140 knots but you can squeeze up to 160 (185mph) out of it in certain conditions, although it's incredibly noisy. Cleverly, those engineers at Boeing have carefully managed to design it so that most of the sound is in the cab rather than outside; that's why we issue ear plugs to all our pax (passengers).

It can perform loads of manoeuvres that other helicopters just aren't capable of, so it's a dream machine to fly tactically. If you make an approach and have to turn into the wind, you can turn through 180° in around fifty metres – that's about half the length of a football pitch, and you're flying at around 120 knots. No other helicopter in the world can do that. You can use its bulk to assist you when stopping tactically – basically, fly in on the approach carrying a lot of speed, but scrub it off quickly by stepping the arse out as you flare, much the same way as skiers do parallel turns. You push the aircraft's tail out one way and then turn it the other way.

In the same way that most modern cars need power-assisted steering and brakes, so the Chinook needs hydraulic assistance to power the flying controls. At sixteen tonnes even without any cargo, it's a leviathan; one of the biggest helicopters in the world. To illustrate the importance of the hydraulic systems on the Chinook, there is built-in redundancy – two systems run in tandem in case one fails, and there's a further back-up system in the unlikely event that both of them break, leak or otherwise fail. They've really thought of everything. It's a truly brilliant aircraft.

The OCF is eight months long, and as with all the other flying courses, you spend a month at ground school followed by seven months of flying. Six hours was all it took for me to solo, which illustrates how second nature the flying side of things had become. Muscle memory kicks in, so it's a bit like doing a car journey on a route you're very familiar with, where you get home and can't remember driving along a certain road. Almost the entire course is about learning to operate the aircraft and work as part of a four-man crew. In the cockpit, you and your co-pilot sit in armoured seats, with armoured panels and an armoured floor. In the back, you have two loadmasters, known colloquially as 'crewmen', and they are essentially responsible for running the aircraft.

Crewmen are vital to the craft's operation. They're responsible for the loading and unloading of pax and freight, for the attachment and safety of loads on the three hook points under the cab, as well as the safe restraint of all cargo. They are trained to navigate the aircraft when we're under pressure up front, and to man the two, or sometimes three, weapons that comprise the Chinook's armament: an M60 machine-gun on the ramp, and an M134 Minigun (also known as a 'Crowd Pleaser') on each door. The Minigun is an awesome piece of kit – it is mains operated and fires between 2,000 and 4,000 rounds of 7.62mm per minute from six rotating barrels. Direct Current versions have now been fitted to cabs in Afghanistan so that in the event of a crash-landing they can still fire by drawing power from the battery. These fire around 3,000 rounds a minute – that's fifty 7.62mm rounds per second! Get hit by a burst and you'll be pink mist.

It's the crewmen's job to talk the pilot down with height and distance calls, which they do by leaning out the door and the ramp so they have visual contact with the ground. This is particularly important at really dusty landing sites, like you'll find in Afghanistan, where the dust cloud generated by the rotors' downwash can completely obscure the pilots' vision at the most crucial time of the descent. They're also our eyes on any threats to the aircraft's safety – be they obstacles, wires and cables, such as you'll find across our green and pleasant land, or tracer fire, RPGs and small arms fire in a war zone. They're able to refuel the aircraft, operate and man the winch, and they're a key link between crew and passengers. In short, they are as important to the safe and efficient operation of the aircraft as the two pilots and it's at the OCF where that really comes home. It's the reason why so much of the course is devoted to working as part of a four-man (or woman) crew.

One of my colleagues on 18 (C) Flight was Hannah Brown, a great pilot and, very quickly, a close friend. We took an instant liking to one another. I thought she was great because there was none of this 'lumpy-jumper syndrome'. She was straight down the line and never played on the fact that she's a girl, like some others do. I respected her and, perhaps just as importantly, enjoyed her company – she was good fun.

On the OCF you're treated like an adult, and there's a work-hard, play-hard mentality. You feel like a pilot there. When I was first strapped in to the Chinook, I was walking on water: at last I was a front line pilot and I could stick two fingers up to all those people who didn't think I'd make it. Don't get me wrong, it's still not the end of the training, so you can't relax. It's just you've reached a point where your experience engenders a sense of self-belief.

It was towards the end of the course that I met Alison. Hannah and I had a night sortie as a two-ship and as I walked into the planning room for the Met brief, I saw this drop-dead gorgeous blonde girl. She was standing at the back, dressed in a nicely-fitted, stylish black dress, and I thought, 'Fuck me, she's fit!' I did some asking around and discovered that her name was Alison and she was a guest of the Officer Commanding (OC). She was a senior civil servant at the Cabinet Office and they'd met on a counter-terrorism conference. The OC had invited her and a few colleagues along to the squadron for a flight. They were going to be Hannah's pax.

There was a party after our sorties. It was Taranto night, the celebration of a famous WWII raid at Taranto where Royal Navy aircraft sank most of the Italian Fleet. When I walked up to the bar I saw Alison in the corner talking to some friends. She looked absolutely magnificent. I'd never believed in love at first sight before, but I was absolutely, hopelessly smitten now. I knew immediately that she was the girl I was going to marry. We've been together ever since.

There was just one thing I needed to resolve before I graduated from the OCF and it concerned my nickname. When I first arrived I was astonished to meet another 'Frenchie'. I thought it was a wind-up at first, until we got chatting and I discovered that, like me, he had a French mother and a Scottish father. His real name was Neil McMillan but we muddled along on the course both being known by the same moniker until the instructors decided enough was enough. They said only one of us could graduate with the right to be known as Frenchie, so a French-off was organised with the instructors as umpires.

On the night concerned, we met in the Mess and undertook a number of events designed to test our 'Frenchness'. These events involved a duel with baguettes instead of swords and eating cloves of raw garlic and live snails (dug up by other members of the Flight from the garden half an hour before). The night culminated in a quiz where the invigilators went to extreme lengths to ensure our questions were equally difficult. I was asked really 'tough' ones like, 'What is the name of the monument at the Place Charles de Gaulle end of the Avenue des Champs-Élysées?' while Neil got piss-easy ones such as: 'Who won the French Open in 1972?'

There could only be one Frenchie, so given that Neil refused to eat the snails and I answered all of my (ahem) incredibly difficult questions correctly, I was declared the winner. The only thing Neil won was the right to call himself 'Frock'!

Apparently, Alison arrived quite late in the evening only to find a very drunk boyfriend wearing some dodgy silk pants (where they came from, I've no idea) and a beret.

I was so delighted to have earned my name back that I ordered a badge with 'Frenchie L'Original' over a Tricolour which, for some reason, really wound Neil up! To this day, I've no idea why . . .

After that, I sailed through my final handling check and passed my night-flying qualification. That marked the end of the OCF for me. There was the obligatory giant piss-up and that was it. Actually, no it wasn't; not quite! I still wasn't combat ready – and my wings? Let's just say they were now half sewn on!

4

ALL AT SEA

I was posted to 'A' Flight, 18 Squadron on graduating the OCF, and although I wasn't yet combat ready, my status felt permanent at last. I'd been at RAF Odiham long enough that I was pretty much in step with its daily rhythm. I knew my way around, knew most of the key personnel in the Squadron – and also at 27 Squadron, which was located just across the base. Hannah had gone to 27 Sqn, so although we were no longer part of the same unit, our paths crossed pretty regularly.

My first sortie as an 18 Sqn pilot was on February 4th 2004, with Paul 'Windy' Millar, a Qualified Helicopter Instructor (QHI) on the squadron. It was pretty much a belt-and-braces assessment to ensure that the OCF had done what it was supposed to and dropped me off the conveyor belt a fully-fledged, limited combat ready Chinook pilot. Also, Windy wanted to get an idea of my ability. Even with the OCF firmly behind me, there were still checks to pass – that's one aspect of flying that never stops. The day you think you can stop learning is the day you have to stop flying.

In May, the Squadron deployed aboard HMS *Ocean*, the Royal Navy's sole helicopter carrier. We were sailing across the Atlantic to support the Royal Marines on Exercise Aurora in the US. It was my first experience of an operational exercise and where I got my Aircraft Carrier tick. That was, to date, some of the most difficult flying I've done. There's a saying among pilots that the three best things in life are a good landing, a good orgasm and a good bowel movement, and a night-time carrier landing is one of the few opportunities in life to experience all three at the same time.

You're in the middle of the Atlantic, you're not using NVGs, and you take off from this absolutely enormous aircraft carrier which, when you're on it, feels like a city at sea. It's got light everywhere; you feel like it's visible for miles. Taking off is easy. You simply come into the hover, slide the aircraft off to the side until you're above the water, turn the tail and disappear into the night; although even that was, er . . . interesting. There was no ambient light other than what was on the ship; there was no moon – just the inky blackness of the Atlantic Ocean forty foot below me, promising almost certain death. It's a disconcerting experience for a pilot.

The circuit is 400ft and it's not like I had to fly a long way out. So I climbed up, levelled off, turned left. You think you've got the correct wind; the ship is going in one direction so in theory it's easy. I looked down and across to get a visual on the massive ship and . . . *What the fuck?* From one mile out, and at just 400ft, it's like someone has turned all the lights off and left a single 40 watt bulb burning in the middle of the ocean. That's what I had to aim for.

The hardest thing by far is when you make your final turn – you have to turn, descend and, at the same time, reduce your forward speed. But at 400ft, descending at 1,000ft per minute, you're going to hit the water in twenty-five seconds if you misjudge it. Initially, you probably wouldn't even notice because there's no demarcation between the sky and the water because it's so dark – until you felt the impact, that is, and sank to the deep. You can't see the water; everything's black apart from this single 40 watt bulb in the middle of the ocean.

To make life a little more interesting, you approach the ship on a bearing of Red 165, the way they do it in the Royal Navy. Red 165? What the fuck's that? You won't get the Navy using a compass for navigation to the ship; that'd be far too easy. No, they have this fucked-up system where Red represents left, 0–180 and Green represents right, also 0–180. So Red 165 should give you the angle to the ship. The idea is to come alongside it, hover next to it until you match your speed. Get the rearmost line on the deck under your arse, and move across. Look for the forward line in front of the cab, and . . . down! It sounds easy when you say it. It wasn't.

The Squadron's part in the exercise lasted over a month, so it was about six weeks since Alison and I had last seen one another. That was hard; we spoke every day but I must have spent a month's salary on phone cards. HMS *Ocean* docked in Jacksonville, Florida and we got a week's leave, so I'd arranged for her to fly out and join me. That's when I asked her to marry me. She said yes. She's the most military-focused civilian I've ever met. Personally, she's all the woman I've ever wanted, and professionally, I've never known anyone like her. She's got real leadership skills, having worked her way up to a senior role in the Cabinet Office briefing Tony Blair and other ministers. She'd clearly impressed a few people because while I was struggling to fly on instruments and worrying about my fledgling career as a pilot, she received an MBE for her work on the Afghanistan Campaign in the wake of 9/11.

Things ramped up pretty quickly after our return from HMS *Ocean*. I did some taskings in Northern Ireland and not long after Christmas 2004, the Squadron went to Iraq, which was my first operational deployment. It was a two-month Det and, to be honest, not a great deal happened. It was like flying a big green taxi; I spent most of my time just ferrying men and equipment around. Aside from a single mission where there was a very remote chance of coming under contact, it was all pretty low-key. The accommodation was first class, nothing like the basic facilities in Afghanistan. We had a bar and a swimming pool and we got to fly. It was Iraq, so in theory it was dangerous, but the flying was good. We'd come back in the evening, go for a swim, have one or two beers in the bar . . . how bad could it be? I thought that was what all operational deployments would be like, but how wrong I was . . .

After a period of leave, I returned to Odiham for some routine flying. It was all about gaining more experience on as many differ-ent mission profiles as possible. Then, on June 20th 2005, after a big work up where I practised all the skills that are required of a Chinook captain, I was declared combat ready. It was all about being able to demonstrate captaincy, satisfy the boss that I could take the aircraft on a shitty night, fly across the UK, do the job and come back safely.

Of course, the real pleasure for me was my wings. They were properly sown in now and that was it; they couldn't take them away from me. Not now. Finally, in June 2005 – almost five years after starting on the journey – I could at last call myself a pilot in the Royal Air Force. I was in!

We'd been tasked to return to Iraq again shortly after I was declared combat ready. In the event though, we were stood down to allow the Merlins to take over in theatre. Shortly afterwards we got the news that we had been earmarked to go to Afghanistan in April 2006, so everything that followed was about us preparing for that.

Some of the guys on the Squadron had been to Afghanistan in the immediate aftermath of 9/11 as part of the operation to oust the Taliban from power, but the landscape was significantly different then. Sangin, Musa Qala, Kajaki – they were meaningless names to us in 2005. There was no back story, no history or association with any particular place. Camp Bastion didn't exist. Also, there'd been just a single British soldier killed in combat operations. Our worries weren't so much focused on the enemy, but on flying the aircraft in an environment in which its performance was a complete unknown.

One of my best experiences of flying came when I did a short detachment to the Falkland Islands in November and December 2005. I was flying with Aaron Stewart, who'd become a good friend while I was on 18 Squadron. He earned himself the sobriquet of 'Tourette's' due to his incredible ability to swear prolifically whenever he gets angry. His vocabulary of swear-words is absolutely extraordinary and he delivers them like a Minigun on a high rate of fire! The two of us did some really good flying in some incredibly testing weather, which took both us and the aircraft to the absolute limits of performance. You really only ever see weather like that in the Falkland Islands.

On one particular sortie, we were supposed to be picking up a JCB as an underslung load and putting it on HMCS *Brandon*, a Canadian Navy ship. We thought it was going to be one of those mini JCBs but it turned out to be the full monty, which weighed about eight tonnes. When we finally got it hooked up and I pulled pitch to lift, we had just a 3% margin in power – right at the limit of the Chinook's capabilities.

Still, at least we couldn't see the effect that the load had on our cab, which isn't the case when you're flying in a two-ship formation and you're both carrying massive underslung loads. You can actually see the other cab 'bow' in the middle as the load exerts downforce on the airframe. It's stressed to such a degree that small waves ripple across the metal skin, in much the same way they'd move across the skin on your arms if you were lifting heavy weights. The cabs are worked so hard they're literally 'sweating the metal'.

It's funny how your mind adapts, almost without you noticing. The first time I flew a Chinook I was amazed at its power, but everything has a limit. Once the engines exceed maximum power or temperature, they'll either blow up or the NR will drop, as they won't be able to provide the energy required to maintain it at 100%. If that happens, the cab will drop like a stone.

This time, all I had to do was finesse the aircraft over the deck of the ship and gently place the JCB on the deck. Easy, right?

Well, as easy at it can be when you're hovering a 99ft long helicopter with only 3% torque in hand, an eight-tonne JCB acting as a pendulum under the aircraft, and two rotor discs spinning at 225 revs per minute just 5ft away from the ship's crane. It would have been all but impossible on any other day in the Falkland Islands (where, even in summer, the wind can exceed fifty knots) but on this particular day it was unusually benign – no more than three or four knots. I learned a lot about flying on that mission that was to prove invaluable in Afghanistan.

Given the Falkland Islands' isolation and its uncontrolled airspace, you can do things there that just aren't possible anywhere else in the world. All incoming and outgoing commercial airline flights are intercepted and escorted by two RAF Typhoon fighter jets. The residents of Port Stanley positively welcome low flying (they phone the base and complain if the jets don't scream overhead at max chat at least twice a week); and at least twice a month the Argentine Navy sails inside the exclusion zone to see just how awake the Typhoon crews are, which heralds a scramble to intercept and chase them away. It's like a playground for the UK military, but it's hugely beneficial from an operational readiness perspective.

We used to do something called the 'Tiger Run'. We would call the RAF Regiment over the radio and say, 'Tiger Run – game on,' and they would then turn on the radar for their Rapier anti-aircraft missile system. The object of the game would be to fly the aircraft as low and fast as possible to see how close we could get to the airfield before they managed to get missile lock on us. To beat our personal score meant flying through some of the gullies that ran in from the west straight into the airfield. The flying was intense and took a lot of focus, but it was to prove hugely beneficial when we got to Afghanistan.

5

DÉJÀ VU

In January 2006 we were briefed that we'd be deploying to Afghanistan as a component of 16 Air Assault Brigade and flying in support of ops by 3 Para Battlegroup, under Lieutenant Colonel Stuart Tootal. We would be flying to Kandahar Airfield and operating between there and a newly-built British base called Camp Bastion. At that stage, I don't think it was much more than a few tents and a dirt runway, but it was growing by the day.

We also knew that we'd be flying on ops with the Army Air Corps' Apache AH-1s. We'd heard mixed reports about them; at that stage they were so new to UK service that the MoD hadn't identified a role for them and nobody really knew how they'd fare. Obviously, we'd never worked with them before and there were all sorts of rumours flying around. We'd heard they were slow and their weapon sensors weren't very good, which, as it transpired, was absolute rubbish because they are fantastic machines. With what I know now, I wouldn't want to fly anywhere without one.

After New Year's Day 2006, there were really only two things on my mind: 'A' Flight's impending departure for Afghanistan; and the big day for Ali and I, which we'd arranged for August. We'd planned on a big do, with our respective families, friends and work colleagues. It was to be a formal gig at the church in Odiham, with myself and the guys from the Flight in full ceremonial uniform, replete with medals, swords and white gloves. But then events conspired to bring about a radical change of plan; Ali told me she was pregnant. That changed things, especially since word started to come back from Afghanistan that things were deteriorating. Suddenly, the whole business of my deployment looked different.

About a week later, we were at home one night and I said, 'Babe, I know your heart is set on an August wedding, but I think we should get married before I go away because we're hearing more and more about how bad it is in Afghan.' If anything was to happen to me, I wanted everything to be alright for Ali and the baby. Foremost in my mind was the case of Brad Tinnion, a British soldier who'd been killed on ops in Sierra Leone – because he wasn't married to his girlfriend, the MoD wouldn't pay her a widow's pension and other benefits she'd have been entitled to. There was no way I was going to let that happen to Ali; her security was much more important than a glitzy wedding or the expensive dress she'd bought. Ali agreed, so we decided on a much smaller service in April, at a Register Office near our home in Brighton.

First though, a hasty training exercise was put together so that the Chinook and Apache crews could get used to working with one another. We spent two weeks at the end of March 2006 flying together. Those two weeks were hard work – I logged a total of thirty hours of day flying and seven hours at night, which was pretty impressive. It was the last piece of proper tactical training we'd have before deploying to theatre in mid-May.

Alison and I married on April 29th, 2006 at Brighton Register Office. It was a very small affair – my parents were there, together with Philip and his wife; on Alison's side it was just her parents and three sisters. I wore my No.1 uniform, Ali a simple but pretty cream and black dress. It was a beautiful day of the sort that recalls the Battle of Britain – blue sky, sunshine and little fluffy white clouds. When we walked out of the Register Office as man and wife for the first time, Mike Woods (my boss) and his wife Lisa, together with Johnny Shallcross (a mate from the Squadron) and his girlfriend, had driven all the way down from Odiham just to throw rice over us. After lunch at a local restaurant, I whisked Ali off for a week's honeymoon in Lanzarote. I got back just in time for a final training sortie on May 11th.

There was no time to sit and reminisce. We filled a cab with some additional fuel tanks that were brimful and went flying. They help create the perfect simulation of a half-full aircraft in a hot and high environment. Lots more power required; lots more inertia. The aircraft wallows and shakes, and you can't stop on a sixpence so you have to plan your flying a lot further ahead.

There was also a lot of last minute admin to take care of. I hadn't made a will, so I had to rectify that. We had to check our dog tags were in order, make sure that next-of-kin details were correct, so that if anything happened the right person would get the late-night knock on the door. I didn't write an 'Open in event of my death' letter. To me, that would be tempting fate!

A lot of the kit we were issued before deployment simply wasn't up to the job, so that meant many of us investing in our own bespoke items either online or at army surplus stores. The holster I was given for my pistol is a good example – it looked like vintage 1960s issue with a lanyard that went through uniform epaulettes, thus rendering it useless when worn with body armour. I replaced that with a thigh holster that I bought myself. I bought a CamelBak – we were only issued with one. Ditto a liner for my green maggot (sleeping bag) and a thermal mattress – the ones we were issued with were absolute rubbish. Ali really went nuclear about all that; she couldn't believe that we had to buy some of our equipment ourselves.

The body armour we'd been given before deployment wasn't really fit for purpose. It was a twenty-year-old design and not of the same standard as a Kevlar soft vest, which can stop a 9mm bullet. The ceramic anti-ballistic plates that stop high-velocity rounds had one major issue: in a heavy landing, the chest plate had a tendency to come up and take your face off. Still, you can only play with the cards you've been dealt. The current vest issued to aircrew is called the Mk60 – although far from perfect, it's definitely an improvement.

There's a line in the Mamas and Papas song 'Dedicated to the

One I Love' that goes 'and the darkest hour is just before dawn'; it underlines how things were at home in the final days before my deployment. There comes a point where you've packed and checked everything twice, you're mentally ready to go, and you just want the whole thing over with.

It's always harder for Ali. I'm leaving to join a family – my Flight – and she's losing a key part of hers. I'm experiencing things first-hand, and although there's a risk, I know what I'm exposing myself to. Ali doesn't. For her, life goes on, but it's different. She has to cope alone, manage the house, work. Meanwhile, the fear is like an unwanted close companion. All she knows is that it's dangerous out there – and for her, that means all of it. Subconsciously, we both start to become more remote, and an unwanted distance opens up between us. In the day or two before I go, both of us wish I was already gone so that the clock has begun to wind down to the day I come home again.

The goodbye is always the hardest part. That's the time when the hold is greatest, when you're trying to break away from a world that you're an integral part of. When the goodbyes are done, you can focus on getting to grips with the job at hand, and each of us has our own coping mechanisms for that. The day or so before you leave is purgatory.

I leave early in the morning. Ali is still in bed. There's a scene in the Mel Gibson film *We Were Soldiers* like that, where his screen wife, Madeleine Stowe, is still in bed and he slips quietly away to go to war. Was that life imitating art, or the other way around?

We're flying from RAF Brize Norton to Kandahar via Kabul, so we meet as a Flight at 18 Squadron HQ, where a coach is waiting to transfer us to the RAF's Oxfordshire-based hub. We've all had a week's leave so it is the first time we've seen one another in seven days. Everyone is wearing their desert gear. The ground is awash with brown and beige, items of kit strewn hither and thither; everyone has been to the barber and a quick look round reveals a sea of heads sporting low-maintenance No.1 haircuts. The mood is subdued; the customary banter and piss-taking strangely absent. People are alone with their thoughts, the warmth of home and the scent of loved ones clinging to the folds of our uniforms.

We arrive at Brize Norton to learn that our aircraft has a technical fault and we're delayed for twenty-four hours, so it's back on the buses, back to Odiham and back home. It's the worst thing possible: Groundhog Day. Another evening meal with Ali – what is there to say? We've said it all already. I shouldn't be here. I feel strangely awkward. Darkness means another sleepless night spent watching Ali slumber and the clock count down. Sleep claims me just as the alarm shatters the silence, heralding another painful goodbye. The events of the previous twenty-four hours play out again. I feel like an actor treading the boards, playing out the same script, in the same place night after night. This one ends differently though; the TriStar is fixed and we depart on time just after lunch. England's green and pleasant land falls rapidly away as the aircraft begins its journey eastwards.

The ageing TriStar that carries us and a couple of hundred assorted infantrymen and support staff is the only way into theatre for the countless servicemen and women deployed there. It's stripped down, functional, bare. The faded decals in the toilets and galleys, all circa 1962, hint at the ageing airliner's previous, rather more glamorous, life. Once people dressed up to fly; now its passengers wear desert combats, Kevlar helmets and body armour for a night-time descent made in total darkness. I'm sure each passenger deals with the darkened tactical approach differently, but there can't be a man or woman aboard who doesn't momentarily dwell on the fact that there is a better than even chance that one or more of their fellow passengers won't be coming home the same way.

For those destined to increase the British casualty list, the route home is rather more high profile: a C-17 Globemaster into RAF Lyneham, preceded by a full military remembrance parade and followed by a procession through the centre of Royal Wooton Bassett, lined by locals who turn out to honour every fallen soldier repatriated back to Britain.

But that all lies ahead. For now, Afghanistan beckons.

PART TWO
BAPTISM OF FIRE

6

A HOSTILE ENVIRONMENT

Those people we know generically as Afghanis or Afghans hail from at least five different ethnic groups and countless different tribes, many of which are spread across Pakistan's Federally Administered Tribal Areas. More than thirty languages are spoken within the country's borders, in addition to the three official tongues of Dari, Farsi and Pashto. Perhaps the only common thread to tie the country's people together is their Muslim religion, which is practised by 99% of the population. The average Afghan feels little or no sense of loyalty to President Hamid Karzai; it is in the nature of many to support whoever looks likely to be the victor of any given argument, battle or confrontation. A deep-rooted system of tribal and ethnic loyalty overrides any sense of nationality, such as that possessed by the average British or American citizen.

Underpinning all of this is the illegal widespread cultivation and harvesting of opium poppies, which are the Taliban's main source of income. Afghanistan produces 90% of the world's opium, the main ingredient in the heroin that finds its way onto the streets of Britain and the US. Despite this, the country could be self-sufficient within a decade if the security situation was stabilised to allow the world's mining companies to invest in Afghanistan's significant mineral resources, which are believed to be worth in excess of three trillion dollars. These include vast reserves of oil, gas, copper, gold and lithium.

It was into that melting pot that we were headed as a component of 16 Air Assault Brigade. Our deployment was born in January 2006, following the then defence secretary Dr John Reid's announcement that the UK would send a Provincial Reconstruction Team with several thousand personnel to Helmand Province for at least three years. The move was coordinated with other NATO countries to relieve the predominantly American presence in the south. Senior Taliban figures voiced opposition to the incoming force and pledged to resist. And resist they did.

Dr Reid expressed the hopelessly naïve view that: 'We would be perfectly happy to leave in three years' time without firing one shot.' Some hope. Within two and a half years, British soldiers had fired a total of 12.2 million bullets.

Our landing in Kabul was uneventful, but because of our late arrival time we had to wait until the following morning to take the short flight via Hercules to Kandahar. We landed at the main base for ISAF forces in Afghanistan around midday; even though it was only May, the first thing that struck me was the heat. Fuck me, it was oppressive! Acclimatising was going to be a bitch.

Kandahar and Helmand, where we would be operating from, is unforgiving territory. It can take over three weeks to acclimatise on arrival. The temperature in the summer months rarely drops below 48°C and reaches as high as 55°C, with humidity consistently around 9%. It's arid, hot and dusty – the sand's consistency is like talcum powder and it clings to everything. Heatstroke can be almost as much of a threat as the Taliban; so too is the dreaded D&V (Diarrhoea and Vomiting), which can strike down a whole patrol within days. You need to take in eleven litres of water a day just to stay hydrated, and there is almost no shelter from the sun.

Incidentally, the heat has other effects on your body's physiology during the acclimatisation period. The heat is an appetite suppressant, but because of the amount of energy that you expend on ops, you need to take in more calories than you do at home. The soldiers at the FOBs, the guys who are engaging with the Taliban, take in around 5–6,000 calories a day. But the heat plays havoc with your digestive and urinary systems – there's almost no desire to go to the toilet. Ten, eleven litres of water each day and you can't remember the last time you went for a piss.

We were relieving 'A' Flight, 27 Sqn when we arrived. After picking up our weapons and other kit, we were met by Sqn Ldr Dan 'Danno' Startup, their OC.

'Welcome to KAF, fellas,' said Danno. Mike Woods, who was OC 'A' Flight for our tour shook his hand.

'Cheers mate, although we're not entirely pleased to be here!' said Woodsy in his thick Geordie accent.

'Sorry about the transport, it's about par for the course round here,' Danno apologised, as he led us out to a vintage 1960s bus that was coated inside and out in dust. All was well as he drove us towards our accommodation, and I took in the vast, sprawling base that is KAF, home to some 8,000 NATO troops. Suddenly, a fetid stench assailed my nostrils. 'What the fuck is that?!' I asked Danno.

'Ah, that'll be Poo Pond,' he said as he rounded the corner to reveal an enormous circular lake about 100 yards across. Facing it on the opposite side of the road were several accommodation blocks.

'Er . . . Poo Pond?' asked Woodsy.

'Yeah, it's that lake there,' said Danno, pointing. 'It's a liquid pit for all of KAF's human waste.'

I stared at the lake's still, brown water and shuddered involuntarily. Nothing stirred. Surely no insect would dare to brave its inky depths. Then I noticed the warning sign hanging from the single rope that cordoned the water off. 'Biohazard: Do Not Enter,' it read. In terms of stating the obvious, that sign was rivalled only by the warning on a bag of peanuts I'd been given on a flight a year or so before that said: 'Warning. May Contain Nuts.' What sort of fucking world do we inhabit now?

'Which poor fuckers live in that accommodation block?' asked Woodsy, as the bus slowed . . . and then turned.

'Er, we did. Now it's all yours. Welcome!' said Danno, and a collective groan went up from everyone on the bus.

The accommodation itself was pretty good, considering: brick-built single-storey blocks with rooms either side of a central corridor. The rooms were air-conditioned and slept four – each berth had a cot and bedside cupboard. At the end of the corridor were the ablutions – a row of about eight showers, sixteen sinks, two urinals and four proper, porcelain flushing toilets. At least the waste wouldn't have far to travel.

'Do you get used to the smell?' I asked Danno, screwing up my nose. I read somewhere that your sense of smell works by analysing molecular particles of whatever odour it detects. Sometimes I wished I didn't read so much.

'Honestly? No,' said Danno. 'But it's not just yourselves. The Harrier Det are in the next block along, so they absorb the worst of the smell.' I laughed – that wasn't going to do the fast jet boys' over-inflated egos any good. How do you know that the man you're talking to is a Harrier pilot? Because he'll tell you himself.

After being given an hour to dump our kit and straighten up, we met up with Danno at The Green Bean, a kind of low-rent coffee shop. In light of the fact that alcohol was banned at KAF, I could see The Green Bean becoming our de facto second home.

Danno did the handover. 'Okay, the set-up is pretty simple. The Chinook Force in theatre is known as 1310 Flight, and we've got a total of six cabs here – nowhere near enough. Two cabs are at Bastion on IRT and HRF and there are two here for taskings, plus another two in various stages of maintenance. The rotation at Camp Bastion is two days on IRT followed by two on HRF (Helmand Reaction Force). On the fourth day, you handle the afternoon's taskings and end up back here at KAF. The taskers will fly down to take over from you. The IRT and HRF cabs are permanent fixtures at Bastion and there will be three crews forward there at any one time, as well as a few engineers to handle routine maintenance and minor repairs.'

Simple as. I was looking forward to this.

First though, there was a mountain of admin to take care of. Our weapons all needed to be zeroed on the range, and we each needed to get Theatre Qualified (TQ) and signed off before we could fly ops. We also had to pick up our morphine. Everybody carries it in theatre, regardless of rank, corps, unit or trade. For those permanently at KAF, rocket attacks were a daily and nightly feature. For anyone forward – well, the risks were obvious. Your personal issue is two syringes of what is basically pure heroin. Get shot, hit by shrapnel or anything else nasty and so long as you don't have a head injury, you slam the auto-injectors straight into your thigh and get eight hours of carefree happiness. That's the theory, anyway.

Woodsy was a good mate and a cracking boss, whose innate confidence did a lot to quell the apprehension that many of us felt about the deployment. It wasn't fear that I felt, more a kind of performance anxiety – the worry that somehow, when it came to the crunch, I might fail. We train hard and you expect the worst, but nobody has a frame of reference for combat if they haven't experienced it, and you don't know how you're going to react when you come under fire. The worst thing in the world would be letting your mates down. But Woodsy made everyone feel better. He was a typical Geordie – straight-talking, and you wouldn't want to cross him, but he was fair, likeable and, professionally, absolutely awesome.

One of the first things he did when we got to theatre was make sure we got our personal go kit sorted; here, the rule book went out the window. It was about what worked. 'What you want is a baseline go bag that contains only stuff that you're going to need,' he said. 'For most, that means first-aid kit, water, ammunition, smoke grenades and survival kit. There's always some fuckwit who fills his go bag up with 100lbs of stuff that, when the wheel comes off, he can't pick up. If you crash or get shot down, you aren't going to have time to sit there planning it and ferreting around for what you need. It's called a go bag for a reason. Grab it, and fuck off.'

He's the only boss I've ever had that did that, and it's one of the things that made him stand out because it was really good advice.

I added some warm kit to mine because the night-time temperature can drop to below 15°C, which is a big difference from the day-time high of 45–50°C. I also added in some boiled sweets for sugar – no point in adding chocolate! In the past, aircrew on ops would have promissory notes that promised a reward to whoever assisted the bearer. They don't do that anymore because trust is a scarce commodity in today's world. Money talks to the average Afghan, and gold in his hand is going to go down a lot better than a promissory note torn out of an Escape Manual!

Woodsy also had us practising egress from the aircraft after being shot down; escaping from the cab under contact, using your rifle to fire and manoeuvre and get into a shelter. We practised that non-stop until it became second nature. Woodsy instigated that, although it's been taken up as SOP (standard operating practice) now. He knew what he was doing and that's one of the reasons he was such a brilliant boss to work under.

I knew it wasn't going to be an easy tour, but with nothing to act as a baseline, I had no idea just what 'not an easy tour' meant in practice. A briefing quite early on quickly put me in the picture.

'Dinger Bell' was a Chinook crewman who had just been promoted and he was doing his operational staff tour in Afghanistan as a Squadron Leader at Joint Helicopter Force (Afghanistan) – HQ JHF (A) for short. He took us to the only place in KAF that was big enough to hold us all comfortably at that time – the church. He'd been in theatre for a while so he knew what he was talking about. And he didn't mince his words.

'Guys, be under no illusions: this is not going to be easy. People here want to kill you and they will try everything they can to achieve that. They hate the Chinooks and Apaches equally and it's their stated aim to shoot one down.'

You could have heard a pin drop. Two days before we arrived, a patrol of French Special Forces operators working with the ANA were slaughtered and the area was apparently littered with dead bodies when 3 Para were sent in to try and rescue the survivors. One of the French guys was reportedly gutted alive. That got our attention. We'd expected things to be shit, but this was far beyond what we'd imagined. I think Dinger's words carried even more weight because they were coming from a guy we all knew and trusted. You could see the worry etched on his face as he spoke to us.

'You can't be too careful, guys. You'll need to apply all the tactics we've practised. You cannot give them an inch. They will try to kill you. And make no mistake; they are sophisticated in their tactics. They might wear pyjamas and flip-flops, but they know what they're doing and are ready for you.'

All this happened on day one.

Welcome to Kandahar.

7

MINDING MY T'S AND Q'S

Nobody could fly in theatre until they'd done their TQ, which basically meant flying with experienced members of the outgoing Flight. They knew the plot; the routes, procedures, the various Helicopter Landing Sites (HLSs). The TQ was the only opportunity we had to learn from the guys who knew how it all worked in practice. We also had to perform a number of both day and night dust landings in the desert.

Dust is a real issue in Afghanistan. As well as blighting everybody's life back at base, because it sticks to absolutely everything, it plays havoc with electronics and machinery. Actually, it's the enemy of everything. It's so incredibly fine – more like powder than sand. It's pervasive, and its micro-fine size means it penetrates into places you wouldn't believe. It plays hell with engines, so the Chinooks have Engine Air Particle Separators (EAPS) fitted in front of the air intakes. Huge suction pumps remove the sand before it can clog things up. The main issue for us is the dust clouds that are created by the immense downwash from the blades as we land. The cloud can start to build at around 80ft and quickly envelop the cab, giving the pilots up front zero visibility just at the time it's most needed. It's known as a brownout.

I was delighted to learn that I'd be doing my TQ with Tourette's who, after our gig in the Falkland Islands a few months before, had moved to 'A' Flight, 27 Squadron. We chatted amiably as we walked out to our aircraft, which sat glinting in the morning sun. Already the mercury was pushing towards 40°C – just another day in Afghanistan.

We walked up the ramp to our cab. I said hello to Craig Fairbrother and Graham 'Jonah' Jones, two seasoned crewmen who comprised the rest of the crew for the day's sortie. Aaron and I took our seats in the cockpit – unusually, Aaron, as captain, was flying from the left, so I took my seat on the right. The controls are replicated equally on both sides of the cockpit so the aircraft can be flown from either seat, although most of the navigation and self-defence controls are on the left. The cockpit is divided by a central console that extends from the control panel and along the floor, in much the same way as the transmission tunnel divides the front seats in a car. On the control panel are the engine instruments – temperature, pressure, fuel etc. On the floor console are all the radio, navigation and defence suite controls.

We were helmeted and strapped in, so all conversation went via the intercom. Aaron called the tower for clearance to start.

'Kandahar Ground, Splinter Two Five, request start.'

'Splinter Two Five you are cleared to start Mike Ramp. Wind two-two-zero at five knots.'

The EAPS means that start-up procedure is slightly different. I hear a whoosh of air through the intercom when I select the EAPS No.1 – that tells me that it's working so I can then start the engine. Once idling, I release the rotor brake and the rotor starts turning. I watch for 7psi on the gear boxes and as I see it, I advance the throttle to 'flight.' The NR reaches 100%. After bringing the generators online, I start no.2 EAPS and the engine and once its at idle, I advance the throttle to flight. Both engines now share the load of driving the rotors. Tourette's does the arming-up check and engages the Defensive Aids Suite.

The Chinook is well equipped with defensive aids, which include a Radar Warning Receiver, an Ultraviolet and Doppler Missile Approach Warning System, infrared jammers and chaff and flare dispensers, which can be manually or automatically fired. Then there's the armament – two M134 six-barrelled Miniguns, one in each front side window, and the M60D machine-gun on the ramp. We're live now, so the system should start throwing out chaff and flares to defeat any threats detected. Craig and Jonah down the back arm and ready the guns.

'KAF Tower, Splinter Two Five. Holding at Mike Ramp, request taxi to Foxtrot.'

'Splinter Two Five, cleared taxi to Foxtrot.'

Foxtrot is a taxiway that's parallel to KAF's main runway 05/23, and it's a departure point for all helicopters. We never use the runway. One, we don't need to, and secondly, it's just too busy. With around ten thousand movements a month, and aircraft of all types from fast jets to airliners and transports, KAF handles almost half as much traffic as Gatwick and that only handles airliners.

I lift the collective with my left hand. Gently does it. The Chinook handles sublimely and needs only the merest hint of input. It's like flying by thinking. I feel the cab straining as the rotors pull it upwards and then the wheels have only the merest contact with the ground. We're airborne. I push forwards on the cyclic and the nose dips. I fly us forwards at little more than walking pace, then land on at Foxtrot.

'KAF Tower, Splinter Two Five ready for departure, Sector Hotel Low.'

It's an unsecure radio so we use different letters randomly to represent whichever sector we want to depart from. This time, 'Hotel' means an easterly departure. Low means we'll be departing at low level.

'Splinter Two Five, Tower, clear take-off. Wind two-two-zero at four knots.'

'Clear above and behind,' says Craig.

'Clear take-off, Splinter Two Five.' Into the hover again and we're away.

'Two good engines, 65% torque, 100%NR maintained, CAP is clear, Ts and Ps are all looking good,' says Aaron, running through the after-take-off checks.

65% torque? That's a product of the hot and high environment that defines Afghanistan. Bearing in mind that we're empty, it's the first take-off of the day and we're carrying less than UK fuel weight, that torque figure means we will be unable to fly on a single engine should one fail.

I make a left-hand turn maintaining low level and head for a wadi on the edge of the Red Desert. We departed at low level and ran out to the south-east from the runway. It's a lovely flat run to get to the wadi and then all of a sudden, out of nowhere, comes the Red Desert. It's that sudden; a literal line in the sand. If we're flying anywhere in Helmand then once we're over that, away from the eyes and ears of any enemy, we'll climb. It's better because it's a more comfortable ride and it's cooler at height, both of which make for happier passengers and crew.

'Okay Frenchie,' says Tourette's. 'I want you to set yourself up for a dust landing in the wadi. It's nice and dry so you should get a good dust cloud there.'

'Okay Aaron, I'm going to set up for a basic one. It's at least eighteen months since I did them on ops in Iraq, so I'm probably a little rusty.'

'Aye, never worry. You'll be grand.'

I start my descent and enter 'the gate'. I'm at 100ft and flying at 30kts and I know that having maintained that speed and height for a few seconds, Aaron will rebug the RadAlt to 40ft – that will give the crewman an audible alarm at 40ft so he can confirm our altitude by sight. I pick a landing marker through the Perspex floor bubble – a bush. The aim is to keep it beneath my right boot. I trim the aircraft to a six degree nose-up attitude and lower the lever for the descent. If the bush's position through the windscreen rises, I'm too low; if it falls, I'm too high. I've put the aircraft in a six degree decelerative attitude, just as I was taught at Shawbury all those years ago, so the speed will start coming down. I let the aircraft do its thing; I don't touch the speed. My job is to keep the 'picture' – the bush – steady.

Aaron calls my height and speed: '100; 30: 75; 25: 50; 22.' 50ft and 22kts. At this point, the crewman is leaning out of the side door immediately behind the cockpit so that he's visual with the ground.

'40; 16,' Aaron says over the intercom, and simultaneously the RadAlt alarm sounds, confirming what I already know. 'Cancel, continuing,' I say, killing the alarm. Jonah starts calling my height and voicing the formation of the dust cloud:

'30 . . . 20 . . . dust cloud forming . . . 15 . . . at the ramp . . . 10, 8 . . . centre . . . 6 . . . at the door; with you . . .'

I see the dust cloud enveloping the nose. The ground is obscured from view and I'm entirely reliant on the crewmen. It's a difficult skill to master, but master it they do. And for us, as pilots, it's all in the voice; its cadence says almost as much as the words and numbers. It is imperative that he gets it right because if he calls 1ft and I'm at 10ft, I'm going to cushion the aircraft to land with a bit of run on – except that at 10ft, I'll go into the hover instead. In the brownout, I'll have no references, so if I drift, I could hit something and crash. The trust is absolute. I'm relying on him to be accurate; he's got to have complete faith in me to get us down. It's a symbiotic relationship.

'3; 2 . . .' I gently, almost imperceptibly, arrest the collective to cushion the landing. 'Four wheels on,' Jonah calls. The rear wheels compress on their suspension as they touch solid ground. I lower the collective to get the front down and hear 'Six wheels on.' We're down. I push the pedals to arrest our forward movement and we stop; exactly where I wanted us to be. In the back, the dust cloud billows up the ramp and through the cab, temporarily rendering visibility down to zero and coating everything in a fine layer of dust.

'Good!' says Aaron. 'Nice one Frenchie. Fancy some pairs landings?'

Nichol Benzie another mate on the flight, was doing TQ in another cab in the same area, so Aaron called him over the radio and set it up. You take it in turns to do the pairs landing, which is a lot more difficult because you want to stay close but not too close – two rotor spans is near enough. The technique is to follow the lead and watch for the second that he puts the cab in a nose-up attitude. That means he's started his descent, and it's important that you get down together because even if there's the merest hint of lagging, you're going to get his dust.

Obviously we have drills to ensure that should either of us have to abort, the right-hand cab will go right or straight ahead and the left-hand one will go left or straight ahead. Whatever happens, the one thing you don't want to do is cross. Not good at all.

So that set the pattern for the next couple of hours. A few more dust landings, single, in pairs. Different variables; landing without markers. By the time we were done, the old muscle memory was back and it was all second nature, just the way it should be. Aaron suggested we do some theatre familiarisation and we headed off to Lashkar Gah and Gereshk so he could show me the HLSs and point out what markers to use to get my bearings on the approach. And later that night, I got to do the whole thing again; on NVGs.

Job done. I was TQ'd and ready for whatever lay ahead.

8

THE GOLDEN HOUR

The morning after my TQ, Craig Wilson and I caught a Hercules down to Camp Bastion to join Nichol Benzie on the IRT. While I'd be flying on the IRT with Nichol, Craig – an experienced squadron pilot – was rostered on to the HRF.

It's a great aircraft, the Herc; similar to a Chinook in many ways. You board from a ramp at the rear and the inside can be configured in a host of different ways depending on if it's carrying pax, cargo or a mix of the two. For the shuttle down to Bastion, it was configured for pax, although the accommodation is about as spartan as it gets. Seats are in four rows – one on each side of the fuselage with a double row running lengthways along the middle, with the seats facing out. Half empty it's manageable, but full up, the knees of passengers on the central seats touch those of the passengers facing them. Add in kit, weapons, body armour and helmets and it's almost impossible to get anywhere near a comfortable position – although being good at Twister would be a distinct advantage.

All the aircraft's cables, wires and pipes are exposed along the inside of the fuselage and the walls are bare metal. As on the Chinook, the designers have cleverly engineered the aircraft to route the bulk of the noise from its four Allison AE 2100D3 turbo-props to the cabin rather than the outside. At least, that's how it seems. The crewmen issue ear plugs to all pax as they board, so it's at least bearable.

It's a short flight from KAF to Camp Bastion, the main forward base for all British Forces in Helmand Province, and Nichol meets us as we disembark from the Herc with our kit. We walk to a battered Land Rover and climb aboard for the short drive to the JHF (A) tent, which is the forward HQ for the IRT/HRF and the Apache Force, which is permanently based here.

Camp Bastion is like a small town in the middle of the flat, featureless, dusty lunar landscape that is this corner of Helmand Province. It's the perfect location for the 2,000 British troops who live and work here – at the sharp end, but removed from it. A perfect paradox.

The living conditions are more basic than at KAF. ISO freight containers are the de facto choice for storage, and air-conditioned tents are used for all the accommodation – for eating, sleeping, working and downtime. Hesco Bastion blast walls are everywhere. The name Hesco comes from the company that makes them – collapsible wire mesh containers with a heavy-duty fabric liner that are used as semi-permanent barriers against blast and small arms fire.

I knew a little about Helmand Province and the Taliban from some of the guys who had been out here earlier on Prelim Ops. Plus I'd done a bit of reading up on the area. Eastwards, the Helmand River creates a ribbon of green through arid desolation. Known colloquially as the Green Zone, it's where the majority of the population in Helmand live. Being where the people and the poppies are, it's also where the battle for hearts and minds must be won. The Taliban revival is at its strongest here: poppies are the most widely cultivated crop in Helmand Province, and it's the money from the drugs trade that finances the Taliban resurgence, buys their weapons and allows them to fight. Ultimately, it is why British Forces are here; not to fight the Taliban per se, but to create enough stability for development to take place.

Helmand Province consists of some fourteen districts, including Nad Ali, Gereshk, Sangin, Musa Qala, Naw Zad and Kajaki, with the provincial capital at Lashkar Gah a short hop from Camp Bastion. The governors for each district live in the District Centres or DCs, and it's in the DCs that the majority of British troops in Helmand are based, either in Platoon Houses, or Forward Operating Bases (FOBs). You can't ensure the security of an area and engage with the local population by hiding inside huge defensive garrisons like Bastion, or even the DCs, so the troops mount regular patrols so that they can build relationships with the local elders. Boots on the ground mean that it is harder for the Taliban to exert control.

It doesn't stop them trying though, and it's led to a pretty tough existence for a lot of our troops, who are being shot at and mortared on an almost daily basis while living in spartan conditions. A lot of the Platoon Houses and FOBs are little more than compounds without electricity or water.

We arrive at the IRT tent and Nichol follows us in as we dump our stuff.

Our role in theatre is to support the guys on the ground at the FOBs and Platoon Houses, principally through taskings such as those carried out by the task line at KAF – resupplies, moving troops, pax and freight from one place to another.

The IRT (Incident Response Team) was a UK military initiative born under the aegis of the UN Protection Force in Bosnia in the early 1990s. Its role then was to deliver engineers, medics and support to any situation where they were needed. The role eventually evolved to mimic that of HEMS London, which was the first civilian air ambulance in the UK to 'transport the hospital to the patient', rather than simply taking the patient to hospital.

That concept delivered a senior doctor and paramedic to the scene of major traumas – traffic collisions, shootings, stabbings – where they were able to perform life-saving surgical and medical interventions, stabilising patients for transfer to major trauma centres. It's well established that the victim's chances of survival increase markedly if they receive care within a short period of time after a severe injury – the so-called 'Golden Hour' of trauma medicine.

The Chinook is the helicopter of choice for the IRT in Afghanistan due to its capacity to transport people and kit and get them where they are most needed – fast. The IRT team includes the MERT

(Medical Emergency Response Team), which consists of up to four paramedics or senior nurses, usually led by a consultant anaesthetist or surgeon. They can be supplemented by two or three members of the resident RAF Fire and Rescue team, equipped with cutting equipment and other heavy-duty hydraulic gear – useful if troops are trapped inside the wreckage of vehicles following IED strikes. Finally, on every flight the IRT carries an element of force protection – soldiers from 3 Para whose job is to deploy as soon as the cab is on the ground and protect the aircraft and the medics as they work to get the casualty on board. The IRT is not an air ambulance; it's a flying, fighting ER.

It's a tough environment for the medics to work in – the back of a Chinook in the skies over Afghanistan has to be the most traumatic operating theatre in the world. It's cramped; it's dark; it's hot and noisy. Also, it's not the most stable of platforms, particularly if we're flying tactically. Then there's the prospect of turbulence, and the buffeting of the wind through the side doors and the open rear of the cab. All this, and then the threat from Taliban fighters on the ground firing small arms, heavy machine-guns and RPG rounds at the cab. At 99ft long, it represents a big and potentially valuable target to the Taliban, who will stop at nothing to bring one down; they're a veritable bull's-eye in the sky.

There's a disconnect on board the Chinooks between us, in the Plexiglass-walled goldfish bowls that serve as the cockpit, and our crewmen in the back of the aircraft. We need to see in front, above, around and below and you can't armour the glass – it's too heavy. The fuselage which serves as home to the loadmasters, though, is Kevlar-walled and floored, giving them and their cargo – be it soldiers, medics or kit – a degree of protection. And they need it; they're there to look after the safety of the passengers and the aircraft.

If they're not manning the guns, the crewmen usually assist the medics in trying to stabilise badly wounded casualties. Often they'll be confronted with a horrific collage of powdery dust, bodies, blood, appalling injuries and piercing screams. Their work environment is loud, dusty, hot, cramped and chaotic. By contrast, we're screened off by a canvas curtain, cocooned in our glass-encased cockpit, connected to the maelstrom behind us only via the audio in our headphones. Amid this disorder, it's our job to remain calm and composed, wringing clarity from the confusion so that we can get the cab and everyone in it back to the relative sanctuary of Camp Bastion where the casualties can be attended to by a full surgical team at Nightingale, the ten-million-pound state-of-the-art medical facility with its own HLS (helicopter landing site).

The IRT is a 24-hour, 365-day-a-year service. It lifts British soldiers, ISAF troops, members of the Afghan army and local civilians. It also flies to treat members of the Taliban. And as dogs play an extremely important role alongside British forces (they are able to sniff out roadside bombs and hidden ammunition stashes, but this also means that they are at risk of being hurt by Taliban fighters or IEDs), it will also recover them too.

Medicine, like justice, is blind.

Dogs injured in Afghanistan are flown to Camp Bastion, just like human soldiers. Humans take priority but injured dogs are rushed back as soon as possible and are taken to a small vet unit at Camp Bastion where two British vets can carry out emergency surgery. If longer-term treatment is needed they are flown to a veterinary hospital in Germany or to the Defence Animal Centre.

You hope for a quiet day when you're on duty because it means nobody needs you, but from what Nichol tells us, days like that are rare. They've been averaging four call-outs per day. It's a dynamic environment; sometimes you don't know where you're headed until you're airborne. And since, more often than not, you're flying in to pick up troops who have been shot or blown up, it's pretty certain that the same people that attacked them will want to have a pop at the big Chinook when it comes in to land.

Two Chinooks and two Apaches were on immediate readiness to respond, and for the duration of our tour on the IRT we would live and sleep in the IRT tent. It wasn't the height of luxury, but it was nothing like the basic privations that the lads on the front line had to put up with either. The tent was air-conditioned, with a Rola-Trac floor and eight cots. To help kill time, we'd have a fridge freezer for keeping food and drink cold; a well-stocked tuck box and kettle, with tea and a selection of coffees; big-screen LCD TV connected to BFBS, the British Forces TV channel, via satellite; a DVD player and library of films; books, magazines and a games console. I don't have this much stuff at home! The duty Apache crew and the MERT each had their own tents with a similar set-up. A short ladder took us over the Hesco wall, down the other side and across the dusty road and directly opposite was the JHF (A) Forward ops tent where we'd get our orders.

We would be living at the mercy of the phone. Two short rings means an admin call, but two long rings means a shout. If you need to shower, you go one at a time and take a radio. Ditto if you need the loo. And the same if you go for meals (although you can go en masse for those).

There were worse places to kill time.

9

HERCULEAN LOSS

It's been a quiet day so far.

'Fancy a brew, Frenchie?' Nichol asks.

'Nah,' I reply. 'But you can get me another bottle of water from the fridge. I'm fucking gasping!'

'Hello Bond, this is Blofeld. Our location now,' says the disembodied voice of the Joint Operations Centre (JOC) Watchkeeper from the radio.

'Fuck it, no time for a brew now,' says Nichol. 'Come on fellas, we've got a shout.'

Jonah and I get into the Land Rover that sits baking under the high afternoon sun outside our tent. Its thin metal skin burns my hand as I open the driver's door. While Nichol and Craig run to the JOC to get the details of the job, Jonah and I drive to the IRT cab to get her going.

I abandon the Landy at the edge of the pan and rush across the hard standing to the aircraft. 'Christ!' I think, as I see the MERT team sorting their kit inside the aircraft, 'I wasn't hanging about and they've beaten us here. Impressive.'

I do a quick walk-around, checking everything is as it should be – latches closed, no leaks, wheels okay, and no seepage of hydraulic fluid on the brakes. I also flick the FM aerials too; I'm a bit OCD about that and part of me thinks, 'If you don't flick the FM aerials you're going to crash, Alex.' I've always flicked them and I've never crashed – so, QED, it must be effective.

Pilots, superstitious? Who knew?!

On IRT, you set the aircraft up when you take over duty, so

58

most of the pre-flight checks are already done – time saved on the ground translates into a faster arrival time. My flying helmet sits on the centre console and my SA80 carbine is strapped to the side of my seat. My personal issue 9mm Browning lives in a holster on my thigh, but to be honest, if it ever comes down to a situation where I'd need to use it, I'd probably be better off throwing it instead of firing it. Everything is as we left it last night.

I climb into the right-hand seat, which I've already adjusted for height and reach, and secure myself into the five-point harness. 'Helmets,' I shout, signifying to Jonah that all conversation now will be via the intercom.

I mentally run through the pre-flight checks. A few minutes later, Nichol arrives with Craig and straps in. The engines are already up and running, the rotors turning, after start checks complete. All good.

'Okay, one of our Hercules C-130s has crashed at Lashkar Gah airfield about fifteen miles from here. We'll route with the AH, which is just starting up. We'll climb to height as soon as we depart Bastion and the Apache will follow us. He'll probably lag behind because we'll be at max chat. When we cross Lashkar Gah we'll turn away from the airfield, so we'll get good "eyes on", then we'll make our descent and run towards the airfield.'

'A Herc's crashed?' I ask. 'What the fuck?'

'Details are pretty sketchy at the moment, but it appears that it struck a mine under the runway on landing and exploded shortly after.'

'That runway at Lash isn't actually inside the base; it's a couple of miles away. The Brits only patrol it when flights are inbound and taking off, otherwise it's down to the ANP, so I imagine the security is pretty lax,' offers Jonah.

'We've got authorisation, so lift when ready,' Nichol tells me.

Ah, the weighty question of authorisation. If it was down to us as crew, we'd lift for every single ISAF casualty the minute we have a location, but it's never that simple to the higher-ups who have to balance the potential loss of a cab, its crew, the MERT and the QRF team against the life or lives that we might save.

They say that with rank goes responsibility and I guess that authorising the launch of the IRT is a graphic illustration of that maxim.

'Okay, we have six QRF and the MERT onboard. Clear above and behind,' says Craig.

'Lifting,' I say, pulling power. The Chinook lifts gracefully and effortlessly into the sky. Fifteen minutes from first call to lift-off.

Nichol calls Bastion to let them know we're on our way: 'Buzzard, Hardwood One Three, airborne on task at this time.'

I've just turned towards Lashkar Gah, which is no more than ten minutes flying time away, when the plan changes.

'Hardwood One Three, Buzzard. Change task. Footballs have been evacuated by vehicle to Viking. You are to route to Viking, pick up footballs and return to Normandy. Confirm copy?'

Nichol okays it and plots me a route to Viking, the British base at Lash, rather than the airfield. The 'footballs' are casualties and Normandy is Bastion. Straightforward enough.

'Okay mate, we're going to approach from the east,' Nichol advises me. 'You okay with it?'

I have a pretty good idea where Lashkar Gah is. I remember some markers on the run in from my TQ, so I say, 'Yeah, all good.'

The early evening haze lends everything a warm glow as I make my run in. The markers are all there: bright pink house; blue school; across the big avenue with a right turn at the big green house; pass the right-hand side of the mast; re-cross the avenue again for a left-hand turn and a quick stop and flare at Lashkar Gah.

Lesson one: Afghanistan isn't the UK, so air density and temperature mean the flare isn't going to be anywhere near as effective in scrubbing off my speed here as it is at home. My hands have just written a cheque that my talent can't pay.

It's a very public way of eating humble pie, but there's nothing else for it: I swallow my pride and overshoot, flying us through the HLS, a quick teardrop around, and I land on with Nichol looking at me, a wry smirk on his face. Oh well, I got us down. And I won't be making that mistake again!

We take on six casualties, all walking wounded but none serious. We're advised that there are more en route from the crash site, so Nichol makes an executive decision that we're not going to wait for them. It makes more sense to drop off the casualties we have and fly back for the others. If all things are equal, we should get back to Viking at the same time as the rest of the casualties.

So I lift and fly us back to Bastion. When I land at Nightingale, the ambulances are already waiting for us and swiftly move the casualties. There's no major trauma – some bruises and shock but that's about it.

More details come in as we sit on the pan at Bastion doing a rotors-turning refuel. The Hercules had flown from Kabul with an armoured car for the governor of Helmand on-board, along with seven aircrew and twenty passengers, including the governor's brother and His Excellency Mr Stephen Evans, HM Ambassador to Afghanistan. It was also carrying a sizeable amount of cash, which was destined for local warlords in exchange for their influence and intelligence. Apparently, the aircraft had barely touched down on the dirt runway when it was engulfed in flames, sending black smoke billowing into the sky. Afghan fire-fighters tackled the blaze, but ammunition in the hold was cooking off and exploding. When the fire was extinguished, all that remained was the Herc's tail section and the burnt-out carcass of the bullet-proof car.

An investigation later concluded that the aircraft was destroyed after detonating an anti-tank landmine buried in the surface of the runway, resulting in aircraft debris puncturing the port wing fuel tanks, leading to an uncontrollable fire. The aircraft captain managed to evacuate all the aircraft's passengers without major injury.

By now, it's early evening. The light is fading but it's not dark enough to warrant using NVGs. Nichol errs on the side of caution and tells the guys down the back to get them ready; if we're delayed for any reason at Lash, we'll need them for the return leg of the sortie.

Refuelling complete, I lift to height and fly us on a different route to Lashkar Gah – if the Taliban have eyes on, it's common sense to vary the direction of your approach. My route in is much better this time around – I pick my markers and come in from the south with a low-level sweeping left-hand turn that scrubs off our speed in plenty of time. This time I don't overshoot, and land on the target with a perfectly executed descent.

Some of the casualties from the crash are there when I touch down, but a handful are still on their way from the crash site, so we end up turning and burning on the HLS for ten minutes waiting for them. We don NVGs for the flight back, although the light's at that annoying level where it's not really dark enough for the goggles to be effective, but it's too dark for the Mk.1 Human Eyeball to see properly. It's not ideal for my first operational 'night' flight in theatre, but then this is a war zone and let's be honest, nothing is ideal here.

It is 22:00 by the time I land on at Nightingale. The casualties are transferred to the hospital and I transition to the pan, where we put the aircraft to bed. So concludes my first operational sortie in Afghanistan where I did something useful.

We're on sixty minutes notice to move on the IRT at night, thirty during the day, although the crews are always much quicker than that.

I remember thinking: 'If it carries on like this I might be able to cope with this Det.'

If. Such a small but significant word.

10

EYES WIDE SHUT

The next few days did nothing to dispel my optimism that my first Afghan Det was going to be relatively benign. I'd had a quiet first twenty-four hours on the IRT, and the following days saw some pretty routine taskings on the HRF. It was all good experience for me, as I was a far less capable pilot than I am now and some of the dust landings took me right to the edge of my ability. It was a steep learning curve, but flying with Nichol really opened my eyes to what was possible. He was, and is, an incredibly skilful pilot.

That first mission on the IRT opened my eyes too, in other ways. Having flown on ops in Iraq, I was used to flying in body armour, with my own sidearm and carbine, but I guess I'd never really considered that nurses and doctors would have to do the same. It's pretty fucked up when you think about it, doctors and nurses carrying weapons, because although they work within the accords of the Hippocratic axiom '*Primum non nocere*' – 'Above all, do no harm' – they may be forced into taking a life in order to preserve one.

I was getting into my stride on the admin front too. Communication with home was quite good, considering. We had email, and every soldier, sailor and airman in theatre got twenty minutes a week of free phone calls (since increased to thirty minutes). Alison and I were luckier than most – because of her role in the Cabinet Office, she had a phone on her desk connected to the Military Network so we could talk pretty much at will.

The next couple of weeks passed in a blur, with quite a few taskings which, although they threatened much, didn't come to anything. They were all instructive and educational in their own way though, whether in terms of improving my skills as a pilot or opening my eyes to the weird and bizarre reality of life in Helmand Province. I flew a sortie on May 25th with Nichol which had me a bit worried, because it was the first sortie I'd flown where there was a clear and present danger from the Taliban.

A 3 Para platoon had gone out on a recce just north of what would later become the HLS at Sangin. They were patrolling in vehicles and a Pinzgauer High Mobility ATV had become bogged down at a wadi where it crossed the Helmand River. It was causing Lt Col Stuart Tootal, the 3 Para CO, a rather large headache, and we were in the frame to be his painkiller.

The mission was a good example of the 'small picture' effect, and the frustration that it puts on those of us at the lower end of the command chain. There were probably very good reasons why Col Tootal wanted the vehicle recovered, but we couldn't for the life of us imagine what they might be. To me, the solution seemed simple, and I said as much to Nichol as we were flying in towards the stricken truck: 'Can't we just drop a bomb on it and deny it to the enemy that way?' He was of the same view, but those at the JOC had other ideas.

So we flew on in tactical formation with the Apache, call sign Ugly Five Zero; our mission, to deliver some troops from the JHSU (Joint Helicopter Support Unit) to assess what the options were for recovering the Pinzgauer. We were flying well above the threat from small arms fire (SAFIRE), but there are other threats, and the Apache was picking up a lot of what we call ICOM chatter – basically, radio traffic between Taliban groups. The radio intercepts told us that the Taliban were moving into position and were about two klicks away; they'd been seen with weapons and heard saying that they wanted to have a go at the aircraft.

Nichol was the handling pilot. For me, it was my first experience of being under direct threat and it wasn't a nice feeling. Knowing that there are some demented, well-armed fuckers on the ground who want to shoot you out of the sky – and that they're close by – is not something you'd wish on your worst enemy. Well actually, given that the Taliban are my worst enemy, maybe I would.

The mission just didn't make sense to me. Why question the wisdom in scrambling us to rescue wounded troops because of the threat to the aircraft and crew, yet send us into the jaws of death to rescue a £40,000 vehicle that had already been 'cleaned' by the crew that abandoned it? All the doors and windows had gone, so it was little more than a chassis with six wheels, a back end and a steering wheel. Why go into the hover to try and pick up a worthless vehicle when there was a better than even chance we'd be taking fire, risking the four of us and our £15,000,000 cab? It was madness.

The ICOM chatter was increasing, the sun had dipped below the horizon, and we knew that if we didn't pick the vehicle up, it would only pass the problem on to someone else. Bastion was telling us that if we didn't do the job, they'd have to send in reinforcements to spend the night guarding the vehicle. What to do? Do we let twenty-four poor sods spend the night outside waiting for an attack, or do we go in and do it as ordered?

Nichol made the call: 'We're going to do this. I'm going to do a zero speed approach right next to the truck; we'll throw a strop out to the Joint Helicopter Support Squadron guys, it'll take them a few seconds to attach it to the hook and then we can lift.'

I was gripped with fear; convinced that we'd be sat there in the hover and some Taliban fighter would come out of the bushes and release an RPG straight through the arse of the aircraft. I had no frame of reference for this, so my mind played all sorts of tricks on me, none of which were remotely useful. It's fight or flight, but what do you do when every cell of your being is telling you 'flight', yet running isn't an option? You get on with it.

Nichol did an absolutely beautiful landing; absolutely fucking nailed it, putting the aircraft right next to the Pinzgauer. The crewman already had the floor hatch open with the hook ready. He chucked the strop under the aircraft, the JHSU ran out, secured the truck, and as soon as they were back in he raised the ramp. No fucking around. As soon as the guys were back on board, Nichol pulled power and did a beautifully smooth straight up and right. It was a beautiful bit of flying, no corrections required.

I've no idea how but we got away with it. I think it was down to how quickly it all happened and the fact that it was done so well. The enemy simply didn't have time to get into position. We were all the way there and halfway back by the time they arrived. I was hanging out of my arse when we shut the cab down back at Bastion, but I'd turned a corner and learned something. The threat was becoming more real and I knew it was only a matter of time before we took fire. It's a cliché, but I knew we'd have to keep being lucky, whereas the Taliban only needed to be lucky once.

It was around this time that the Taliban intensified their attacks on the towns of Now Zad and Musa Qala, and it was being reported that Now Zad in particular was about to fall. The governor of Helmand province, Mohammad Daoud, urged Brigadier Ed Butler, the commander of 16 Air Assault Brigade, to defend government positions in both places.

Butler was reluctant to do so because Lt Col Tootal's 3 Para were already overstretched, and it was tactically unsound to see the small force that he had available being tied down to two fixed positions in remote outstations. Daoud threatened to resign over the issue, which would have caused the UK government – who had pressed for his appointment in the first place – some embarrassment. Butler was in an impossible position; in the end, he had to relent, dispatching B Company, 3 Para to protect Now Zad and a small force to Musa Qala. We were starting to feel the pinch as both 3 Para and the Chinook Force had finite resources available. There were a total of just six Chinooks available in theatre, so helicopter hours were scarce, and 3 Para were dangerously overstretched.

We'd been engaged to support their move into the newly established Platoon Houses and were flying supplies in, using underslung loads. We were flying as a four-ship: two Chinooks – Splinter

Two Five (Nichol and I) and Splinter Two Six; and two Apaches to support us – Ugly Five Zero and Ugly Five One.

We were increasingly glad of the Apaches that accompanied us on every mission. The Apache helicopter is a revolutionary development in the history of war. It is essentially a flying tank – a helicopter designed to survive heavy attack and inflict massive damage. It can zero in on specific targets, day or night, even in terrible weather. It's a terrifying machine to the Taliban, who call it 'The Mosquito', and for whom it vies with the Chinook as the aircraft that they would most like to shoot down.

The Apache's main function in battle is to close with the enemy and kill them, and it's a particularly personal form of killing for the pilots who, along with snipers, are the only two combatants to get a detailed look at the faces of the men they are about to kill. A sniper fixes his quarry in the crosshairs of the sight on his bolt-action rifle; the Apache crew watch theirs in close-up on a five-inch square screen in the cockpit before they pull the trigger. The main fixed armament is a 30mm M230 Chain Gun under the aircraft's nose. It can also carry a mixture of AGM-114 Hellfire missiles, and Hydra 70 rocket pods on four hard points mounted on its stub-wing pylons.

One of its most impressive features is the helmet mounted display (HMD), which has a clip-on arm that drops a monocle-like screen in front of the pilot's right eye. Instrument readings from around the cockpit are projected on to it and, at the flick of a button, a range of other images can also be superimposed underneath the glow of the instrument symbology, replicating the Apache's camera images and the radar's targets.

The monocle leaves the pilot's left eye free to scan the world outside the cockpit. The HMD has one other major advantage: at the flick of a switch, it enables the Apache's weapons systems to slave to either pilot's line of sight. In each corner of the cockpit, sensors detect exactly where the right eye is looking and lock the weapons systems to the pilot's eye-line. At the HMD's centre is a crosshair sight, and as the pilot's eye moves, so too, for example, does the Apache's 30mm cannon, which swivels to point wherever the pilot is looking. Look at the target, pull the trigger and that's where the rounds will land. If the Chinooks represented Cold War technology at its best, the AHs were the latest word in cutting edge.

A few hundred metres south of the DC at Now Zad was a small hillock with commanding views over the town, which had previously been manned by the Afghan National Police. It was known by everyone as ANP Hill and we had to drop off some pax there. First though, we had to drop an underslung load at the Patrol House in the DC. It's a sortie I'll never forget because I witnessed an incident at ANP Hill that really opened my eyes to one of the uglier elements of Afghan culture.

I was flying from the right-hand seat with Nichol on the left, and made my approach to Now Zad. We landed first while Splinter Two Six remained in the overhead to offer us an extra degree of protection. As I came in to drop the load, we were completely enveloped by what seemed to be the biggest dust cloud in the world! The target compound was ankle-deep in really powdery sand, and the height of the walls and the compound's size both conspired to channel the dust vertically. What normally happens is that it builds gradually from the rear, but with this it was like someone had thrown a switch and we went from no dust with clear visibility to a complete brownout. How I managed to put the load down in the middle of the compound without breaking anything is anyone's guess, but I was pretty chuffed about it.

Having dropped the load, I rapidly transitioned away and thought myself lucky that I was first aircraft in and not the second. As Splinter Two Six came in, they got exactly the same as us, only worse, because they also had to contend with the dust cloud that we'd whipped up as we departed. Still, things aren't meant to be easy – they just 'are', so you do what you have to.

With both underslung loads dropped, we landed on ANP Hill, turning and burning while our pax – a mortar platoon from the

Ghurkhas that would be manning a position there – walked off. Almost out of nowhere, we were surrounded by a wall of people. It was the first time that the Chinooks had been into Now Zad, so I guess we created something of a spectacle. Dozens of women and children came out to look at the aircraft.

There was an ANP patrol milling around. Some of them engaged with the Ghurkhas that we'd dropped off, while others just stood and watched us. Then one decided he wanted to take a picture of us and started walking towards the aircraft from the front. Bear in mind that we're on a hill, so the tips of the forward rotor blades were about four foot off the ground at their lowest point. Spinning at 225rpm, walk into one of those, as this clown was close to doing, and they'd cleave your head from your shoulders as easily as a hot knife through butter.

Everything happened in slow motion. We were frantically trying to motion to this ANP fellow, who was completely oblivious to the dangers and to our attempts to attract his attention. Fortunately for him, one of the British troops on the hill saw what we were doing and unceremoniously grabbed the Afghan policeman from behind and pulled him to the ground. There was no time to explain what he was doing – it was grab him or watch him die, so this Brit basically saved the guy's life. But the policeman didn't quite see things that way. He'd been trying to be clever, showing off about how close he could get, but he'd lost face in front of his mates. Worse, the women and children in the crowd saw it too.

Predictably, the guy's mates were all laughing at him, much as I guess would happen had the characters in this particular saga been British or French. In that case, the guy who'd been dragged back would probably just have got up, thanked the guy who saved his life and laughed it off. Not this guy.

Instead, he headed towards the women and children who, although still about seventy metres away from us, were gradually edging closer. And what happened next stunned me. Instead of telling the women to get back, the ANP attacked them, using their AK-47s and batons to hit them. Faces, heads, bodies, legs

– they didn't care where they hit them. Bear in mind, these were the very people they were supposed to be protecting. They went about their task as though born to it, and the attack was vicious. But hey, they demonstrated their masculinity and I'm sure the guy who lost face felt a lot better. So that was alright then.

Nichol and I were incensed, but we were completely helpless; framed by the windscreen and with the sound muted by the noise from our aircraft it was like watching a particularly misogynistic and violent snuff movie. I'd have happily drawn my weapon and shot the guy; fuck the consequences. We'd come with the best of intentions, all about hearts and minds and winning over the local population, and this is what we had to confront: not only the evil of the Taliban, but the pig ignorance and violence shown by the narrow-minded idiots in the ANP. And they were supposed to be 'onside'! What really got me was the knowledge that to those in the crowd, we were now guilty by association. That I really found hard to accept. It left a really sour taste in my mouth.

11

EMERALD BEAUTY

Much of what followed was a series of relatively straightforward taskings out of KAF; straightforward, but never mundane. How can anything be mundane when you tackle every sortie as if you're going to war – armoured up, armed and with eyes on stalks waiting for the shots that are going to blow you out of the sky?

It's amazing how quickly you adjust. Even at this point of the tour, less than two weeks after arriving, I could already see how much I'd advanced. Not just in terms of my flying – I was acquiring more and more knowledge of extreme tactical manoeuvres and becoming more proficient in executing them – but also in terms of my mindset. I had a frame of reference now; I'd flown missions where intelligence said the Taliban were waiting for us, and although nothing had happened, you only know that with the benefit of hindsight. For each sortie I flew with the expectation of something happening. It was a tick in the box; I'd done what I'd trained to do and I hadn't been found wanting. Some people might call it courage. But what is courage, after all? I've heard it said that bravery is being the only one who knows you're afraid. To me, that isn't bravery, it's leadership. It's what being an officer is all about.

Every sortie I flew, I flew aggressively. That might sound nonsensical, but just as you can drive a car aggressively, so you can fly an aircraft like that too – even one as big and heavy as the Chinook. I had good teachers in the captains I flew with and I'm a perfectionist – if I learned a new trick, or another aggressive way to scrub speed off in as short a distance as possible, I honed it until it was second nature. Every mission was about doing it to the best of my ability, learning something from it and acting as aggressively as possible so as to deter the enemy from having a go. Every day we stayed alive was a day that we learned something.

The view from the office was something I never tired of either. Despite the risks – aviation per se is a risky business; military aviation the riskiest of all – I still feel privileged to do what I do and one of the best aspects of flying in Afghanistan was the ability to forget, if only for a few seconds, the reality of the conflict we found ourselves in and just take in the majesty and breathtaking, forbiddingly beautiful vista of Kajaki from the air.

The Kajaki Dam is a particularly important asset in Helmand, providing as it does the water that irrigates the Helmand Valley, and satisfying the demand for electricity for the whole province. Along with Musa Qala, Sangin and Now Zad, it came under increasing and prolonged attacks from the Taliban, who were effectively laying siege to it. Night after night, they would launch mortar attacks against the small contingent of the Afghan National Army (ANA) and the private security team led by an American contractor who defended it. Colonel Tootal was under pressure to bolster its defences but simply didn't have a spare company to deploy there: they were all committed elsewhere.

The stunning beauty of Kajaki has to be seen to be believed, and is a startling contrast to the arid, dusty landscape that surrounds it. The dam itself was built by the US in 1953 and further developed in 1975. It holds back the melt water that flows from the Hindu Kush in a mammoth lake of the most intense aquamarine hue. The water then flows through the single working turbine, generating enough power to serve the demands of those in the valley, and emerging in a torrent of foaming white water that feeds into the crystal clear waters of the Helmand River.

Its remarkable beauty belies an incredibly violent past, although the signs are there if you look carefully enough. The minefields laid by the Soviets delineate the surrounding countryside and are as deadly a threat now as when they were laid. But the most chilling element of the Kajaki complex is a building just outside the perimeter known as the Russian House.

When the Soviets retreated towards the end of the war, a detachment of young soldiers who had been holding the strategically important dam were cut off. They fought wave after wave of attacks by Mujahideen fighters, but eventually they ran out of ammunition and were overrun. The Afghan fighters broke through the barricades to the ground floor and brutally butchered the soldiers they found there; it's said that they were flayed alive while their friends and colleagues upstairs had to endure the agony of their screams. It's thought that those upstairs were fed into the fans of the turbine. The walls, ceiling and doors bear witness to the last few bitter, desperate hours of the fight, pockmarked and scarred with scores of bullet holes and shrapnel damage.

These days, the handful of defenders at Kajaki enjoyed a miserable existence thanks to the Taliban's regular mortar attacks, and the ANA were starting to get jittery. My first run-up to the dam came about when I was on the IRT and we got a call to pick up an ANA soldier with a minor bullet wound. The flight from Bastion to Kajaki takes about half an hour or so. Once we were across the Desert North of Bastion, we'd transition to height and fly over the Green Zone, which is quite stunning when viewed from altitude. The Helmand River snakes across the landscape and a sea of green radiates from its banks to a distance of about 10km or so – lush, verdant vegetation and crops. The locals and Taliban both depend on it. But either side of the Green Zone lies arid desert – a flat nothingness.

Shortly after leaving the Green Zone behind, the route takes you through the Sangin Valley, and it's around here that the topography starts to change. Suddenly, sharp crags appear as the valley floor rises up to a series of vertiginous peaks. The ground looks barren and dry, a canvas of ochre, beige and sand as far as the eye can see. Suddenly, the landscape changes dramatically and you're confronted with the majestic beauty of Kajaki Lake. The colour of the water – a rich, vivid aquamarine that changes from a deep emerald to turquoise, depending on the position of the sun – takes your breath away and is perfectly framed by what appear to be luscious sandy shores. If they ever get the security situation in

Afghanistan squared away, Kajaki would make the perfect holiday destination. There'd be no shortage of ex-RAF aircrew wanting to set up jet-ski schools on the lake.

You drop down low as you turn on finals for either of the two bases at Kajaki – Broadsword and Lancaster – and with the sun high in the sky, you get a perfect shadow of the aircraft below you in the water. It's a tricky run in – there are a lot of wires to negotiate, a sharp descent downhill as the land falls away beneath you, and a ruined crane (another hangover from the Soviet occupation) to avoid. It requires some highly technical, precision flying; otherwise you could find yourself too high and too fast, with the aircraft literally running away from you in the latter stages.

The ANA we picked up on that first sortie had a highly suspect bullet wound to his foot and he became the first of many. With the Taliban subjecting the defenders to a nightly barrage of mortar fire, I think that some of the ANA decided that some self-inflicted minor gunshot wounds were just the thing to get them a break from the action. Either that, or their weapons hadn't been zeroed in years and the sights were way, way out of line.

Eventually, Col Tootal would have to find the numbers from within 3 Para to properly man the bases at Kajaki, but that was a few weeks away at this stage. At the time, he simply didn't have sufficient men to provide a company, so he came up with what was quite an audacious and effective plan to neuter the threat from the Taliban mortar team.

A small force of two mortar teams, a platoon of infantry and a machine-gun section was hastily assembled and smuggled into the base under cover of darkness. Then they waited for the Taliban's next barrage of fire. They didn't have long to wait. Once the force had been fired on, they returned fire and their salvo landed directly among the Taliban mortar team that only a few minutes previously had sought to cause death and destruction among the men defending the dam. Several of the Taliban were killed outright, with many wounded. A few of the survivors sought refuge in a reed bed along the banks of the River Helmand, but they ran right into the sights of the machine-gun section, which quite happily opened up on them. Those who weren't cut straight down by the barrage of 7.62mm rounds ran straight out into another salvo of mortar rounds from the team. When the firing stopped, twelve Taliban fighters lay dead and several others lay severely wounded. They'd been caught with their trousers down and 3 Para made them pay the ultimate penalty. The attacks against the base stopped and for a period of several weeks the small force defending Kajaki had room to breathe. By the time the Taliban had regrouped, Col Tootal had deployed 'A' Company, 3 Para to defend the base. The Taliban's days of free rein around the dam were at an end.

I called Alison for a chat at the end of May and she answered the call with the news I'd been waiting for: 'We're having a boy!' She'd been for a scan and we were going to have a son. I was ecstatic; from that moment on, my world changed irrevocably. Every day became about survival – even more so than before. Surviving each day so that I'd be able to fly home and watch my wife give birth became the ultimate focus for me. When I put the phone down, I could barely contain myself. I ran straight to the crew tent where Woodsy, Craig and Nichol were kicking around.

'It's a boy!' I shouted, to which, almost to a man, they said, 'Oh, has she given birth then?' Morons!

12

POKING THE HORNETS' NEST

Operation Mutay was 3 Para Battle Group's first major pre-planned operation since deploying to Helmand Province. Its aims were simple: a cordon and search op focused on a mud-walled residential compound about 3km east of Now Zad, in an area consisting of dense orchards, irrigation ditches and inter-connected walled compounds.

Intelligence indicated the compound was the base for a Taliban High Value Target (HVT). It was thought it was being used as a weapon and ammunition dump, bomb-making facility and safe house for insurgent commanders all rolled into one. The intel also suggested that the majority of the Taliban HVT's fighters had melted away following the arrival of British troops in the Now Zad DC. The intel was wrong.

We knew something was afoot on June 3rd, the day before the operation was planned, because there was a lot of coming and going and all the Flight's captains kept disappearing. Nichol Benzie finally briefed us later that evening; we received our orders for the operation, which would turn out to be one of the defining battles of the Paras' tour, with a six-hour firefight that involved almost everyone.

The plan involved a hundred or so men, encompassing 3 Para's 'A' Company and Patrols Platoon and a platoon of the Royal Ghurkha Rifles, together with some Afghan National Police. The Ghurkhas were based with the ANP in Now Zad District Centre so they, together with Patrols Platoon, were tasked with moving forward and establishing an outer perimeter. Our role was to insert

'A' Company into the compound, which they would then assault and capture. Air support would be provided by the Army Air Corps Apaches together with A-10 Warthogs and B-1 Bombers from the US.

We were all quite keyed up because this represented a break from the usual diet of taskings and IRT – something proactive. It was also to be the Apaches first offensive op in theatre. The briefing, led by Lt Col Tootal at the JOC, was packed with everyone from 'A' Company there, right up to the level of Section Commander. On the RAF side, there were the crews for the four Chinooks that would be inserting 'A' Company – Nichol Benzie and Mike Woods; Andy Lamb and Chris Hasler; Dave Stewart and Mark Heal; and Craig Wilson and me. The IRT crew was also there – they'd be on standby to scramble for any medevacs (medical evacuations). There were also four Apache crews – at any one time there would be two in the air, with two on standby at Bastion to provide continuity of cover when they needed to return to rearm and refuel.

Stuart Tootal introduced the orders, which basically boiled down to us inserting 'A' Company, who would flush out any HVTs at the compound. Any that were missed would be picked up by the troops manning the outer perimeter. The lift was planned for 12:00hrs and our mission meant each of us carrying a third of 'A' Company – roughly thirty men each. Nichol and Woodsy's role was to provide an airborne Command and Control platform for Lt Col Tootal.

We left Bastion on time the following day in a gaggle formation of four Chinooks, with the two Apaches (call signs Ugly Five Zero and Five One). As soon as we were over open desert, the crewmen in each cab test fired their Miniguns and M60s and made sure they were cocked and ready.

We flew a straight route north-north-west towards Now Zad and then held at a point about 10km south of the target, waiting for the Ghurkhas and Patrols Platoon to get into position. Nichol and Woodsy took up a position on overwatch at altitude while we, together with the two remaining cabs, dropped to low level and used a steep hill to mask us from any potential dickers while we held, flying in a figure of eight.

As it turned out, both the Ghurkhas and Patrols Platoon had encountered heavy resistance as they drove towards their respective positions and became involved in rolling contacts. We had our own issues, though nothing like as dangerous as people shooting at us from close range, like the guys on the ground were experiencing. Because the three of us were in a tight figure-of-eight holding pattern, our respective DAS kept mistaking the other cabs for missiles, so whenever we passed one another we were all pumping out flares. That was easily dealt with, but it was an obstacle we could have done without.

You can imagine after about twenty minutes of holding the tension is starting to build and the adrenaline is kicking in. We are on radio silence so there is no banter between the cabs and not much between the crews; we are all focused on what we have to do. Finally, we get the call to go. We are number two in the formation so we slot in behind Andy's cab on a north-easterly heading with 50ft on the light and 40 on the noise at about 120 knots. You have to strike a balance on a job like this – we would prefer to fly quicker but that would mean a rougher transit and it's no good delivering the troops so shaken up that they're not ready for combat.

When we are three minutes from the drop point, the crewmen in the back of the cabs give the troops a three-minute warning so they can organise themselves and their kit – check weapons and ammo and basically get themselves ready to run straight out the back as soon as the ramp drops. Craig gives the crewmen their Fire Control Orders.

'Okay guys, you are clear to engage any target you see is dangerous. I would rather you wait for my orders or advise me of potential threats first. However, if the delay caused by you doing so means that a potential threat is going to endanger the aircraft, you have

Sitting in the cockpit of a Mk3 Chinook at RAF Odiham. Note the cyclic control by my hands, and the collective lever by my left leg. September 2010.

Captain Jo Gordon, an Apache pilot from 653 Squadron Army Air Corps, stands beside her aircraft at Camp Bastion. The Apache AH1 is at the cutting edge of technology and can detect, classify and prioritise up to 256 potential targets in a matter of seconds.

An Apache AH1 approaches Camp Bastion after providing overwatch on a mission involving the Chinooks just visible behind. RAF Chinooks in Helmand Province always fly with a wingman for protection, and an Apache AH1 to provide heavier firepower in overwatch.

The breathtaking beauty of the topography surrounding Kajaki Lake. Its emerald crystal-clear waters feed into the Helmand River, which rises in the Hindu Kush and runs for over 700 miles through Afghanistan.

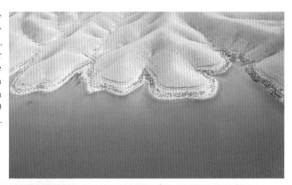

Members of the Joint Helicopter Support Unit at Camp Bastion prepare to attach an underslung load to a Chinook for a resupply run to Sangin.

Carrying essential supplies for Operation Ghartse Palang as an underslung load on short finals to FOB Inkerman.

The view from the office at 120ft as I fly over the sluice gate on finals to land at Kajaki. Note the side of the mountain to my right.

Banking hard left over Kajaki Lake for the approach to the HLS at Lancaster on a routine sortie to insert some troops.

Fast and Low over the surface of Kajaki Lake on a routine sortie to drop some troops at the Broadsword HLS.

...rewman Flt Sgt Galvin takes in the view as his Chinook departs the Forward Operating Base Kajaki Dam, which is just visible below.

IRT Tent. Our home for the 24–48 hours that we spend on IRT duty. Our detritus lays all around, the TV plays to an empty tent. Everything is left as it was when the call came to scramble.

The rear of the IRT cab, loaded with the MERT's life-saving kit. The MERT is the most advanced first-response airborne combat medical team in the world.

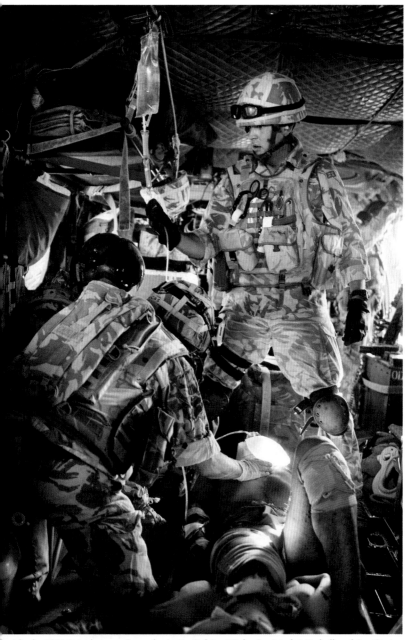

Inside the IRT, British Army Anaesthetist Lt Col Ian Hicks, Sgt Mark Mitchell and Sgt Gavin of the MERT attend injured ANA Sgt Quem Abdulh en route to Camp Bastion. Sgt Abdulh suffered multiple shrapnel wounds from a roadside bomb.

Yours truly, standing next to my cab on the 2008 Det. Note the Minigun in the door behind me.

My crew for the first half of my 2008 Det. From left: Flt Lt Pete Winn, Sgt J Fulton, FS Mick Fry and yours truly.

my authority to open fire without reference as per the Rules of Engagement.'

The RoE are something that most people back home never think about, but they define every element of how we operate in theatre. Adherence means you stay legal. Failure to observe them leaves you personally liable to murder charges and court martial. The firing of weapons in theatre for any given scenario has to be cleared by lawyers in the Army Adjutant General's Corps, and we operate under clear legal constraints; the RoE give us clearly defined parameters as to when we can engage those identified as enemy and pre-planned ops have to be cleared in advance. The lawyers want to know everything before they'll grant us authority to operate under less restrictive rules – what's the worst-case scenario in terms of collateral damage, risk to civilians etc. Ultimately, we can return fire at anybody firing at us, but with certain provisos.

Mostly, it's all about proportionality, and that means using the most appropriate weapon for the job. It's not so much of an issue for an infantryman armed with an SA80, a 9mm sidearm and some grenades, or even for us, given that the cabs only have machine-guns on them. But it's a real issue for the Forward Air Controllers who direct and coordinate close air support. They can bring a disproportionate weight of firepower to bear on any target, so it's imperative that they are meticulous about what they use and how it's directed. It's all about using the minimum force to achieve the objective, which basically means that you can't use a 2,000lb bomb or Hellfire missile on a lone Taliban gunman if you've got a less destructive weapon available.

The target compound that we're headed for is L-shaped. About 30m due north is a field roughly 150m wide, 100 deep – Chris and Andy plus Craig and me will be landing there, while Dave and Mark will be landing at a smaller field about 200m to the south-west. I wanted to line our cab up on a south–north heading so that when the ramp came down, the troops could run straight off with their weapons pointing toward the target compound rather than landing front or side on, where they'd have wasted valuable seconds looking for it.

I brief Craig on the run in, having acquainted myself with the route via intel pictures and maps: 'Okay, you want to turn left now, head west and maintain low level. In ten seconds you're going to see a track – there you go – and you're looking for three buildings close together.'

'Roger that. Got them.'

'Okay, I've got the compound. At the next compound turn right and head north.'

We're running in to the target with a minute to go now. I can see the village building up below as more and more compounds appear closer and closer together, often linked one to the next. There are no women or children around and I feel the hairs on the back of my neck stand up. It's nothing I can put my finger on, more a general sense that we're in the 'Badlands' and people are going to start shooting at us.

We're on the approach now. Craig says, 'Okay, I'm going to delay to see what dust we get from Andy as he lands on, then we'll slot in.'

Andy goes in and there's no dust whatsoever so we go straight in next to him. Craig flies in carrying a lot of speed but it's tactically sound – it's more aggressive and dynamic but a moving target is harder to hit. He flares the aircraft, standing it on its tail and using the belly of the cab to scrub off speed.

'Okay mate, 50ft and 22kts, you're in the gate. Commencing the approach; 40ft and 16kts.'

The rear crew come in with height calls: '20ft; 10; 8; 6; 5; 4; 2.'

We're bracing ourselves for a dust cloud that doesn't come. A slight bump as the wheels settle on and the suspension compresses slightly and a metre or so of run on. Craig applies the brakes, the rear ramp goes down and, in less than five seconds, all thirty of the fully-armed and kitted up Paras who were sitting in the cab have charged off. Their blood is up; they sense the enemy and they want to get at them. They're off the cab like rats up a drainpipe.

It's the first time I've landed in an enemy compound and I can feel my heart pounding in my chest. It isn't always about what happens; more often it's about the expectation, the foreknowledge there are people out there with weapons locked and loaded and pointed at you. The Taliban are synonymous with Rocket Propelled Grenades or RPGs – a weapon we very much fear because they could really ruin our day.

RPGs are exceptionally light, portable and easy to operate. The launcher is little more than a 3ft steel pipe with a grip and trigger about halfway along and a cone at the rear to dissipate the blast that a round produces on launch. They fire unguided rockets carrying a high-explosive warhead that detonates on impact. They were designed as anti-tank weapons, but being inert and non-sentient they don't get hung up on what they're used against. One of those hitting a Chinook is either going to break the cab in two or blow us out of the sky. Neither option is particularly appealing. The downside for the operator is that they're inaccurate over distance, so he needs to be quite close to the target to have any chance of a hit. That means he's going to be exposed and visible.

My eyes are darting all over the front and sides of the aircraft looking for threats – enemy gunmen or RPGs lining up or coming out of the wood line immediately ahead of us.

'Come on,' I say out loud. We're a sitting duck here, except we're loaded with ammunition for the guns and 1,600kg of fuel, so we're like a duck sitting on a bomb.

As soon as the Paras' feet touch the ground, the radio sparks into life with calls of 'Contact, Contact!' as they're engaged. So much for the intelligence that said resistance should be light to non-existent. There are enemy in various positions and the Paras are taking heavy fire from inside the compound. We're immediately behind them so that means we're taking fire too.

'Scan your arcs, guys. If you see a threat, take it out,' Craig warns the crewmen. It's daylight, so tracer doesn't show and you can't hear the telltale 'crack' of rounds coming in over the noise of the blades. The only way you know you're taking fire is either from the 'tink' sound that rounds make when they penetrate the skin of the aircraft, or the spiderweb of cracked glass that occurs when they hit the windscreen or chin bubble. Basically, you're either going to be dead or wise after the event. I think the only thing that saves us that day is the fact that we are shielded from view of the enemy by the height of the compound wall.

'Ramp up, clear above and behind,' from the back. And not a second too soon.

'Pulling power, lifting,' says Craig and we're up.

Due to concerns over dust from Andy's aircraft, the brief is for us to depart to our 12 o'clock for a sharp left-hand turn followed by a climb to fly south at height, but Craig decides that, as there is no dust, he's going to depart with a right-hand turn and fly over a 1,500ft high range of hills to the East of Now Zad and hold in this area. It's a spur-of-the-moment decision, made on impulse, that quite possibly saves our lives. As we later learn, an enemy team were dug in with an RPG at around the point where, had we departed and turned left as briefed, we'd have been flying at 50ft at around 20kts. Had we followed our planned route, we'd have been low and slow, directly over them at the most vulnerable stage of our departure, giving the RPG firer an unobstructed shot at the cab's underside. It would have been like shooting fish in a barrel. Unfortunately for the Taliban, the team was overrun and killed by Paras.

Meanwhile, Lt Col Tootal had discovered that the Chinook is a far from ideal Command and Control platform, due to its poor comms fit (no secure radio at that time) and poor visibility. Nichol therefore landed near to where 'A' company had been inserted and the 3 Para CO joined Major Will Pike, 'A' Company's officer commanding on the ground, where he felt better able to coordinate events. Nichol was called in to extract a Taliban prisoner so he returned to Bastion.

We fly a holding pattern for a while in case we are required to perform a medevac, but our fuel level gets dangerously close to bingo so we return to Bastion and shut down. The plan is for us to stand down and be ready to lift again three hours later to extract the Paras but as the aphorism goes, no battle plan survives first contact with the enemy. At this point, all the ground units – Patrols Platoon, 'A' Company, the Ghurkhas and ANP – are engaged in protracted firefights with large numbers of determined enemy forces.

There is no proper pan at Bastion at this stage, so the cabs just sit on what is essentially a large gravel pit. We don't know when we'll be required so we stay close, removing our helmets and body armour and wearing our flying suits tied around our waists. We gather by our cabs and chat among ourselves, releasing the pent-up tension that's left over when the adrenaline subsides. We debrief, talking about how well the mission went, what lessons we've learned, what we can do better next time.

Mark Heal and Dave Stewart missed their target and ended up landing in the wrong compound about 300 metres away from where they were supposed to be. Nobody died; their element of 'A' Company worked out where they were and made their way over the ground to their starting position, but it's an easy mistake to make out there – it's an exceptionally difficult place to navigate in and you're relying on the GPS, which in Mark and Dave's case was running on the wrong setting. Aviation has to be a no-blame culture. That way, every-one is honest about their mistakes and you learn from them. It can, and does, happen to everyone.

We see the first two Apaches return for rearming and refuelling so we know that the fighting is pretty hardcore. This is the first time the Apaches have been used in anger out here but word is that they have impressed both the pilots and, perhaps more impor-tantly, the guys on the ground. It was reported that there were many in the MoD, Government and the military who wondered where the Apaches could possibly fit in the great scheme of things. They had the potential to be another military white elephant, but very quickly they are proving themselves adaptable, fearsome and indispensable.

Eventually, we get the call and lift off to return to Now Zad. About ten miles out, I see a massive cloud of black smoke hover-ing in the haze. I'm wondering what has caused it and thinking there must have been the mightiest firefight. Is it a vehicle? Is it on our side, or the enemy's? It turns out that it's a very dry field that has just taken the wrath of an Apache's 30mm HE cannon. Several Taliban lay dead in it and the tinder-dry stubble has caught fire.

By this point, Craig and I have progressed to the west side of the town at height and are looking down on events below, when I become aware of a voice over the radio coordinating close air support down on the ground. Its call sign is Widow Seven Zero, a Joint Terminal Air Controller or JTAC, known colloquially as a Forward Air Controller. The call sign belongs to Flt Lt Matt Carter, an officer in the RAF Regiment attached to 3 Para who will go on to be awarded the Military Cross in part for his actions on this mission.

He was with Patrols Platoon. They had come under heavy contact from a number of enemy combatants based in and around a farmhouse. The platoon had got to within a few metres of the house but then became pinned down in two groups behind two walls, separated by a gap of about fifty metres. He was trying to call in some air support to deal with the guys in the farmhouse but was unable to at that stage because he couldn't be certain of the Paras' exact locations. Also, the walls they were taking cover behind were only thirty metres away from the house so they were Danger Close – missiles, rockets and cannon don't discriminate between friendly and enemy forces. The only way he could be sure was to run through the gap to see for himself.

The Taliban started firing at him as soon as he started running but he made it across in one piece and slumped down behind the wall. Although he could see the house clearly from where he was, the Apaches were a lot higher up and further away – around two kilometres from his position. It was imperative that they identify the Taliban's position accurately and, given the proximity of friendly forces to the target, the choice of ordnance was vital too; there's a real chance of fratricide with rockets at that distance, due to their spread on impact, and it's even close for the 30mm cannon – although the 30mm is accurate to within three metres, Carter's position relative to the target was still outside of what's considered safe distance back in the UK. So he had to get it right.

Back in the cab we can tell he's having a lot of difficulty getting his message across to the Apaches. We can hear the intensity of fire that he's taking down there, because every time he keys the mike we can actually hear the RPGs flying over his head and the frantic sound of the guys around him returning fire, the sound of heavy machine-guns engaging and the noise of rounds zipping past and hitting the ground next to him.

Lt Col Tootal's voice comes over the radio. 'This is Sunray. Can any Chinook to the west of Now Zad assist Widow Seven Zero and describe where the Engagement Zone is?'

'Sunray, this is Splinter Two Four. We're visual over the engagement area,' I call looking at my map. 'Ugly Five Zero, Splinter Two Four. The enemy is in the vicinity of Blue Five, repeat Blue Five.'

'Roger that, Splinter Two Four, Blue Five.'

The Apaches now have a rough idea of the vicinity of the farmhouse, but Matt needs to be sure that they have a dead-on, accurate fix on the position of the target. He and the Paras involved in the firefight are so close that if the fire is remotely off target it will wipe them out instead of the Taliban.

'Ugly Five Zero, Widow Seven Zero. Confirm, it is the compound south of my position. Distance 200 metres. Three enemy.' As he keys the mike, I hear the 'whoosh' of an RPG followed by an explosion. Things are desperate down there. The Apaches still can't identify the specific target that Matt wants taken out. 'Ugly Five Zero, Widow Seven Zero, wait one,' says Matt.

He explains his predicament to Captain Mark Swann, the head of Patrols Platoon, and they come up with a rather unconventional idea: they're going to mark the building with a Light Anti-Tank Weapon (LAW). A Para called Bashir Ali ('Bash') picks up the LAW and prepares to fire it at the enemy position. As he does so, he's struck in the chest by several 7.62mm AK-47 rounds. They hit his body armour and ignite some tracer rounds in a magazine on his chest webbing, which catches fire.

The impact knocks Bash off his feet and a quick-thinking buddy pulls him into cover and rolls him in the dirt to extinguish the flames. Incredibly, he is unhurt. He dusts himself off, picks up the LAW and positions himself once again in clear view of the enemy, the rocket launcher on his shoulder.

Matt informs the Apache of his plans. 'Ugly Five Zero, we're going to mark the building with a LAW.'

'Widow Seven Zero, Ugly. Confirm . . . with a LAW?' asks the pilot, surprised.

'Roger that, with a LAW,' says Matt. 'Standby.'

Bash fires. His aim is dead on and the warhead explodes against the firehouse sending a huge pall of black smoke and flames skywards.

'Widow Seven Zero, Ugly. We have the building.'

'Ugly, look south from that building and thirty metres away you'll see a wall with a load of Paras behind it; that's us. You're clear hot, initials Mike Charlie.'

Whenever a JTAC calls in anything that's Danger Close, he has to give the pilot his initials to indicate that he's taking responsibility for it if it goes wrong. In effect, the ordnance he calls down is his but it's fired by proxy.

'Widow Seven Zero, Ugly Five Zero. Roger that commander's initials are Mike Charlie. Visual with target, engaging now with 30mm. Keep your bloody heads down!'

A hail of 30mm cannon shells rain down on the house, killing or injuring everyone inside it. Matt and the Paras then move forward and clear the house, but all they find are splashes and pools of blood on walls and in the dirt, some flip-flops and the detritus left by the enemy. No bodies. The Taliban try to take their casualties and dead with them, just as we do.

From our vantage point above the town, we see everything happening below us; the radio calls colour in and add detail to the picture. I'm greatly impressed by Matt – by his coolness under pressure and his ability to think outside the box. Clearly others are too (partly for his actions in Operation Mutay, and his bravery in exposing himself to enemy fire to call in air support, he is awarded the Military Cross).

By now, we're low on fuel again. The ground units are still involved in firefights and pushing forward, so we return to Bastion to refuel. Several hours later we get the call that they're ready for extraction so we return and, after a short time holding off station, we get a new grid reference. The guys are falling back under contact so they cross the wadi and dig in on the far side to put some open ground between them and the Taliban. I'm anxious as we make the approach. As always, we're a big, slow target and rounds are flying.

Andy goes in first again and kicks up the mother of all dust clouds. He lands next to a wall, which is protecting the waiting Paras from enemy fire. There's no modern expertise, no complex engineering in the compounds and the walls that define them. It's two-thousand-year-old technology – mud, straw and dung baked in the sun. It's hard as concrete and utterly impenetrable to almost all of our weaponry. Small arms fire literally bounces off it, leaving barely a dent.

Craig does an amazing piece of flying as, due to the brownout from Andy's cab, we're going in blind. He manoeuvres the aircraft gently using the Doppler (an instrument that tells you how you are drifting), the altimeter and the artificial horizon to descend, and gets us down perfectly. The troops board and we take fire but nothing hits us – the Taliban are at least 600 metres away and it's a tough distance to hit anything unless you can work out angles, the effect of gravity on rounds and take it all into consideration. We get out without a scratch, as do all of the ground troops.

When we get back, we're invited to the debrief. It's a first, and we all feel honoured to be included. We're aircrew, they're soldiers and it's really all about them, but there is a huge amount of mutual respect. Listening to what the guys were involved in is humbling in the extreme. It's an open and honest exchange with the ground units going over the events, the various contacts and asking what they did right, what they did wrong, and what they could improve upon. We hear some astonishing stories.

One of the guys mentions that he was driving a Pinzgauer when he saw a man pop up out of a ditch running parallel to the track, level an RPG and fire at him. The warhead flew between his arms and legs as he was holding the steering wheel and exploded harmlessly against a wall several tens of metres away on the other side. What saved him was the fact that the doors had been removed from the Pinzgauer before the patrol to allow some ventilation and this allowed the RPG to pass straight through. Another Para was walking along and a Taliban gunman stepped out of a compound about twenty metres away and opened up on him with an AK-47. Twenty metres and nothing but empty space between them and the Taliban had the element of surprise. He emptied his magazine and every single round missed the Para, who raised his SA80 to his shoulder, sighted on the target and fired two double taps. Four rounds hit the attacker, who dropped to the ground like a marionette with its strings cut, dead.

In another incident, Major Will Pike and his second in command exchanged fire with a Taliban fighter who ran off through a compound (as Colonel Tootal said, 'You know it's a bad day when the commanding officer and his 2i/c are firing their weapons!'). They chased him into a building and were peering around the compound entrance when some women and children came out. Suddenly, the Taliban popped up and started firing over their heads; Will and his 2i/c couldn't fire back, so they waited until the civilians had all got out and went inside. At the end of the entrance, there was a door. They counted: '1-2-3-go!' and burst through, levelling their weapons. One of them had a stoppage; the other heard the dreaded 'Dead Man's Click' that signifies an empty magazine. They were back out quicker than they came in, just as the Taliban fighter unloaded a full AK-47 at them. In the meantime, the stoppage was cleared and a magazine changed. As soon as they heard the firing stop, they were back through the door where they unloaded on the gunman, killing him.

Over twenty Taliban were killed during Op Mutay, a fact that was verified when Colonel Tootal received a report a day later that twenty-one Taliban fighters had been buried in a cemetery in the Sangin Valley. Not a single British soldier was killed or wounded, although luck clearly played a huge part as Bash, Matt Carter, Will Pike and the driver of the Pinzgauer, among others, can testify. It was supposed to have been a three-hour operation; it lasted over eight hours. In the event, nothing much came of the operation – we found some money, a quantity of opium resin, which the Paras left behind in line with UK policy at the time. A few weapons were recovered, but nothing to indicate the major cache that the intel had predicted, nor the High Value Target.

Maybe the intel was wrong. Maybe the HVT melted away before the Paras arrived, taking the weapons and ammo with him. Who knows? What was never in doubt was that everything changed that day and nothing has ever been the same since. However we were regarded up to that point, however much progress we might have made in terms of hearts and minds, we'd opened Pandora's Box and we couldn't un-know what we'd learned. Whatever our preconceptions of the Taliban were, here was the reality: they were brave to the point of foolhardiness, well-armed, ruthless and tactically aware.

The genie was out of the bottle and we were confronted with an insurgency that would quickly develop into a major conflict. War, for our generation, isn't always a conventional conflict fought between two armies. Ours is an asymmetric war; well-equipped and trained forces on one side, men in flip-flops and pyjamas on the other. We play fair and fight according to the rules of the Geneva Conventions. There are no rules for those we fight though. For them, anything goes. Nothing is off-limits. They don't care if they kill or harm civilians to further their cause – they'll even go out of their way to do so. Their desire to 'down' a Chinook extends to their planting IEDs in civilian markets because they know that the IRT will be scrambled to help.

It's a war where the Taliban masquerade as civilians; where they will place mortar tubes in crowds of women and children and launch attacks on coalition forces knowing that our moral and ethical code prevents us from returning fire. It's a war where a man will take his five-year-old child along as cover while he plants an IED. The Rules of Engagement that dictate how and when we open fire on the Taliban prevent us from fighting on an equal footing. These are the things we have to bear in mind, the things our infantry have to be aware of, in the heat of battle.

One thing was certain. After Op Mutay, things were very, very different.

13

WHITE LIGHT SPELLS DANGER

The morning of June 11th dawned with Craig Wilson, Jonah, Rob Chambers and I down at Bastion on IRT/HRF for four days. It had been a quiet day with nothing much to mark it out as being different. Yet by the time I would next go to bed, I'd look back on a marathon sortie that saw us repeatedly taking fire, and some audacious flying which would eventually lead to Craig being awarded the Distinguished Flying Cross.

It's around 19:00 hrs when the phone breaks the silence: two long rings. I grab the receiver and listen: 'You've got a shout. A T1, Kajaki. ANA, gunshot wound to the leg.'

When ISAF troops are wounded or ill and the IRT is required, the radio call coming from the point of origin is known as a nine-liner; nine lines of text requesting the medevac, each line giving a vital piece of information starting with the grid reference and call sign of the requesting unit. The next piece of information is the number and condition of the casualties given using a T-code. A T1 means immediate threat to life; it means urgent evacuation and surgery required. T2 means surgical intervention required within four hours. T3s are less serious – evacuation within twenty-four hours. Nobody likes T4 – it means the casualty is already dead.

We get to the cab and Craig gives me the details. We look at each other: ANA, Kajaki, T1? We share the same thought. Regardless, we still put everything we have into the call – we try not to be judgemental and work on the basis that if someone says we are needed, then we are. None of us wants anyone to die on our watch; certainly not through something we've done.

The reasons that drive men to risk their lives in battle are many and varied but one of the most important covenants is the knowledge that, if they get hit, they'll be looked after. Rapid, timely evacuation to immediate medical care and surgery and don't spare the horses. We are the exponents of that covenant, picking the guys up from wherever they've been wounded and delivering them into the care of the world's best trauma surgeons – within minutes, in some cases. If we are scrambled, we go. We put everything into it, whether the guy at the end is a British or ISAF soldier, an Afghan civilian wounded in battle or, in some cases, a member of the Taliban.

We are there and back to Bastion again in an hour and five minutes, which is bloody quick, all things considered. We make the return flight on goggles as it is fully dark by then, and after shutting down, a debrief and some food, I decide on trying to get some sleep; you grab it where you can on the IRT. I grab a radio so I can stay in touch and have a quick shower, get dressed again and go to bed. I keep my boots on, but leave my pistol in its holster hooked over the end of the bed – it takes valuable minutes to put my boots on if we got a shout, but I can strap my firearm on as we run for the Land Rover.

I lay my head on the pillow and shut my eyes. It feels like no more than five minutes have passed when the phone interrupts my dream. Two long rings. I swim up from the depths of sleep and snatch it up, only half awake.

'British soldier at Sangin. He's a T1, bleeding heavily, so make it quick.'

I check my watch; it feels like five minutes' sleep because that's all it was. Oh well. I grab my holster from the bed and secure it to my right leg. The others know the drill and are ready to go as soon as they hear the phone ring. Make it quick? We are. We're airborne and en route with our Apache escort within thirty minutes.

This was probably the first time that a cab had been to Sangin which, at this stage of the war, was not under siege as it would become later in the month. However, a patrol had been sent out from nearby FOB Robinson to recover a Desert Hawk Unmanned Aerial Vehicle (UAV) that had crashed near the Helmand River. The patrol had been dicked by the Taliban almost as soon as they left their base and, having failed to locate the UAV, were ambushed on a track as they returned. Lance Bombardier Mason of I Battery, 7 RHA was hit in the chest. The patrol medic alone got through six SA80 magazines defending the casualty while waiting for assistance.

A relief force led by Capt Jim Philippson of 7RHA was put together and despatched to assist the patrol that had been bogged down in a firefight, but sadly Philippson was killed outright by Taliban fire as he manoeuvred across a field to get to the patrol's location. He was just twenty-nine.

Another relief force was raised to assist both patrols and it too came under contact. Sgt Maj Andy Stockton of 18 Battery was hit by an RPG round which took off the lower half of his arm. Despite this, he continued to return fire with his pistol.

All this is going on while we are being despatched to pick up the first casualty, Lance Bombardier Mason. All we know at this stage is that the Taliban are still in the vicinity and the firefight is ongoing, so there is a bit of nervous tension in the cab as we fly towards the grid. Craig is captain of the aircraft and the handling pilot. I'm in the left-hand seat doing the nav. I feel tired, having been woken by the call just as I'd dropped off, so I guess my cognitive function is a little less than 100%. That's my excuse anyway – how else can I explain my interpretation of what happens next?

We are transiting to the HLS and I am looking at the Apache escorting us thinking how glad I am to have it along when, completely apropos of nothing, I see the most beautiful shooting star arcing between us; it's absolutely awesome – I've never seen one last as long as this one. Then my cognitive function kicks in: a shooting star at 4,000ft, climbing up instead of descending? Get a fucking grip, Frenchie; it's a rocket! And then I work it out. Someone has fired a Chinese 107mm rocket at us and missed.

Those things are evil – they're already breaking Mach 1 as they leave the firing tube. If they're aimed in the right direction, you're toast. That really wakes me up and refocuses my mind.

The Apache goes on ahead to check out the HLS and comes over the radio to report that it is 'cold' – good to go in. Craig says, 'I'm putting 100 on the light so bug the RadAlt to 80 on the noise. I'm going in fast and low, into the bottom of the wadi and we'll look for the grid.' As Craig flies the approach, I am talking him down on his height and speed so he can remain visual.

We crest a hill and drop to low level. Craig makes a steep turn and, after a quick look at the grid, I see the marker held by one of the soldiers – it's our signal.

'Yeah, I've got it,' Craig confirms and then greases us down in what has to be one of the most beautiful landings I've ever seen at night, particularly as I can see nothing whatsoever of the landing site in the last few seconds. It is a perfect zero speed landing and if ever a zero speed landing was required, it's now. When the dust clears, both Craig and I have an ANA soldier literally five feet in front of us. And between them and the front wheels of the aircraft there is a one-metre deep ditch – literally three feet from the wheels. Directly behind us there are another three or four ANA just feet from the ramp. They've performed a perfect demonstration of 'All Round Protection', except they've fucked up their drills and made the landing site so small that only a perfect zero speed landing would prevent total disaster. And luckily for everyone that's exactly what Craig delivered.

In the cockpit, I am anxious for us to get airborne again. A bizarre thought comes into my head that I can't chase away: 'If an RPG hit us now, would it hurt?' The troops on the ground run forward with Lance Bombardier Mason on a stretcher. He's only eighteen – no more than a kid really – and is bleeding profusely. The entry wound is on his left shoulder. The bullet has hit the back plate of his armour, bounced off and come out through his chest, missing the main arteries to his heart by millimetres.

The Apache comes over the radio. 'Guys, you need to lift. Enemy have got the HLS zeroed and are setting up to launch.' I can hear the sound of the AH's 30mm chain gun raining fire down on enemy positions across the airwaves.

'Ramp up,' says Jonah, just in time.

'Lifting,' says Craig.

'Clear above and behind.' And with that, Craig pulls pitch and we lift into the sky. Seconds later an RPG slams into the ground exactly where our cab had been.

'Fuck, that was close,' I say out loud.

'Thanks for that, Captain Obvious. I don't know what we'd have done if you hadn't been here!' Jonah quips. That breaks the tension: laughter fills the space over the intercom.

We always ask the medics what sort of exit they want, as we can climb to height and transit back with a more stable run; it takes longer because you lose speed on the climb and descent, but it's safer. Or we can fly at low level; it's significantly faster, but it's a lot rougher.

The doctor's voice tells us all we need to know about our casualty: 'We'll go as fast as we can on this one; we're just trying to stabilise him.'

We make the flight back in record time and the medics are waiting for us as soon as we land. We later hear that our casualty was back in the UK within forty-eight hours, stable and on the road to recovery, which gives everyone a lift. It's a lovely feeling when you know you've made a difference and someone has lived who, had we not performed as we did, might have died.

We start shutting down. Craig and I discuss the sortie. The blades are still spinning.

'Mate,' I say, 'that was the most amazing fucking landing I've ever seen! It was tighter than a gnat's chuff in there and you nailed it.'

Craig being Craig plays it down. 'Nah, it was nothing special. You'd have done exactly the same.'

I nod in agreement, knowing full well that I'd never have been able to execute a zero speed landing in the dark like that one.

'I just hope we don't have to go back there tonight – with the Taliban having the HLS zeroed now, I wouldn't fancy revisiting it!' Craig says.

Just then I feel a tap on my shoulder. I look round: Woodsy has walked up the ramp and is standing there with a sombre look on his face. My heart sinks.

'Guys, I'm really sorry but you're going to have to go back.'

Craig and I just look at one another and shrug. There isn't much else we can do. The Taliban are waiting; they saw us on the last mission and fired at us. Now we're needed again so we're going back. It isn't a nice feeling.

'What have we got?' I ask.

'A patrol went out to support the one you've just picked the casualty up from, and was engaged. You've got a T1 with serious injuries – potential traumatic amputation to his arm.'

We spend a few minutes debating our strategy. We need another Apache to escort us for starters, as the one we'd had for the first sortie remained on station to support the guys on the ground and is still in contact. We debate using one of the vehicles that had been hit in the ambush for a diversion, with the AH firing at it and causing an explosion so the enemy would get their heads down, but that isn't an option. In the end, it's decided to move the casualty to an alternative landing site.

I am the handling pilot for the first leg of the return – aside from anything else, I think Craig could do with a break after the last sortie. Our Apache has gone on ahead to recce the new landing site, so we hold off in an orbit about fifteen miles or so from the grid and remain visual with him. We have quite a wait. Long enough, in fact, that the standby Attitude Indicators topple because I've been flying circles at the same altitude for so long the gyros are confused.

One of the most impressive elements of the Apaches is their ability to engage the enemy from distance. The imagery they can see on their screens from the Target Acquisition and Designation Sight system they're equipped with is quite incredible – its array of lenses includes a 127-times magnification day TV camera that can read a car number plate from over 4km away. It means they can rain fire down on an enemy that can't see them, and that's exactly what they were doing as we sat in orbit and watched.

The firefight is clearly still going on because both Apaches are now involved. I watch transfixed as both aircraft are illuminated by the muzzle flash from their 30mm cannons, which are delivering hell to the enemy on the ground. Those M230 cannons fire 10 armour-piercing High Explosive Dual Purpose (HEDP) rounds every second, and they fragment on impact like a grenade. You really wouldn't want to be on the receiving end.

'Have some of that, motherfuckers!' I say out loud.

'Quite!' says Craig.

I have a thought: 'Er, how much fuel do we have?'

Craig does the calculation. 'About twenty minutes of playtime.'

'How long ago did we get the call?'

'About forty-five minutes, an hour at most.'

'Okay. So we've got a T1 casualty down there who's already been moved to an alternative LS and he's been bleeding badly for at least forty-five minutes. Actually, it's going to be longer than that – that's when we got the call. What are our options if we don't get clearance to go in before we reach our minima?'

'Er . . . nearest refuelling site is at Gereshk. Let me see . . . twenty minutes there, fuel another twenty minutes and then twenty minutes back. Another hour at least. The guy is never going to make it out alive.'

Craig tries to raise one of the Apaches over the radio, but they are both still busy engaging the target area and trying to clean out the enemy. Eventually, he gets through.

'Ugly Five Zero, Hardwood One Three. We're going to position further up so that we can get on station quicker once you clear us in. We're almost bingo fuel.'

'Copy that, Hardwood One Three.'

I've just started flying us in the direction of the LS when the AH comes back over the radio:

'Hardwood One Three, Ugly Five Zero. We've got a grid for you but we'll need another few minutes to suppress the area because it's still hot.'

'Negative Ugly Five Zero,' said Craig. 'We're bingo fuel; it has to be now or not at all.'

The radio goes quiet for a few seconds, like the AH pilot is thinking.

'Okay, Hardwood One Three. You're clear in, grid reference 41SPR71405 46516. One of the ground units will mark the target to aid you with a visual reference.'

Craig takes over flying for an aggressive approach. I'm calling distance and speed again and we're both looking for the marker, which we see ahead of us as we've been briefed. We land on, the ramp goes down and Rob leans out into the night looking for the casualty. His voice comes over the intercom, 'Er guys, there's nothing fucking moving out there. I'm going off to see what's happening.' He grabs his rifle and walks off but is only gone for a few seconds. He's not happy.

'Fuck! It's the wrong fucking landing site!'

'What do you mean, wrong landing site?' I ask.

'Wrong landing site − as in, we're not supposed to be here. Some idiot didn't remove his fucking marker when we picked up the first casualty earlier. For fuck's sake, let's get the fuck out of here!'

After all the debate getting the casualty moved to an alternative landing site, we've landed on at the last place in the world that we want to be: the same landing site we took fire at earlier.

'Hardwood One Three, Ugly Five Zero, you want to get out of there. The enemy looks like they're preparing to fire on your position.'

'Clear above and behind. Let's get the fuck out of Dodge,' says Jonah but Craig is ahead of the game; he is hauling the collective upwards as soon as he hears the word 'above'. And as we lift, it's like Guy Fawkes' Night down below us. The Taliban seem to let loose everything they have onto the spot where seconds before we'd been turning and burning.

'For fuck's sake,' says Craig, echoing what we are all feeling. 'How lucky was that?'

'Lucky?' says Rob. 'What's lucky about landing on a hot HLS twice in one evening?'

'Lucky because we must have landed on at exactly the moment

the Taliban had their heads down or were reloading. Lucky because the fuckers missed again.'

It's bizarre, the first time you come under fire. Your head is so full of the job at hand that you don't get a chance to be scared – you go into automatic mode and you're working flat out doing what you've been trained to do.

Almost as soon as we take off again, we see another marker for the correct HLS. Craig pulls a couple of tight turns and flares the cab to reduce airspeed for the descent.

'100ft, 80 knots, you're in the gate,' I say and the guys take over in the back with height and dust cloud calls.

'At the ramp,' says Rob.

'20, at the centre,' says Jonah.

'10, 8, 5 . . . at the front door.'

'4, 3, 2, with you . . .'

'1. Two wheels on . . . six on. We're down.'

'Ramp going down,' says Rob. 'Okay, the medics are off, the QRF are out now in defence.' The swirling, blinding dust cloud settles and clears and I can see again. I look over my shoulder to the rear cab and I can see a figure walking up the ramp . . .

'I don't believe this,' I say to Craig. 'The T1 . . . the guy with his arm hanging off? He's walking up the ramp unassisted, smoking a cigarette. What the fuck are these guys made of?' Andy Stockton's arm is all but missing below the elbow, and what remains is only held on by a few strips of muscle. He must be in agony, but he looks for all the world like he's taking a stroll through the Sussex countryside.

Once again, I'm amazed at the conditions that the MERT guys work in. It's dark in the back – no lights means less chance of us being hit by ground fire (there's no point making the enemy's job easier) so the only illumination is from green glow sticks. It's hellishly hot, dirty, dusty and cramped. The dust grates at your throat as you swallow. We're used to it – as Chinook pilots it goes with the territory. But these guys are medics, many of them drawn from the TA where their day jobs see them working out of climate-controlled, clinically clean, safe and hygienic hospitals. What a contrast. All that, yet they work uncomplainingly, in impossible conditions, and perform miracles on badly injured soldiers.

The biggest killer in military penetrating trauma is blood loss; lose enough and you can't get oxygen from the lungs to the brain. It's also an avoidable killer. In Vietnam, over 9% of the men who died did so through bleeding out from an arm or a leg. Nobody should ever die from bleeding out via a limb injury and with the advances in knowledge and equipment the medics now have in theatre, almost nobody ever does.

Soon after, the QRF and the medics return and we get the all clear from Rob at the ramp.

'Lifting,' says Craig as we transition away.

'How'd you like us to fly this?' I ask the doctor.

The answer comes back the same as before: 'Fast as you can, please. We need to get this guy back asap. He's lost a lot of blood.'

Once again the medics are waiting for us as soon as we land on back at Bastion and, within minutes, they have Stockton stabilised on a table in the operating theatre. He's lost his arm but they have saved his life.

By now it is around 04:00 and all of us are done in. If it's tough for us, you can't imagine what it's like for the crewmen. I honestly don't know how they do it. They have different but interchange-able roles and they may swap about on the same sortie, but basically the No.1 crewman is the primary interface with the outside for loading and unloading. The No.2 crewman will generally stay at the front of the aircraft and is more involved with the mission; he'll do the radios, look at navigation and give a tactical review of what's going on. When we've got the MERT on board, they're doing all that plus whatever else they can – putting on tourniquets, applying pressure to bleeding arteries. To be honest, I think they have the hardest job of all and they don't get enough recognition for it.

Craig and I are sat in the cockpit waiting for the rotors to slow down so we can apply the brakes and stop them altogether. We've been up since the previous morning at 08:00 and flying since around 20:00 the previous night, so we're beyond tired. My whole concept of time is skewed as I sit there. It's a concept too far for a brain that's been on the go for eighteen or more hours. Right now, my bed – even in the IRT tent – is all I want. I'd trade a week at home for it, right here, right now.

Woodsy appears. He's not smiling. I look at Craig, who looks back at me, our faces impassive. This is Groundhog Day.

'Guys, it's bad news, I'm afraid. I'm really sorry but you're going to have to go back to the same area. That patrol has got a KIA – Captain Jim Philippson.'

My heart sinks. It had to happen sometime – someone had to be the first; but why now, why him? He's the first British casualty of our deployment to Helmand Province. It hits hard. It's difficult to believe now, looking back across a sea of Britain's dead in Afghanistan that numbers over 360 at the time of writing, but Capt Jim Philippson was the first to die in Helmand from enemy action.

'There's more to it than the KIA,' Woodsy continues. 'There are a lot of guys bogged down in a firefight with enemy forces that have been there since the first T1 you picked up yesterday evening. We need to insert a company of troops in support so they can flush the enemy forces out. And don't feel obliged or think you'll be judged if you turn this down; you've all worked more than hard enough. I can always raise the other crew.'

We look at each other – Craig, Rob, Jonah and me. We've all got the beginnings of a beard. The shower I'd taken before getting into bed seems like another life ago. We are all stinking, wide-eyed and knackered. Jonah, Rob and I nod.

'No, we'll do it,' Craig says. 'There's no point breaking in another crew when we're already this far down the line. Keep them fresh for duty as rostered. We'll do the insert.'

Back in the UK, it'd be illegal for us to fly this tired, for this long. But then again, we wouldn't be flying as low as we do here either. Here, Concealed Approach and Departure means we can fly at whatever height and speed we want. In the UK, when we say height commensurate with safety of the aircraft, it means when I'm flying at 20ft I'm flying at 10 knots. In Afghanistan, if you're flying at 10ft, you want to be flying at 150 knots! That's what's going to make it safer. We're stretching all sorts of rules and regs but we're in a theatre of operations during a war and people's lives are at risk. We're willing and just about able. Different rules apply.

We take off again at first light flying as part of a three-ship formation with two Apaches in support, freshly armed and re-fuelled. A whole company is spread across three Chinooks with Craig and me in one cab, Nichol leading the pack from another and Scot Eldridge flying the third. In the event, it is pretty straight-forward; we drop our element of A Company, 3 Para and are then diverted to FOB Robinson along with Nichol to repatriate Capt Jim Philippson's body to Bastion.

We are more than a little ragged by the time we lift from FOB Robinson. It is like looking at the world through a veil, like we are six degrees of separation removed from events; they are happening but there is a weird kind of lag to everything, as though space–time has become distorted.

My hand is on the switch ready to arm up the Defensive Aids Suite as per normal, the minute we are about to lift, when out of nowhere, Craig yells, 'For fuck's sake Frenchie. Fucking arm up the cab!'

I feel myself tense up. His manner and words are completely contrary to the concepts of crew resource management, but more to the point, his behaviour is completely out of character. Craig is one of the nicest, most laid-back guys I know – certainly not the sort to throw his weight around.

The thought occurs to me, 'If I did it any faster, I'd have to defeat the laws of physics,' but I know that Craig's outburst is born of intense fatigue; nothing more and nothing less. I'm not the sort of person to take shit from anyone and I stare angrily at Craig for a second. But when I see the stubble on his face, his lips cracked and bleeding, how caked in dust he is and how bloodshot his eyes are, I realise that it was the distorted perspective of fatigue that made him react that way. We all look the same – tired, yet fired up because we still have a job to do. The symptoms of that Det Tourette's we all suffer from when in theatre are always worse when sleep is lacking. Craig was just sounding off – that's how it affects him. As for me, I feel calmer so I just let his rant slide. It's funny how fatigue affects us all differently.

When we eventually shut down the cab, it's twenty-four hours and thirty-five minutes since we'd started duty. It is for the missions we've flown this night that Craig is later gazetted and awarded the Distinguished Flying Cross.

14

NOT SO 'PLANE' SAILING

The week following that mammoth IRT duty with Craig was a nice antidote to the madness of those twenty-four hours. There were no stand-out missions, just a raft of routine taskings around the Helmand Triangle – Bastion to Lashkar Gah to Gereshk and back to Bastion again. Underslung loads, mail and parcels for the troops – we'll move mountains to deliver those because it's the greatest motivator and morale booster known to man.

I'd also received my own motivator and morale booster in the form of a chat with Woodsy, where he informed me that I'd be going home early from the Det so I could spend some time with my very pregnant wife. That was the good news. The bad news was that there was no free space available on a TriStar out of theatre any time soon.

KAF is tolerable but it's no place for a holiday and, away from the routine of flight planning, taskings and deploying forward to Bastion, it soon becomes dull. The food's okay but the bullshit is relentless – speed restrictions, senior officers from non-front line units insisting on correct attire, caps worn, being properly shaved etc. When you've just returned from an operational sortie or you've been on the IRT for twenty-four hours, being shot at, and you haven't eaten, you're not overly concerned about the finer aspects of personal admin, such as shining your boots or dragging a razor over your stubble. It's one of the reasons that Bastion was preferable – aside from the fact that it was a British base, the only people there were operational. There was none of the bollocks about wearing the right shorts with the right sandals or wearing your uniform shirt outside of your trousers. It was about getting the job done, and you were surrounded by like-minded people.

REMF – the acronym for Rear Echelon Mother Fuckers – is a sobriquet applied to any non-forward based jobsworth. You didn't have far to go to find them at KAF. In fact, you didn't need to find them at all. They'd find you. Alongside the enforcers of bullshit, the term also encompassed those who had convinced their friends back home that they were single-handedly taking the fight to the enemy and getting shot at on a daily basis. Kind of difficult when they were paper pushers and admin clerks who never set foot outside of, or flew above, the relative safety of Kandahar. Some of these guys were so far from the front they could send their laundry forward.

I quickly became bored of the good food, the gym and the TV, and I'd read all the books I'd brought with me. I also started to feel a little paranoid about the regular rocket and mortar attacks that were a feature of life at KAF. They weren't aimed – the launch system that the Taliban was using was far too primitive for anything like aiming – but they were no less dangerous for that. It was more a case of 'fire and forget' from anywhere in what became known as the 'Rocket Box' – an area of vegetation and crops outside the wire which the Taliban could rock up to in a truck, fire their ordnance and drive away before we could respond.

I knew the chances of being hit were minute, but so are the odds of winning the lottery and people play that every week. Chance and statistical probability are all well and good, but a million-to-one chance is only relevant if you're not the 'one'. I couldn't think of anything worse than surviving the fire that had been aimed at the Chinook, only to die in a random rocket attack while I was killing time, waiting for a flight home. So I resolved to do something about it.

One of the biggest frustrations for all military personnel deployed anywhere involving a flight are the movers. Sure, they have a job to do, but it's the attitude of many of them that pisses people off.

Their job is logistics and that means freight – people or cargo – and making sure that the right bit or the right person goes on the right aircraft to the right place. The trouble is they are a little bit possessive about aircraft. They always refer to them as 'my aircraft', like they own the fucking thing, and they come over all high and mighty and dictatorial; but bless them, they have to get their kicks somewhere. Their insecurity at never really moving outside the safety of the perimeter wire usually manifests itself in an unhelpful, aggressive manner. The default answer is generally 'no', regardless of the question.

As per usual, they were being no help whatsoever in my attempts to get on a C-17 to fly home. Ostensibly, it should have been a straightforward proposition. After all, the Boeing C-17A Globemaster III strategic heavy-lift transporter – to give its proper name – is one of the most modern and capable aircraft in the RAF's inventory. It's also by far the biggest. The cargo compartment can accommodate most large wheeled and tracked vehicles, tanks, helicopters such as the Apache, artillery and weapons. Three Bradley armoured vehicles comprise one deployment load on the C-17. The Challenger 2 main battle tank can be carried with other vehicles or it can swallow a Tornado F3 fighter jet. Several flew in and out of Bastion every week and all I wanted was space on one heading home to Brize Norton.

Again, it should have been easy because the crew area on the C-17 is pretty large too. A staircase leads up to it from the cargo deck and opens into a crew rest area behind the cockpit containing two seats and two full-size bunks, which can be curtained off for privacy. Through a doorway is the flight deck itself, again one of the largest in aviation. Of interest to me was one of the two observers' seats directly behind each of the pilots' positions.

I tried every avenue available from KAF, but the movers blocked my path at every turn, treating me like an idiot and saying things like, 'Sorry sir, I can't get you on my aircraft because there's no room.' Like one single body and extra kit bag would tip one of the world's biggest aircraft over its weight limit. In the end, I did what I should have done from the off. I called the duty officer at 99

Squadron in the UK who operate the C-17 and it was sorted. One phone call and the man said yes.

That said, I hadn't reckoned on the determination of the movers to fuck things up. I was stood at the ramp down at Bastion, dressed in uniform with my bag all ready to board, when one of the movers told me, 'Sorry sir, you won't be able to travel on this aircraft as they are repatriating a UK national who was killed in action last week.'

That UK national was Captain Jim Philippson.

'I was one of the pilots involved in the mission to bring his body to Bastion last week,' I tell him.

The mover's face fell; it was like someone had pricked a balloon. All the bluster and self-importance seemed to rush out in a puddle on the floor.

'Ah, sorry sir,' said the REMF. 'I didn't realise you were aircrew.' Like that should have made a difference! I didn't have time or energy for a fight though. All I wanted now was to get home.

When the C-17's pilot walked across the ramp, I recognised him at once. It was Guy Givens who I knew from my days at 101 Squadron at Brize. He took one look at me and smiled.

'Frenchie mate, how are you?'

'I'm good, mate, thanks. Been an interesting tour but I'm looking forward to getting home.'

'Get yourself up to the cockpit then, you can have the jump seat behind me. Make yourself comfortable and I'll be right with you.'

The sense of excitement and apprehension I felt was palpable. After what had been quite a stressful tour, I was going home to Ali and I couldn't quite get my mind around it. It's recognised that the guys on the front line need a break between here and home and if they're lucky they get it in the form of 'decompression' – a few days in Cyprus where they get to drink, swim, fight, have barbeques and generally get all the rivalries, resentments and pent-up aggression out of their systems before going home. For everyone else, it's front line to front room in twenty-four hours or less and it takes some getting used to.

I must have bored the tits off Guy all the way back, but I don't think he minded. It's one of the biggest indicators of how different things were at the beginning. At the time, there were no embedded journalists and almost nothing of what was happening in theatre was getting out. All the information so far had come from private emails between those in theatre and their loved ones at home. Eventually, things leaked out into the media, but at this point the war was really only just starting and, even within the RAF, there wasn't a great deal of understanding of what it was like, so I was being asked all sorts of questions by the crew.

I loved that whole trip. One, because I was going home, but also because flying there in the cockpit of an RAF C-17 piloted by a mate is the best way to travel. We chatted, we caught up and then, when we were done, I unrolled my sleeping bag and lay down on a bunk to sleep. I woke up about an hour out of Brize Norton to a cup of steaming hot coffee and a full English breakfast served from the galley. It was the perfect welcome home.

15

ANOTHER PERSPECTIVE

It took me a while to settle after I got back, but you accrue a month or so of leave on Det due to the time you spend being operational, so I was taking things a day at a time and just enjoying being back with Ali.

After a week or so, I went over to 'B' Flight, 27 Squadron. They were due to fly out a few days later to take over from us in theatre. Hannah Brown had been posted to 'B' Flight straight from the OCF, so I wanted to see her and give her and her colleagues a heads up on how things really were on Det. It was all pretty informal. As I was back three weeks or so earlier than the rest of my squadron, they invited me over and asked me what the tour had been like. So I pulled up a bar stool and told them. When they left a few days later for the handover for their two-month stint, I felt confident that they'd have an idea of what life on the ground would be like.

Those in the military outside of the Chinook Force, particularly soldiers, tend to only notice the headline figure of our time on deployment: two months. Their tours last for six months. Some people see an iniquity there. But those headline figures hide the real truth, which is that while soldiers aren't liable to deploy for another two years after they return, aircrew deploy every eight months. Basically, we spend four months out of twelve in theatre on a rolling basis. Some have completed eight or nine detachments now – that's up to eighteen months of one's life on high-density combat ops in Afghanistan. That said, I still wouldn't trade with a soldier. They earn every penny they get and more. I have the utmost respect for what they do and the conditions they endure, but I feel a lot safer up in the air flying a Chinook.

It was early September when Hannah and the rest of the Flight arrived back at RAF Odiham, so after taking leave entitlements and everything else, it was mid-October when I next saw her. By then, much had changed for me. Ali and I had moved into married quarters – a lovely detached house just around the corner from Woodsy. I'd become a dad – Alison gave birth to our son Guy that October – and I'd moved from 'A' Flight, 18 Squadron to 'C' Flight, 27 Squadron. Although Hannah and I were on different Flights, we were based in the same building, so it wasn't long before she sought me out to tell me about her Det. This is what she told me . . .

'We flew out from Brize on July 8th and I flew my first pre-planned operation on the 14th. Craig Wilson did my day and night TQs – they were my first two flights. My third was Operation Augustus just two nights later.

'Operation Augustus was a strike mission with the objective of killing or capturing a Taliban leader who intel said was based in two compounds a few klicks north of Sangin. It was a big op because it was believed that the Taliban commander had a hardcore of about fifty fighters who would fight to the death to protect him, so Lt Col Tootal committed "A" Company and Patrols Platoon. He also used "C" Company who he had to pull out of Gereshk where they were based at the time.

'The plan was to fly in "A" and "C" Companies to assault the compounds and kill or capture the Taliban commander and his fight-ers. They would then be supported on the ground by Patrols Platoon, 3 Paras' Mortar Platoon and a company of Canadian infantry mounted in light armoured vehicles to provide a cut-off.

'By the time we arrived, Woodsy and the rest of "A" Flight had amassed over a hundred hours flight time in theatre, so there was obviously a massive amount of experience there compared to what we had having just touched down. So the Brigadier asked Woodsy if "A" Flight would agree to stay on to undertake the mission, mixing some of the 18 Squadron crews with some of us on 27 Squadron who had just arrived. He agreed.

'It was a huge op, using five Chinooks for the insertion, with close air support to be provided by the Apaches, a B-1 bomber and an AC-130 Spectre. Colonel Tootal had convinced the US to provide a couple of Black Hawks which he would use as a Command and Control platform. The insertion would happen in two stages, with three helicopters in the first wave, and two in the second. We'd be really pushing the envelope in terms of power – each Chinook would be carrying forty-odd Paras with all their ammo and individual kit plus a quad bike. Also, due to the resistance that we expected to receive, each cab had a third crewman so that every weapon was manned – an M60 on each door and one on the ramp.

'Nichol Benzie (18 Sqn) was to lead the formation, flying in the No.1 cab with Russ Norman (27 Sqn), and I was earmarked to captain the No.2 cab with Woodsy as my co-pilot. However, due to my lack of experience in theatre, I offered my seat to Glen Militis (27 Sqn), who was supposed to be flying the No.5 cab. I was like, "Come on, it makes sense – I've only flown twice since I got here," and he agreed. So that was No.2 sorted – Glen and Woodsy. Chris Hasler (18 Sqn) was captain on No.3 flying with Adam Thompson (27 Sqn). Nelly Bauser (27 Sqn) was flying No.4 with Jonny Shallcross (18 Sqn) and I would be flying in No.5 with Andy Lamb from 18 Squadron.

'You can't exactly disguise a nine-ship formation of Apaches, Chinooks and Black Hawks in the middle of the night, but you can try to confuse any potential dickers, so we flew south in the opposite direction of the target for about twenty minutes. As soon as we were over open desert, Andy gave the order for the crewmen to test fire their weapons and then he gave the fire control order. We'd been briefed that there were no friendlies at the HLS; therefore anyone we saw was to be treated as hostile. We were "weapons live" so he authorised the guys to engage as soon as they established a firing point for any incoming fire.

'You know how it's drummed into us that no battle plan survives the first contact with the enemy? We didn't even get to first contact before things started unravelling. Colonel Tootal started to receive intel from a Predator UAV that was picking up movement at the grid. The plan relied upon us getting in undetected, so we were flying in a holding pattern away from the HLS while the 3 Para CO decided whether or not the op was a go.

'While this is all going on, I was frantically crunching some numbers because the fuel gauges were showing us with far less fuel than expected. The fact that we were flying at the absolute limit of capacity and the time we'd spent flying a holding pattern had both taken their toll, and I realised we had just eight and a half minutes of fuel left. We needed eight minutes to get back to Bastion, so I told Nichol that we had just thirty seconds of playtime left. Longer than that and something would have to give – the mission, or us reaching Bastion. It was tight.

'Nichol radioed the Apache and put him in the picture: "Either we go now or we're all going home." The AH checked out the picture with its thermal camera, picked nothing up and I guess Tootal made the call – it was a go.

'Nichol went in first, and as soon as he made his approach, it all kicked off. Tracer started arcing up towards us and the sky was alive with danger – the glow of red and green tracer, RPGs exploding, Dushka heavy machine-gun rounds. It was absolute mayhem. So much for the surprise – the Taliban were there and they'd known we were coming. We'd been forced into an upwind holding pattern so the noise of five Chinooks flying in circles had carried down to them. Great!

'Once Nichol was committed, so were Woodsy and Chris Hasler – less than three aircraft would have meant the troops in Nichol's cab would have been completely outnumbered.

'The Apache came over the radio with frantic cries of "Abort! Abort! Abort!" just as we were about to start our approach, so Nelly in No.4 and Andy both heaved on the collective. You should have heard the creaks and groans of the cabs as we demanded more and more power from the overstressed engines. We banked away throwing our Paras around the cabin in the process as they were standing like commuters on a tube train at rush hour.

'Those in the three lead aircraft got out, straight into a wall of fire. There seemed to be firing points everywhere. I looked down and saw tracer streaking towards Nichol's cab from both sides. All three guns on his aircraft were engaging targets, as were the Paras as they streamed off the ramp. Until they were all clear there was nothing Nichol could do but sit there. Somehow nothing hit his aircraft but, as he took off, his cab became the filling in an RPG sandwich as one shot over his aircraft and another passed just feet below its belly.

'Woodsy's aircraft was immediately behind and it started taking fire. A hail of bullets streaked along the side, impacting the fuselage; I realised immediately that it was the one I should have been in originally. Poor Glen! He did me a favour by taking my place and got shot up for his trouble! I'm not superstitious and I'd had no premonition of danger or anything like that – it was just the way it worked out. Luckily, Glen didn't hold it against me, but it was weird seeing it all happen and knowing that I should have been there – it sent a shiver down my spine. One of the Paras on board wasn't so lucky and took a round straight through his shoulder, but even that wasn't enough to keep him down. I know these lads are hard, but what the hell do they make them out of? Even after being shot, he still wanted to get out and join his mates in the fight. In the end, an officer had to physically restrain him to prevent him getting off, and order him to return to Bastion for treatment.

'Chris Hasler was the last one in and he came in fast and steep, pulling up the nose and using the cab's underside as a brake to scrub off speed. He started taking rounds from firing points and I could see both door guns and the M60 on his ramp firing back at targets through 360°. His troops got off and I think there must have been a breakdown in communication somewhere because as he started to lift, Matt Carter – who was the JTAC for the mission – was still on the ramp with his signaller. Realising that without him the operation would have no close air support, he and his signaller jumped into the darkness from about 15ft as Haz was lifting. They were both carrying about 90lbs of radios and kit and landed on their backs in a ploughed field, winded but otherwise safe. His decision to jump was decisive in the mission's eventual success.

'Nelly's cab got away okay but, as we flew away from the area of the landing site, we could see all of the firing points as they engaged Nichol, Glen and Haz's cabs. Two of my crewmen – Craig Wadeson and Dave Neale – engaged targets on the ground with the M60s. No pun intended, but it was a real baptism of fire.

'Our fuel state was perilous, so we diverted to Gereshk with Nelly to refuel. It was while we were away that Matt Carter managed to gain the initiative for the op which was in danger of getting bogged down before it got under way. He called in support from the AC-130, which is an amazing piece of kit – basically a converted Hercules C-130 with the ability to fly slowly and loiter for extended periods. More importantly, it has massive firepower in the form of 40mm cannon, a 25mm Gatling gun and 40mm and 105mm howitzers.

'Once Matt gave them a grid they were able to see everything through the extensive high-def array of low-light TV and infrared and radar sensors. They told him, "We can see exactly where you've deplaned; I can see all enemy firing points. There are four around a machine-gun . . ."

'Matt talked them on to the compound. The Spectre completely annihilated all the different positions with 40mm grenades and 105mm shells. One of the Apaches took care of a position with a Hellfire missile and all the firing stopped.

'By the time we returned to the HLS it was completely cold and the Apache cleared both of us straight in. Watching the forty-four Paras we had in the back run off the ramp was a sight to see – they were all off in something like fourteen seconds, which was amazing when you consider they were all kitted up and weapons ready. I'd never seen anything like it!

'With all the Taliban killed, the Paras regained the initiative and were able to search all the compounds and complete the mission. When we landed back at Bastion the atmosphere was incredible. It could all have worked out so differently but in the end, aside from the Para who'd taken a round through his shoulder and a few breaks and sprains, there were no serious injuries and no dead on our side. A huge number of Taliban were killed and a quantity of weapons and rockets recovered, although there was no sign of the Taliban commander.

'That was a real red-letter day for us, because it was the first time that the Chinook Force had ever done anything like that. I mean, we'd flown kinetic ops in Iraq but it was nothing like this where we were being opposed at the HLS. It was also the first time a Chinook had taken rounds in theatre. All things considered, I think we got away very lightly. I have to admit though, it was pretty exciting!'

By the time the end of the year rolled around, the tempo of ops in Afghanistan had increased significantly. Thirty-nine British servicemen had lost their lives with scores more severely injured. Corporal Bryan Budd of 'A' Company, 3 Para was posthumously awarded the Victoria Cross for bravery displayed in a firefight with the Taliban at Sangin. His colleague, Corporal Mark Wright, was posthumously awarded the George Cross for his actions in trying to save the lives of injured colleagues after they entered a minefield.

Closer to home, the Chinook Force at RAF Odiham hadn't gone unnoticed. Three of 18 Squadron's pilots received the DFC – Chris Hasler, Craig Wilson and Royal Marine Major Mark Hammond, who was attached to 18 Squadron on an exchange. Woodsy and Nichol Benzie both received a Mention in Despatches, as did two crewmen – Sergeant Daniel Baxter and Sergeant Graham Jones. Joint Commander's Commendations (JCC) were awarded to Sergeant Samuel Hannant and Sergeant Darrell Harding, both of 18 Squadron, and Flight Sergeant Andrew Welham-Jones and Flight Lieutenant Glen Militis, both of 27 Squadron.

16

EUROTRASH

One of my best friends on 'C' Flight, 27 Squadron is Rich Hallows. He's from Essex, but his sparkling blue eyes and blonde hair mark him out as the epitome of the Aryan dream. Thus he was known to all and sundry as 'German'. We've got similar taste in music and cars and a similar outlook on life, so we did quite a bit together back at Odiham. I'd bought myself a 5.0 litre V8 TVR Chimaera, and Rich had a BMW M3, so track days were a regular diversion for us and we'd often swap cars. Basically, he's a good bloke.

Our OC on 'C' Flight was a Squadron Leader known by all as 'JP'. He's a brilliant leader, one of the most impressive pilots I've ever met and a good man to be around; I learned so much about flying from JP. He is also a good mate.

I guess it was inevitable with German and me working together that it wouldn't be long before JP christened us; the opportunity was just too good for him to ignore. There was a mission coming up and he just said, 'I think we'll send Eurotrash on that one,' and the name stuck.

Much had changed by the time we returned to Kandahar in early July 2007. The Royal Marines' 3 Commando Brigade had taken over from 16 Air Assault Brigade who I'd deployed with the previous year, and they in turn had handed over the lead to 12 Mechanised Brigade in April. The principal infantry units were the Royal Anglians and the Grenadier Guards, who we would be supporting on operations.

The Platoon House strategy that saw so much of 3 Para tied

down in remote bases across Helmand had been abandoned in favour of more Forward Operating Bases, which meant that ISAF forces could exert an influence over larger areas through regular patrols. A good illustration of the limitations of the Platoon House strategy is the siege of Sangin. Just after I left theatre in June 2006, 'A' Company, 3 Para was deployed to secure Sangin following increased Taliban activity in the area. The operation was only supposed to last a few hours but the troops ended up staying until the end of their tour after the Taliban effectively laid siege to their District Centre base. Daily attacks – sometimes up to seven times a day – punctuated a tour that saw a number of losses to the Paras, who also ran low on food, water and ammo.

On April 5th 2007, a major operation involving some 1,000 ISAF troops was launched to take control of the town. Advance warning was given and they advanced into Sangin almost unopposed after it was abandoned by most of the insurgents. The British built two new FOBs a few miles away in a move that drew most of the Taliban attacks away from the town itself, allowing some degree of governance and normality to return.

Also in April, the number of British troops deployed in southern Afghanistan was increased from 3,300 to 5,800 men, indicating a longer-term commitment by the UK Government. Heavier equipment was also deployed including Warrior and Mastiff armoured infantry fighting vehicles and GMLRS multiple rocket launchers. The new task force was commanded by Brigadier John Lorimer.

A permanent force had been based at Kajaki Dam after 42 Commando launched Operation Volcano in February 2007, clearing a safe zone around the dam and driving the Taliban out of mortar range. The Taliban's main fortified position in the village of Barikju was cleared without casualties.

Musa Qala, which had been held by the Paras in 2006, had been ceded to local tribal elders in a negotiated truce. The deal was intended to see neither British nor Taliban forces in the town in an effort to reduce conflict and civilian casualties, but the Taliban reneged on the agreement, overrunning the town with as many as

300 troops in February 2007. When we arrived in Helmand it was still under Taliban control. They imposed their own extreme fundamentalist interpretation of Islam, closing down schools, restricting women's movements, levying heavy taxes, and hanging those inhabitants they suspected of being spies. Men were attacked for not having beards, music was banned and women were beaten for not wearing the burqa.

This was the background against which we arrived; although, aside from being a little bigger and busier, KAF was the same old dusty and annoyingly anal place it had always been. One of the first things I did was head over to the Survival Equipment Specialists to pick up my Mk61 LCJ. In addition to the plate armour on the front of the jacket, it also features a series of horizontal webbing tape loops to which you can attach various items of equipment. Having flown with my sidearm in a thigh holster on my previous Det, I realised it was too restrictive and uncomfortable. With the Mk61, I could strap my weapon and magazines to the front. Our admin and TQs were quickly dispensed with and we were up to speed and flying ops in no time.

My first few sorties were pretty routine admin runs, which are about as 'everyday' as life gets in theatre. I was flying with Squadron Leader Morris Oxford, a great guy who's been on the squadron for years and has a wealth of experience. For someone so seasoned, this was his first Det as a pilot, so he was limited combat ready. That said, he wasn't exactly green – he'd previously been a Chinook navigator and had been the Qualified Navigation Instructor at the OCF, so he was a safe pair of hands and a great guy to fly with. I liked flying with him because, as the captain, I could concentrate on what I needed, secure in the knowledge that there was nobody better qualified to handle the nav side. For all that, he was a cracking pilot too.

We were blessed with our two rear crewmen who had a lifetime of experience between them: Jim Fowler, an affable guy who's good to have around and knows what he's doing, and Bob Ruffles. Bob is like everyone's dad and he's got over 5,000 hours on Chinooks, so is as useful a crewman as you could ask for.

If the ambient temperature had been hot on my previous Det, this one was off the scale. It's around 09:00, July 25th and we're at KAF preparing for the day's sorties – admin taskings, flying people and cargo all around Helmand Province. We have a series of sorties to fly that will see me add another seven hours flying time to my logbook by the time I shut down the airframe at Bastion this evening, our starting point for the next day's flying.

Morris has got one of those all-singing, all-dancing Breitling Pilot watches with a thermometer built in. When we get to the cab to do our pre-flight checks, he takes it off and leaves it on the centre console.

'And today's forecast for Kandahar is it's going to be hot!' I say to Morris, as I walk down the cab and off the ramp to do my walk-around. I pick up my Mk61 jacket and strap it on to me as I'm walking. It's early but the temperature is already insufferable, a good sign that things can only get more uncomfortable. It takes an average three weeks to acclimatise, so I know it's going to get a lot worse before it starts getting better.

Back on the cab, I slot a fresh magazine into my SA80 short carbine and strap it to the side of my seat in its allotted place. I'm flying from the right seat today, so I stow my CamelBak on the right side of the cockpit.

It's a tight cockpit, which makes for some interesting contortions to reach the seats. To access it from the cab, you stoop and walk through what is essentially a narrow corridor, about 2ft long. I stretch my right leg across the seat, behind the cyclic, and find the floor. Then I bend my head so I miss the overhead console and push my body forwards, dragging my left leg and swinging it over the centre console. Hunched over, I can now slide my body down and I'm in the seat.

I grab the centrepiece of the five-point harness, find and connect the two straps that attach to the bottom – one either side – then reach over my shoulders for the top ones. Attach those and I search for the pigtail – the cable that I'll plug into my helmet that will connect me to the aircraft's intercom and radio system. I'll leave my helmet on the centre console for now. I adjust the pedals – there are four settings – I always take the second one from the top. Move my seat forward a notch and then set its height. I adjust it so that I have the perfect picture for a three-degree glide path on the approach, which means that the 120kts marker on the airspeed indicator is just disappearing under the lip at the top of the dial.

I look in the mirror and I can see the crewmen in the back sorting out the cabin. They're making sure all the equipment is secured and in place, and our personal kit is stored properly. They start putting on their helmets and attaching their pigtails. At that point, I shout, 'Helmets!' and reach across to the centre console to pick mine up, securing the chin strap and connecting the pigtail. All conversation from now until the end of the sortie will be via the intercom.

It's then that I notice Morris' watch, which is still on the centre console. It's reading 68°C! Obviously, the vast expanse of glass – there are windows above, in front, to the sides and under our feet in the cockpit – mean we're in direct sunlight and there's the greenhouse effect, but even so. There's no acclimatising to that sort of extreme heat, but you just have to get on with it.

It's difficult to describe what it feels like. What's hot? 30°C is enough to make the news during an average English summer; 40–45°C is the average daytime temperature in the UAE during summer and is the reason that all sensible Emiratis abandon the state for cooler climes until autumn. 80°C is the temperature of the average sauna – and you strip naked to sit in one of those. Most people sit in a sauna for five to ten minutes and then take a cold shower. We sit in uniform shirt, trousers and boots, body armour that weighs 15kg, sidearm and spare magazines, helmets and flying gloves. Nothing is easy in Afghanistan; there's a reason it's called a 'hostile environment' and it's not all about the bullets.

We run through start-up. Battery on, pressurise and start the Auxiliary Power Unit. Set the engine control lever to 'Ground Idle' and then start the number one engine.

Time to engage the rotors. 'Clear rotate,' I say and the reply comes back from Bob, 'Clear all round.' The blades start moving and I start counting them to ensure they are at the same interval. One-two-three; all good. They speed up until they're a blur, beating out their loud, hypnotic rhythm. I advance the number one throttle all the way to 'flight' and the blades mesh together, working their magic. I bring the generator online and start the number two engine.

Watch the Ts and Ps (Temperatures and Pressures) build. Ts and Ps on both sides are looking good – I'm looking for 100% NR, all good, no captions on the CAP (Caution Advisory Panel) that I can see. Check the gearboxes, fuel pumps are working correctly. That's after start checks complete. Morris reaches across to the centre console and arms up the self-defence kit, nav kit and radios while I carry out the pre-taxi checks.

'Swivel switch for the wheels at the back is at lock, parking brake is on.'

'RadAlt: 50 on the right with a light, 40 on the left with the noise.'

'Altimeters: 1,016 (that day's pressure) set; I've got 2,920ft on the pilot side, 2,940ft on the co-pilot side, within limits.'

'Instruments: instruments are all set and correct with no undue flags. Morris, you've crosschecked them, putting the director for the GPS live, selecting TACAN (tactical air navigation system) on the HSI needle. You have command of both HSIs.'

'Light: master on. Normal. We've got steady, bright, top red, searchlight is normal, searchlight is coming on and bright star IR is off.'

'Fuel: we have 2,850. Four on four flow cross feed off.'

'Radios: we're on stud one on the ground, we'll go to stud two for the taxi. VHF is back up 1,221 for the tower on the victor, 51.4s on the Fox Mike.'

There's one more thing to do before I call the tower for clearance. I address the guys in the back. 'Right fellas, usual brief. On my cab, it's first names only. I'm not sir – I'm Alex or Frenchie, this is Morris, you're Jim and Bob. All clear?'

'Clear Frenchie.'

'Okay. If we are engaged, there are two calls. "Tracer" and "Contact". Tracer is ineffective enemy fire, Contact is effective. My rules are if it's tracer or contact, call it, identify it and get the guns on it. As soon as either of you identify rounds coming towards the aircraft – that is, we're under contact – and you can identify firing points, you are clear to engage. You have my authority to engage without reference to me first if we come under fire. Clear?'

'Clear, Frenchie.'

So long as it's an aimed shot, I have no problem with that. The responsibility rests with me, but what I don't want to happen is for us to come under fire and for a crewman to ask me, 'Am I clear to engage?' In the three seconds or so that it takes to ask and for me to reply, any aimed rounds could have taken out a critical system, one of us or the entire cab. Equally, in that time, the crewmen could have missed a window to take out the threat. To me, it's a no-brainer.

I make the call for departure: 'KAF Tower, Splinter Two Four. Four on board, holding at Mike Ramp. Request taxi to Foxtrot for a westerly, low-level departure.'

'Good morning Splinter Two Four. Clear taxi to Foxtrot. Visibility is five kilometres, wind two-five-zero at ten knots.'

'Taxi Foxtrot.'

I ground-taxi and reposition us to Foxtrot, a taxiway that's parallel to the main runway at KAF, and then make the call for take-off clearance: 'KAF Tower, Splinter Two Four ready for departure, Sector Hotel Low.'

'Splinter Two Four, clear take-off.'

I run through the pre-take-off checks:

'100% torque NR, torques are matched; LCTs are ground, auto; AFCs coming on.' Morris selects both AFCs ON for me.

'One good; two good,' he says.

'CAP, all clear. Ts and Ps are all looking good. Fuel, we have got 2,750kgs. Brakes, holding on the toes; swivel switch at lock and both whites. Okay, clear to lift?' I ask.

'Yep, clear above and behind,' from the back.

'Pulling pitch,' I say as my left hand raises the collective.

Feedback comes via two senses; I feel the aircraft shake as sixteen tonnes of metal are lifted skywards, and I hear the note of the two Lycoming engines increase as they respond to my demand for power.

'We have two good engines, 68% torque, 100% NR maintained, CAP is clear. Ts and Ps are all looking good,' says Morris.

'Transitioning,' I call as I accelerate away. Then, 'Above the light and noise,' and I'm finally free to settle into the cruise, flying at 50ft as we head towards Lashkar Gah, our first pick-up point.

And so begins another day in paradise.

17

ANY TIME, ANY PLACE, ANYWHERE

The following morning saw me waking up in Camp Bastion for some more tasking on the HRF. Bastion, like KAF, is a work in progress, and while still recognisably the same place that I remembered from last year, it's significantly bigger. More troops, more tented buildings, more phones provided by Paradigm for us to call home on – conveniently situated in private booths in air-conditioned ISO containers. Work is under way to build an 8,000ft-long concrete runway in place of the dirt landing-strip that existed previously. Sadly, one of the biggest changes is to the simple yet poignant war memorial erected by the Paras in 2006; too many names have been added to the brass plates that adorn its base since my last visit.

It's a pretty routine day for us – I'm flying the Helmand Triangle with German so we are Eurotrash once again. After lunch, we do a run-up to Kajaki and are routed to Gereshk by Bastion Ops on the way back to pick up a British soldier who's been shot. He's categorised T2 and we make contact with the Apache that is in orbit near the HLS, providing ongoing fire support to troops involved in a contact.

'Ugly Five One, Beefcake Two Five, inbound to recover one T2. Can you confirm the LS is secure and cold?'

'Beefcake, Ugly. LS is volcano [i.e. hot] at this time, repeat volcano. Hold off until further notice.'

'What's our fuel status?' I ask German.

'We've got about ten minutes playtime before we're bingo,' he replies.

I call Bastion and advise them that we may not make it in. It's a tough call, knowing that a guy's on the ground and needs us but we can't get in to lift him and may yet need to bug out. Bastion scrambles the IRT while we fly an orbit about three minutes out from the HLS awaiting clearance. It's going to be tight. Nine minutes pass; I call up the AH.

'Ugly, Beefcake. Any change?' I ask.

'Beefcake, negative. Maintain hold, will report change.'

'Ugly, we are bingo fuel, returning to Bastion. IRT en route from Bastion to take over,' I advise them before dipping the nose and flying us home. About five minutes west, as I'm heading towards the desert east of Bastion, I see the IRT cab pass us on its way to our previous target, crewed by Morris (Mo) and JP. Later that night, we catch up in the crew tent.

'Boss, Mo, how'd it go with that IRT shout to Gereshk earlier?' I ask them. I pull up a chair and listen to their account:

'It was interesting, to say the least,' says Morris. 'It'd been fairly quiet; in fact, we hadn't been scrambled at all until that point. We'd just been taking it easy in the crew tent as we weren't long back from lunch. JP had his head down and I was reading when the call came in.

'JP was captain, so he went to the JOC to get the nine-liner while I went to straight to the cab with the crewmen and began start-up. The call came over as a straight T2 – a British soldier who had taken a round through the left side of his torso.

'I think the firefight must have calmed down just after you left because we were on our approach about ten minutes after we passed you. We had trouble getting comms with the ground call sign but the Apache escorting us said, "You're cleared in, LS is ice." The ground units popped green smoke for us and we started our descent.

'We came in from the south and the HLS was an area that had trees and bushes on three sides. It was going to be an extremely tight squeeze for us but, as you know, there's nothing unusual in that – just another day in Helmand, right? You know JP though – he's a pretty unique pilot so he managed to get in there seemingly with no difficulty whatsoever. Christ, the guy makes even the most impossible manoeuvres seem easy.

'So there we are, landed right on the green smoke. We're turning and burning, the ground party has gone off the ramp to find the T2, and JP and I were quite happily sat there, scanning the horizon within our respective look-out arcs for any incoming. I happened to look out of my left-hand window and I noticed some Afghan troops there. They were firing and doing that Afghan thing of ducking down in a crouch and firing their AKs above their heads in the general direction of where the enemy might be. You know how it is – it's like there's a slight lag between your eyes seeing something and your brain analysing what it is they're seeing and making sense of it all.

'I looked to my right and I said to JP, "I've got some Afghan troops just under the disc on my side." As I said it I looked past JP and I could see the same thing on his side. "Ah, it appears you've got some on your side too. Er . . . your guys seem to be firing JP," and I looked down at my side again and sort of did a double take as it dawned on me. We'd landed right in the middle of the firefight – literally. And suddenly we were doing that "shrink down in your seat" thing where you try and make yourself into as small a package as possible – not ideal seeing as neither JP or myself are the smallest of people. We ended up doing that cockpit bullet-dodging dance, where you start moving and bobbing your head around, trying not to keep it in the same place in case somebody is aiming at you!

'Talk about wrong place, wrong time, do you know what I mean? Of all the places we could have put down, we've landed on right in the middle of the ANA and the Taliban having a pop at one another. Vulnerable? It felt like we were sat there with a huge fuck-off target painted on us and the words "Come and have a go if you think you're hard enough" written alongside the cab. I hate that feeling – all you can do is sit and wait for the guys to get on and give you the "Clear above and behind" so you can raise the collective and get the hell out.

'After what seemed like an age, although I'm sure it was no more than about two minutes in reality, they found the T2 and walked him on to the back of the ramp. He was bandaged across his left shoulder – I think he'd taken a through-and-through. That was the first time I'd seen the troops fighting in mufti. Most of the British troops were shirtless, in helmet, shorts and flip-flops, wearing their body armour over bare skin; it was that hot. Poor guys, it must be unbearable for them living and fighting in those conditions. I have the utmost respect for them.

'Once we got the guy on board and got the all clear, I don't think we've ever lifted so fast; JP did an over-the-shoulder departure away from the firing line and we got back to Bastion with no further incident. What really made this one stand out was their JTAC, an elderly RAF officer. He was a Flying Officer – I guess given his age, he'd come up the ranks and taken a commission. He arrived back at Bastion earlier this evening and came and found us.

'"Are you the guys who flew in to pick up the T2 at Gereshk earlier?" he asked, and I nodded. "I've got to tell you, the boys thought that was fantastic, utterly brilliant. You've got their eternal respect now, do you know that?"

'I was like, "What do you mean?"

'"Well, you know that field that you landed in? It's just in front of where the Sergeant Major had been driving his quad bike with a trailer on the back. The trailer had gone over an IED which blew it to pieces and that woke the Taliban up and they launched the fire-fight that you landed in the middle of. I was trying to raise you on the radio to tell you to hold off as it was too hot but the next thing we know, you've arrived in the middle of the firefight, picked this guy up and disappeared. Well as far as the troops are concerned, the guys think you're brilliant; they reckon you're going to come in regardless of what's going on and pick them up – any time, any place, anywhere! You've no idea what a morale boost that was for them!"

'With that, he made his excuses and left. I have to say Frenchie, I know that the guys on the ground value the service the IRT delivers, but I had no idea how much. It might have been more by accident than design, but I think that little error with us landing when the LS was hot has raised our stock with the boys on the ground.'

'Fucking hell, Morris!' I say. 'Bet you were glad to get out of there! Kind of makes you appreciate the simple and bizarre calls we get, doesn't it?'

'Yeah, always interesting those, although not for the casualties obviously! We've had some really weird ones. I know Elle Lodge on "A" Flight got a shout to pick up a guy from a FOB who'd been doing press-ups in his tent and a dog ran in and head-butted him really hard. How weird is that? Similarly, JP and I picked up an Afghan kid that had been kicked in the head by a donkey – the boy survived but he was in a really bad way.'

'Yeah,' I reply. 'I picked up a T1 from one of the FOBs, a British soldier who'd been stung by a hornet. He'd gone into anaphylactic shock and it was really touch and go.'

'Can't remember who it was, but one of the IRT crews was recently scrambled to pick up one of the Army's sniffer dogs that had fallen ill. That really gives some indication of just how important they are to the overall mission here,' offers German. 'Also, Alex Townsend had one that really fucked every one off; you hear about it?'

'Don't know. What's the story?' Morris asks.

'Fucking outrageous. You know how we had that spate last year of the ANA and the ANP shooting themselves in the foot? I think it was an update on that. Guy had swallowed some caustic soda or something. It came over as a T1 and when they got there, the guy just walked on to the ramp. He'd drunk the caustic soda the night before, didn't say anything at the time and then mentioned it in the morning so he could get off the front line for a while.'

'Those ones really piss me off mate,' Morris says. 'You're risking the cab and twelve people at least – the MERT, the QRF team and obviously all the crew – and you break your neck and it's all for nothing.'

There's nothing like a good moaning session to get everyone going; we're really cooking on gas now! I throw something else into the conversation.

'The ones that really get me are those that fuck with your head. I had a T2 that I picked up from Now Zad, a Taliban IED maker. Quite ironic really; he'd blown himself up making a bomb. What really bothered me about this one was that when he'd blown himself up, some of the shrapnel hit a little girl who was nearby, severely wounding her. We couldn't pick her up due to the rules that only allow us to pick up ISAF troops, the Taliban and civilians hit by crossfire between us and the Taliban. We had no remit and no authorisation or responsibility to pick her up.'

'Fuck man, that's just wrong,' German offers.

'Personally,' says Morris, 'I'd have left the Taliban guy to die and taken her instead.'

'Me too mate,' I say. 'Me too. But it's one of the realities of war I guess; the Taliban was of immense value from an intelligence perspective. She was "only" a little girl so he was hooked up and she wasn't. It's an impossible decision to make because, either way, the outcome would have been potentially bad.'

'That's realpolitik in action my friend,' adds Morris. 'It ain't pretty, but it's the way it is. I'm just glad it's not our call. It's way above our pay grade. Did Hannah tell you about the Taliban gunman she was called out for on the IRT?'

'Dunno. What's the story?' I ask.

'It was somewhere near Gereshk. He'd been captured after he'd been wounded in a firefight and he absolutely did not want to get on board. He was trying to fight the stretcher-bearers even though he was restrained. They found a razor blade on him when they searched him. He'd obviously wanted to hurt them even though they were trying to help him.'

'Is it just me that feels more of an affinity for the Brits we pick up?' I ask. 'I always felt a greater level of concern when it's a UK national or British soldier that we pick up.'

'No, it's not just you mate,' say German and Morris. Morris goes on, 'I guess it just hits closer to home – you can identify with them more, you have some sort of picture of their existence and their life back home so it has greater gravitas, more meaning.'

'That's exactly it,' I say. 'It resonates more because there's an instant affinity based on shared experience and culture. It doesn't matter how I try and rationalise it and if I'm honest, I feel a bit strange that I feel like that, but it's not something you have any control over, is it? It's just the way it is.'

'You know how we pick up so many children?' asks Morris. 'What amazes me is how they always tend to arrive with a rela-tive – usually a father or grandfather – and if it's a girl we're picking up, they're always more concerned about her status and her religion than they are with letting the doctors deal with her injuries. The medics are trying to lift her dress up to treat severe leg injuries or traumatic amputations and she's trying to cover herself up because her father's stood there. That always strikes me as a terrible shame; one of the cultural differences that we don't seem to be able to bridge.'

Just then the phone goes: two long rings. The guys have got another shout.

German and I make our excuses and head back to our tent. One more day down; another day closer to home.

18

SIX DEGREES OF RISK

We finished the month providing IRT support to Operation Chakush, a British-led NATO operation which had started about a week earlier in the area between Heyderabad and Mirmandab, just north-east of Gereshk. Chakush, the Pashto word for 'hammer', was designed to kick the Taliban out of the area and keep them out, and it involved around 1,500 mostly British Forces drawn from the Light Dragoons and 1st BN Grenadier Guards together with some 500 ANA.

We were seeing a lot more ANA-led ops against the Taliban on this Det, assisted of course by UK troops from the Operational Mentor and Liaison Team, or 'OMLT'. Nevertheless, it showed that the Afghans were taking a hand in dealing with problems themselves, which in itself was a remarkable improvement on how things had been previously. Even this early on in our tour, I'd already noticed quite a difference compared to my deployment in the summer of 2006. We weren't necessarily coming under fire more frequently, but we were flying a greater number of IRT missions. What it illustrated was that the Taliban were evolving and had started to adapt their tactics – there was a massive spike in their employment of IEDs.

The Afghan National Army had been leading an operation attacking two compounds near Sangin with a trench system between them, and one of the ANA soldiers had taken a round. It was late at night when we got the call to scramble; he was categorised T1.

As per usual, we were up and away in no time. As captain, I went to the JOC to get the details while Rich, Jim and Bob went straight to the cab to get her up and running. Rich was the handling pilot, while I was doing nav.

We were flying on NVGs, which always makes for an interesting experience. The technology behind this vital bit of kit is something of a paradox, as it's both amazingly simple in concept, yet complex in application. At its most basic level, the goggles work by converting whatever light there is into electricity, boosting that electricity, and then turning it back into light. It's easy to take a small electric current at one end and produce a bigger flow at the other – it's what amplifiers do, although you probably most commonly associate them with electric guitars or sound systems.

In practice, NVGs gather all available ambient light – cultural, moonlight, starlight and infrared – through a lens on an image intensifier tube (IIT). Light is made of photons (particles of light) which the IIT converts into electrons (subatomic particles carrying a negative electric charge). Those electrons hit a very thin charged disc called a photocathode, which amplifies them, releasing millions more electrons, and they then hit a phosphor screen, which converts them back into photons. As there are now millions more photons than originally entered the lens, what you see is a much brighter monochromatic green two-dimensional version of the original scene.

Although the photons that hit the IIT are carrying light of all colours, these colours are lost when the photons are converted to electrons. The phosphors on the screen are deliberately chosen to make a green image, because the human eye can decipher more different shades of green than any other colour. As NVGs display a two-dimensional image, there's no perception of depth, which can make flying quite a challenge since distance and closing speeds are very difficult to assess. It's something you get used to though.

Initially, we were held off by the Apache escorting us as there was a firefight going on, but we got clearance within about ten minutes so we started our approach to the HLS.

Rich flew a tactical descent to scrub off speed and line us up with the target that we'd identified, and suddenly it all kicked off. The ANA heard us coming in so they laid down a weight of fire to suppress the Taliban who were intent on shooting us down. That prompted the OMLT in their Warrior Fighting Vehicles to join in, so they opened up on the compound with their 30mm cannons. That was great in one sense, but it was fucking scary at first: all we could see were loads of lines of red and green tracer being directed against these two compounds.

Through the NVGs, everything has an ethereal, slightly unreal quality and in some respects you feel quite detached, but it's still bizarre seeing all this ordnance being fired, knowing that, although it looks quite pretty, it would ruin your day if it were to hit you. AK-47s and RPGs are the weapons of choice for both the ANA and the Taliban, so it seemed like thousands of 7.62mm rounds were flying back and forth, with RPG rounds being traded in both directions and a sizeable amount of 30mm to boot. The image through our NVGs was almost painfully bright and it seemed like the sky was alive with rounds. The air was thick with lead.

The HLS was really dusty, even by Afghan standards, and I remember thinking, 'I'm glad I'm not flying this!' Rich did a beautiful landing and he put us down in the exact spot we needed to be in. We were just behind the line of friendly forces so we were pretty well protected. The ramp went down and the QRF guys fanned out in a protective cordon while the MERT ran off to find the casualty; Rich and I just sat there with the rotors turning watching the fireworks.

I guess it was still pretty risky – we were within range of fire from the Taliban, but the ANA were so effective at suppressing them that we never really felt under threat. It's funny how your perception changes and, with it, your attitude to risk. I guess it's all relative, but even when you're taking fire, it's a matter of degrees. It's one thing being stood at close quarters having someone trading fire with you, but when there's distance involved and difficult angles it's another story altogether.

I don't recall feeling scared once we were on the ground, and that made me think again of how much easier life is for those of us in theatre than it is for our loved ones back home. To them, you're going to Afghanistan so they're worried sick. They don't know the parochial aspects of life out here – most of what people at home know is gleaned from the media.

Sex sells, which is this case translates as bullets, bombs and guns. So the TV news, magazines and newspapers rarely show the casual side of life in theatre because it's dull – the public are fed a steady diet of high-octane ops, with reporters being filmed looking like Rambo in chinos, minus the weaponry, diving for cover as the bullets fly. Ross Kemp speaks breathlessly of the dangers, taking cover in a ditch somewhere in Helmand as the section he's embedded with tries to fight its way to safety. In short, those at home know that when you go to Afghanistan it's more than likely going to be bloody dangerous.

Compared to being at home, yes it is. But the reality is that you're six degrees of separation from mortal danger, all depending on where you are and what you're doing in theatre. Those degrees start inside the wire at Bastion, where the biggest danger is from the sun or the dreaded D&V rather than bullets, RPGs and IEDs. The risk is marginally greater at KAF with its regular rocket attacks, but even then it's not really anything to worry about. Although we're airborne and we get shot at, it's a known quantity; I'm in a familiar environment, we're a moving target and to a degree, as pilots, we're masters of our own destiny because we can fly tactically – making ourselves harder to hit. To most of us, the risk is negligible compared to that experienced by the real heroes – the guys and girls living in the FOBs out on the front line who patrol and are close to contact with the Taliban every day. That's how we were able to sit in the cab while the rounds flew, watching the display through our NVGs, and waiting for the casualty to be brought on board.

We couldn't have been on the ground for more than about two minutes. The MERT team reappeared with the casualty, the QRF came back on, and as soon as the ramp closed we got the familiar call of 'Clear above and behind' from Jim. We never, ever chase them with calls of 'How long?' We're a crew, we work together, and it's a given that nobody wants to stay on the ground one second longer than we need to. Helicopters belong in the sky and that's where we want to be so, while it varies from boring to downright fucking scary to be sat on the ground in the goldfish bowl that doubles as a cockpit, we know that the crewmen will tell us we're good to go the second it's appropriate.

We got back to Bastion without incident and delivered the casualty to Nightingale, but I don't think we'd even sat down in the IRT tent when the next shout came in: two casualties – Afghan nationals, both categorised T1s. A suicide bomber had walked up to an ANP checkpoint near Gereshk and blown himself up. It's a quick run from Bastion to Gereshk so we were there and back within thirty minutes.

We shut down, got back to the IRT tent and twenty minutes after landing we were all in bed for, unusually, an uninterrupted night's sleep.

19

THE FIFTH PASSENGER

There's a book out there called *The Eighth Passenger* by Miles Tripp and it's a stunningly eloquent and articulate account of his life as the bomb aimer on a Lancaster in World War II. It's so called because the Lancaster flew with a crew of seven; the eighth passenger was fear.

There is a mission that German and I flew early in August that really brought that home to me. Fear was my fifth passenger on that sortie and for me, it perfectly illustrated the maxim that it's not always about what actually happens; we're all wise after the event. How we feel is more often dictated by what's known at the time.

The mission involved us supporting a major offensive over four days with the objective of putting some pressure on the Taliban in the Upper Gereshk Valley. The aim was for ground troops to probe and patrol through the Green Zone to try to reduce the number of attacks on FOB Inkerman, which was being attacked every day at around 13:00 hrs with multiple mortar rounds, RPGs and small arms fire. The guys inside were living a miserable existence.

We were flying as a four-ship gaggle – two Apaches to support two cabs; Eurotrash in one, JP and Morris in the other. For this particular mission, almost two companies of Royal Anglians needed moving over a short distance of something like a mile and a half. They were on the eastern side of the Helmand River and needed to be somewhere on the western side, because they wanted to investigate what intelligence suggested was a Taliban front line combat hospital.

The plan was to land two Chinooks in a cultivated field that was completely surrounded by trees. Tactically, it was far from ideal because the HLS was looked on from all four sides and the trees provided perfect cover for the Taliban, but that's how it had to be; the troops we were lifting were at that location. Once we had them aboard, we would fly them across the Helmand River and land in the middle of a field full of maize. That field was just at the bottom of a hill, which was where the building they were going to investigate was sited.

The mission was risky and my biggest concern was the fact that the sortie was over such a short distance. Given the density of Taliban forces in the Green Zone, if we were landing inside, loading troops and flying them just a mile and a half, we'd be low and slow for most of the flight – the worst combination of all. We'd be lucky to fly at more than eighty to a hundred knots, making us an inviting target, and if Taliban forces were anywhere close, they'd have to be fast asleep or blind and deaf to miss us. To make matters worse, we had a huge number of troops to move – almost two companies' worth – so we were looking at three separate trips to get them all across.

JP was flying the lead cab and he'd come up with a plan routing us along the western side of the river. Sangin is on the eastern side of the Helmand River with a wadi running east to west on the northern side, and on the western side there were some pretty steep cliffs with some very deep cuts – steep-sided, deep valleys really. The plan was for us to set down on the flat desert floor about three miles or so out on the west side of the river and, once cleared in, to approach the pick-up point by flying along the valley floor, which was just deep enough that you could fly a Chinook and it would be completely hidden from view. That element would turn out to be one of the most exciting bits of flying I've ever done in theatre; it was just like the scene in *Star Wars* when the Rebellion Alliance pilots are flying the X-Wing fighters through the Death Star's canyons as they try to destroy it.

As we come in, I can see there are some British troops in position on top of the cliffs. They are out of sight to any Taliban forces in the Green Zone. They've approached from the desert side and are in Jackals; they are there to cut off any Taliban who escape once the main thrust of the attack on the hospital has come in from the west. I see that one of the Jackals is on fire following a mine strike; it does not do anything to calm my nerves.

The Apaches are on station providing overwatch; they clear us in. We have a time on target – it's all calculated by JP, who is a brilliant tactician, so we know it's going to be dead on. We are familiar with his methods – 'You're going to come in on this heading at this speed for this amount of time, and then throttle back on this heading on the approach.' Let's say you normally fly the approach at 120kts for three miles. You decelerate for the last mile and you'll average 60kts, so you'll be in the gate at the target. So JP has worked all that out to the last second and, as usual with him, that's where we are; time on target is exactly as he'd planned.

The wadi we are flying through on the run in is very narrow and very deep so JP goes in ahead. Because we want to arrive close together, I am as close behind his cab as I dare – certainly no more than twice the span of our rotors. And when I say that valley is narrow, there can't be more than the width of one rotor either side of us, so there is no room for error. Luckily it's dead straight, because there isn't enough width for us to effect a tight turn – the rotors are simply too close to the valley walls. Tactically, you could argue it isn't brilliant, but it is the best option and with the Apache on overwatch, as good as it gets. JP has chosen this particular wadi for the run in because it is stripped of vegetation, so there is absolutely no cover and nowhere for any Taliban to lie in wait.

The sense of speed and noise is awesome – obviously, you need a frame of reference to feel and see speed, which is why 160kts at height doesn't feel particularly fast. Over the ground you get some sense of perspective, but where we are – in a narrow valley, flying at speed below the level of the ground on either side, just a cab's height from the floor – it is breathtaking. With our two cabs flying so close and in such an enclosed space, the noise outside must be deafening.

We're getting close now, I can see the Green Zone starting to appear ahead and below me as I look through the floor bubble, and suddenly the AH calls us on the radio.

'Beefcake Two Four, Ugly Five One, we're picking up ICOM chatter. Be advised Taliban forces may be moving long-barrelled weapons and RPGs near your location. ICOM seems to be saying they should concentrate on the helicopters.'

I turn to Rich. 'For fuck's sake, we so don't need to know that.'

He shakes his head. 'What the fuck use is that? Talk about stating the obvious. So he's basically telling us that the Taliban are out there and might be waiting for us. And we can do what about that, exactly?'

We know there are people out there that have the weapons and desire to shoot us down, it goes with the territory, but you keep your awareness of that fact at the back of your mind where it belongs. Otherwise it gnaws away at you and the fear builds. If the AH had said he had the Taliban in his sights and was about to engage, fair enough. Telling us that there were Taliban forces waiting for us – what good was that to us, other than to divert our focus just when we needed it to be on the job at hand? I know the AH crew were only trying to help, so I can't blame them too much; I guess you're damned if you do, damned if you don't.

So we're running in and I can really feel my heart pumping. My senses are amplified and the adrenaline is flowing now, I'm wired on it. I've got that metallic taste at the back of my throat and I can feel my palms sweating into the calf-leather flying gloves that encase my hands as I work the cyclic and collective.

The end of the valley is in sight. JP has aimed to get us into the southern end of the target because the Green Zone is at its narrow-est there, meaning there's less cover for the Taliban to hide in. He makes sure we take the shortest route in and immediately we're out of the wadi and over the Helmand River.

'JP's going to come hard left. The target is currently in your 10 o'clock, one and a half miles, heading 010,' says German. 'Past this tall hedge in the 10 o'clock, visual?'

'Visual,' I reply, and it's an effort just to say that one word as I'm concentrating on the low-level flying, JP, the enemy, the navigation, my fear and, most importantly, not fucking up the approach.

I fly a really tight left-hand turn to slow us down for the target. The Apache is in contact with the troops on the ground and they've popped smoke, so we have visual on their location. JP goes forward and right, so I go slightly to his rear and left. We want to get in as fast as possible, so I keep our speed over the ground high and leave it to the last minute to slow down. As soon as we are on short finals, I flare, then bank the cab, booting the pedal; the idea is to use the belly of the aircraft as an airbrake. We pirouette nose down, I add a touch of forward cyclic to stop us climbing and with the tail at a 40° angle to the ground, all the speed falls away. It's aggressive flying, but it works – I want to be as unpredictable as possible because anything I can do to make us more difficult to hit has to be good.

We land on and it runs like clockwork. The troops are waiting for us in the field ready to move, and their mates who we are going to move on the second lift are fanned out along the treeline, defending the LS. Our pax are on in double-quick time – it seems like we are on the ground for less than thirty seconds before I hear the crewman say we're ready to lift. I pull power and we're away.

With just a mile and a half to run, we're at the drop point in no time. I see JP make a tight right turn with loads of flare on the descent and I'm thinking, 'Fuck, he's landed in the jungle there!' because it's a maize field and the vegetation is so high and thick. It's incredible to watch because his downwash flattens everything as he sinks groundwards. It's just like the parting of the Red Sea.

There's no way we are going to get into the same field – it's just too small to accommodate us both. I pick a field to the left.

'BANG!'

'What the fuck was that?' asks Rich as the centre windscreen cracks and we see a mass of blood and feathers. 'Bird strike,' I say, my nerves already on edge. 'That helps!' I flare the cab for the descent. The maize goes wild, flattening in our downwash. I spot a small sapling in our 1 o'clock and it flattens too until the downwash subsides and it fights back, popping up just high enough to miss the forward disc.

Things have changed since Vietnam, where the Hueys would come in to clearings too small to land in, and the pilots would use the disc to chop the trees down and make it larger. The tensile strength of the blades is different – the Huey's were solid steel whereas the Chinook's are lightweight and far less durable by comparison.

The ramp is down as soon as we hit the deck, the troops run off and, within seconds, we lift again and are away. The rest of the mission runs like clockwork and we land back at Bastion, tired but pleased at a job well done.

I'm exhausted – partly because the flying has been so intense, but it's more than that. I feel wrung out with the stress. Okay, the mission went without incident in the end, but how the hell did we get away with it? All the warning signs were there; we were in Taliban territory, we were big and bold, low and slow in places, just waiting for it to happen. There was nothing we could do; we were a big fucking target in the sky. All it needed was a few Taliban with their heads turned skywards, RPGs on their shoulders and that would have been it. Even if they couldn't see us coming, they must've heard us. And there was the ICOM chatter that they were laying in wait for us with weapons ready. What the fuck was wrong with them? They missed a huge opportunity, and we ended up scoring an impressive goal in their backyard.

I was already on edge, but the ICOM chatter had me even more focused and my senses amplified. Every nerve cell in my body felt alive, alert to the danger. My heart was pounding like it was ready to jump out of my chest and all along I felt like I was just waiting for the rounds to hit us. So while all that was going on, I had to be 100% focused on flying the aircraft, getting my passengers down safely and making sure we were where we were supposed to be. I had no spare capacity and as soon as we turned for home, I felt all the adrenaline disappear, leaving me utterly drained.

I think back to the briefing before the sortie, learning that the pick-up and the drop-off points were so close together, right in the middle of the Green Zone. It seemed like a suicide mission.

There was no way to vary our route in or out, so we just had to get on with it and the fear was my constant companion throughout, like a fifth member of the crew with nothing to offer.

We do the missions because we feel compelled to – because the guys on the ground have an infinitely more dangerous job than us and they rely on us. Partly it's also down to good leadership, and in JP we had that and more. He was someone that we trusted implicitly. Also, there was a good chance he'd been privy to intelligence I hadn't seen; the bottom line is there were clearly good operational reasons for the mission and I knew JP would have looked at the plan upside down and back to front. He would have deconstructed it, looked at it in its component parts and worked out how best to put it back together, so I had faith that the profile we flew was the best one under the circumstances.

I always try and rationalise things but, if I'm honest, that's one sortie I can't explain.

20

A VALIANT SOLDIER

August 11th 2007 is a day I'll never forget. Rich and I, together with crewmen Jim Warner and Bob Ruffles, were on the third day of a four-day stint in Bastion, which had been dominated by trips to and from FOB Inkerman to extract a significant number of British casualties. The base, which was home to 'C' (Essex) Company Royal Anglians, is situated about eight klicks north of Sangin and acted as a buffer between the town and the Taliban for whom it seemed to be some form of ordnance magnet.

Every day was the same. Sometime between 13:00 hrs and 14:00 hrs, the Taliban would launch concerted attacks on the base, employing every weapon at their disposal. Those inside the base got used to a daily diet of recoilless rifle, RPGs, rockets, mortars and small arms fire, and in giving as good as they got, they took a number of casualties. In the two previous days, we'd recovered at least eleven troops, including the body of Private Tony Rawson, who had been shot dead while on patrol. His Company Commander, Captain David Hicks, had written a very moving eulogy for him.

Whenever a British soldier is killed in theatre, Brigade HQ immediately enforces Op Minimise, a blackout of communications across the entire country. Phones, email, Paradigm text and internet are affected simultaneously. When it happens, and it can be at any time of the day or night, an announcement is made to that effect by Tannoy at each base and FOB. If you're in the middle of a call or surfing the net, you won't get a chance to say goodbye – Op Minimise has the immediacy of a power outage.

Its purpose is to allow the next-of-kin informing process to begin and not be inadvertently or wilfully undermined by members of the casualty's unit advising the family, friends or media before the military can track them down. How long that takes can vary – Op Minimise might last a few hours, it could last a whole day, or during summer (when the UK's casualties are at their highest) Op Minimise can be called back-to-back, meaning we can go four, five, six or more days without being able to contact our loved ones. Of course, as soon as Op Minimise comes into effect, every Brit in Afghanistan knows that somewhere in the country a commanding officer is making the call that will set in chain the sequence of events that will lead to someone's partner, parent or sibling getting the dreaded knock on the door.

The morning of the 11th had been quiet, so we'd taken the opportunity to enjoy lunch as a crew together at one of Bastion's DFACS (dining facilities), although the radio was always close at hand. Sadly, life at FOB Inkerman wasn't so sunny. At around 13:30, just as we were arriving back at the IRT tent, the Taliban had launched another attack on the base and a mortar round had landed on a fuel tank, causing multiple injuries. An RPG had also found its mark, hitting an observation tower in the middle of the base, severely wounding Captain Hicks. We got the call just after 14:00: two long rings, which by now sounded to us like the clanging chimes of doom. Like Pavlov's dogs, we responded through conditioning; we hated the sound, but it produced a surge of adrenaline in all of us.

I'm captain, so Rich and Jim head straight for the aircraft to get her spun up, while Bob and I head for the JOC to get the details. There is no need for us to wait for the Apache on IRT duty to escort us; the crew is already overhead at Inkerman helping out the beleaguered guys inside with some close air support. As per usual, by the time Bob and I reach the cab, we're pretty much good to go. The MERT is already on board, busily sorting kit out and hanging up IV drips. The QRF sit ready and waiting, their weapons resting between their legs, business ends pointing downwards – that way, any negligent discharges aren't going to take out vital systems.

Back at RAF Odiham on a routine tasking, it takes us around forty-five minutes to start the aircraft and get airborne. On the IRT, we've got it down to just a few minutes. There are lives at stake and every second counts; we do everything we can to make a difference, and in the dynamic, constantly changing environment that is a war zone, getting airborne in the shortest time possible is one thing we can influence. I brief the crew as soon as I don my helmet and connect the pigtail.

'It's a bad one, guys. FOB Inkerman. We've got two T1s, four T3s and a walking wounded to pick up. The LS was still hot when I left the JOC and the Apache was letting loose with everything it has, so it could get interesting on the way in. Everyone okay?'

'All good, Frenchie,' the crew come back. German fires up the engines and with the all clear from Jim at the ramp, we lift into the afternoon sunshine and turn north.

'OK, same drill as usual,' I say as we climb to height. 'No rank bollocks on my cab. I'm Frenchie or Alex, this is German, you're Bob and you're Jim. You have my authority to engage without reference if you identify a firing point. Clear?'

'All clear, Frenchie,' from the back.

Before we climb to height on the transit north of Bastion, there's a linear feature which we know as the deconfliction line. With that in our six o'clock, the guys in the back can test fire the guns – aside from the Apache, they're our last line of defence, so if they're going to fail, you want to know before things heat up, not at a crucial life-or-death moment. Hence, on every sortie, the aircraft's weapons are test fired.

'Checking weapons,' says Jim at the ramp.

'Checking weapons,' says Bob on the Crowd Pleaser.

'Work away, fellas.'

Jim opens up with the ramp-mounted M60. It's a gas-operated, air-cooled, belt-fed, automatic machine-gun with a maximum rate of fire of 550 rounds per minute; on its own, it's pretty impressive as it fires a line of rounds out into the sky over Helmand. Then Bob lets fly with the door-mounted M134 Minigun – compared to that, the M60 sounds like an *X Factor* loser against Whitney Houston. The noise the Crowd Pleaser makes as it spits out up to four thousand 7.62mm rounds a minute has to be heard to be believed. A spout of flame erupts from the front as the six barrels rotate and fire a line of red-hot rounds earthwards. It's a great weapon to have.

We come in through the Sangin Valley and fly a holding pattern over the western side, waiting to be called in by the AHs. The site is still hot as hell and we wait for a lull in the fighting so we can put down. The Apaches are doing everything they can to speed that moment along and are directing a huge weight of fire at the Green Zone. The 30mm cannon fire a stream of High Explosive (HE) shells earthwards and then they let loose with their flechette rockets. These weapons are truly awesome in their destructive power, especially against multiple personnel out in the open; once in flight, each rocket releases eighty six-inch tungsten darts travelling at 2,460mph. They'll shred anything within a 50m spread and if they hit a human target, their supersonic speed creates a vacuum that will suck up everything in its path. They are just the thing for the fuckers who are causing all the misery at FOB Inkerman.

The site is still hot, but we know there are seven casualties down there who are depending on us. The AHs are raining fire down to suppress the enemy below in an effort to get us in, so it's in our hands.

'Guys, we could wait 'til the end of tour for this LS to go cold. Are we all happy to make a move with it still hot?'

All three of them agree. We're going in. 'Ugly Five Two, Doorman Two Four, request you keep the pressure on. We're going in,' I advise.

'Roger that, Doorman. We'll keep their heads down,' I hear against a deafening live soundtrack of 30mm cannon fire.

'Okay, Rich. There are two or three triangular-shaped hills there that are almost like the pyramids at Giza. They're your marker for a left-hand turn to end up on a south-west track. That'll put us a mile and a half out from the LS.'

'Got it.'

Rich flies fast, aggressive and dirty as we make the approach at low level. His favourite technique to arrest our speed is a series of steep, acute turns and he's expert at it; the tail goes left, right, left, right as our speed drops. I'm 'eyes out', looking out the window, but I look at the engine instruments briefly to scan the Ts and Ps and that's when I notice the NR is at 114%! In all my hours of flying, I've never seen it that high. 110% is the limit, and I've never even seen it that high, let alone 114%!

It's weird because normally once you get above 104% – still within limits – the gearbox protests by making a noise that sounds like God shouting, and you feel a shed-load of vibration in the aircraft caused by the blades slapping the air. Normally, push the aircraft this hard and you know all about it. This time? Nothing. The aircraft is flying with NR of 114% and it's as smooth as a baby's bottom. There's no time to tell Rich to correct it, so I pull on the collective to create some lift to bring the NR back within limits.

Rich looks at me. 'Fuck, Frenchie! Thanks for that.' He's as stunned as I am.

'No worries. Twenty seconds to go. HLS is on the nose. You visual? Speed is good, good rate of descent. Everyone secure?' I ask.

As Rich sets us up in the gate at 100ft and 30kts, the LS is still taking fire. Suddenly the Defensive Aids Suite detects a threat. Some sort of weapons system has engaged us and the DAS has picked it up.

BANG! BANG! BANG! BANG! It fires out a series of flares.

'60ft, 30kts,' I say as Rich brings the nose up.

Jim and Bob take over the talk-down and within seconds I feel the rear wheels land on.

'Two wheels on . . . six wheels on,' from the back.

The ramp goes down and the doctor heads out to meet the troops who are already with the casualties and heading for the aircraft. At the front, Rich and I are busy scanning everything and doing all the checks we can so that as soon as we get the nod, we can lift; we know the crewmen are busy and they'll signal to us to get the hell out of Dodge the minute they can.

The threat from incoming mortars is a real worry for me. How much longer can our luck hold? The casualties take longer than I'd like to load but, with seven of them, that's to be expected. I look down and see a pair of feet in the 2ft narrow 'corridor' that leads from the rear of the cab to the cockpit. Something's wrong though; they belong to an ANA who is laid on his back and his toes are pointing down towards the floor, not up as they should be. Both ankles are broken.

I catch Jim's eye. 'This guy's in a bad way, mate,' he says. 'I'm just putting a tourniquet on him and it's my tourniquet cos we've run out of them in the back.'

Fuck me, it must be bad; I've never heard of that happening before. I look towards the ramp and a scene of absolute bedlam greets me: six wounded British casualties and a wounded Afghan soldier on board – two T1s, four T3s and a walking wounded. I can't ever remember a time before when we had that many casualties in the cab. There are stretchers taking up every spare inch of floor space and almost nowhere for the QRF guys to go. IV drips hang from every point, the floor is awash with blood; I can almost smell it. It's a scene of utter devastation – broken bodies and medics working like crazy in the dark, cramped dusty cab.

'Ramp up, clear above and behind.'

That's all we need to hear. 'Lifting,' says Rich, pulling up the collective. He pushes forward on the cyclic to get the nose down and we disappear, as low and fast and dirty as we can, manoeuvring all the while to make ourselves as difficult a target as possible. We're engaged again; the DAS fires flares off to tempt away whatever threat it's detected headed towards us.

The number one priority on lifting is to get the aircraft out of the engagement zone. Rich turns an immediate left as we depart, along the wadi at low level – Sangin's to the right and we don't want to get too close to that without getting some speed up.

The team are trying to stabilise Captain Hicks. I ask Bob how he is.

'He's taken a head wound, Frenchie. They're doing CPR on him at the moment.'

They manage to revive him, but I'm in awe of the crewmen. Already overworked with running the cab and managing the aircraft, they're up to their elbows in all of the worst aspects of conflict – the bloodied, battered bodies of young soldiers. It's hard enough for us looking in the mirror and seeing the guys working on them, but there's no escape for the crewmen – they're up close and personal. I look at the MERT team working on Capt Hicks; he has multiple arrests but each time they perform CPR he comes back. I will him to hang on. We all want him to live.

We run down as fast as we can down the east side of Sangin, along the east side of FOB Robinson, and once we clear that we do a right turn towards the south-west, north of Gereshk and a straight run for Bastion, avoiding all the danger areas. With the nose dipped, we are wringing every single ounce of power the cab has, flying at the aircraft's VNE or Velocity Never Exceed. The ASI shows us at 160 knots – even more at times.

The engine is temperature-limited rather than torque-limited in theatre, so there are certain temperature bands that govern how hard you can push it. Continuous does what it says on the tin, as does thirty-minute power. Ten minutes means you can push hard for ten minutes but then have to come back into thirty minutes. Finally, there is 'Emergency' – you can push the engines to the max for five minutes but doing so starts a countdown timer. Once you exceed that, the engine's ready for the bin.

We literally can't fly the aircraft any harder to get it back. We are flying at the top of ten-minute power for nine minutes fifty-nine seconds, and then we lower the lever, get the engine back into thirty minutes and then yank the power back up to the ten-minute band. We try everything we've got. We're flying faster than I've ever done before in a Chinook and it's shaking like a bastard. We can't fly a straight line back – the risk to the cab from ground fire is too great. We have to weigh up the options: save thirty seconds and risk losing the seven casualties, the crew, the medics and the cab, or go the longer way round? It's a no-brainer. We can't go as the crow flies so we take the quickest route we can. It adds maybe thirty seconds to our journey, but it feels like an age. I feel like we're watching an hourglass and the sand's about to run out.

Bastion's in sight now. I can see the wire. Nightingale and the HLS are on the nose. We're seconds away. Rich is working it like a madman; we're digging deep to give everything we can.

'How are things in the back?' I ask.

'I'm sorry mate, I think it's over. He's had a heart attack and they're stopping CPR,' says Bob.

I feel like the bottom has dropped out of our world. It's absolutely heart-wrenching. But there's still a chance, so we don't stop. We don't ever stop until we're on the ground and we've done everything we can. We rip the aircraft all the way to Nightingale and the team are waiting for us. Rich stops the cab on a sixpence, we land on and the ramp goes down. The casualties are off, but we're too late for David Hicks – sadly, he doesn't make it.

We're gutted. All of us. The aircraft is deathly quiet, everyone gathering their thoughts. I've never seen a cab so trashed in the back; there's equipment strewn everywhere, the detritus of the frantic fight to save lives. But we've no time to wallow; we have to prep the cab in case we're scrambled again. We have a great relationship with the MERT because we fly with them all the time. When we drop the casualties at Nightingale, it's only the surgeon who goes off with them – the nurses stay on the aircraft. They clean up the cab, prepare it. Jim and Bob are part of the team – they're all involved. They put on the white all-in-one forensic suits and gloves to protect against contamination and get to work cleaning out the cab and mopping up the blood.

The MERT worked so hard to save those guys. We did everything we could. The aircraft couldn't have given any more. All that, and it wasn't enough. Fuck it! Everything we know, all that medical knowledge and it's not enough. He still died, and what's worse is, it was within sight of the hospital.

I feel powerless; totally powerless. I feel an intense sadness, but it's mixed up with anger. Sat on the HLS you have time to think, to replay events. Did we do all we could? Could we have done more? Would it have made a difference? What did we fail to do?

As pilots, we're tested constantly. We take three or four tests every year, simulator sessions; an off day, one fail, and that's it. Game over. It's the end of your flying career. We don't fail, ever. But suddenly, we've given everything and yet we failed.

The death of Captain David Hicks really hit me hard. I've picked up the bodies of British soldiers who have died before; I've had people die in the cab before, but I've not known their names or seen their faces. This is different because David Hicks wasn't a faceless, nameless person. I knew his name, I saw his face.

Captain David Hicks was twenty-six when he died and, to me, a real hero. He was the acting company commander in charge of fifty men at FOB Inkerman and when an RPG hit the tower that he was in, he received multiple shrapnel wounds. Those wounds made him a candidate for immediate medevac, but he chose to stay even while five others were evacuated, and carried on in command of the outpost.

He reportedly tore off his oxygen mask and refused a morphine injection on the grounds that it might cloud his judgement. He was still insisting on getting back to his men when he lost consciousness. For his actions, he was posthumously awarded the Military Cross. For me, he displayed total leadership all the way to the end. I think he was a rare human being and when you learn all this stuff about him, you question yourself again and again. Did I do everything I could to save him? However much you know that the answer is yes, you still feel responsible; it's human nature. You take ownership because your two worlds collided.

I still live in mine. I wish the same could be said for Captain Hicks.

21

THE TWILIGHT ZONE

After the IRT shift where FOB Inkerman dominated so much of our time, we flew back to the weird hinterland of KAF for some downtime. There was no question that the conditions were better at KAF – the accommodation was brick-built, properly air-conditioned, and the ablutions were much better than the converted ISO containers at Bastion.

The trouble was, living at KAF was like living in the Twilight Zone. While Bastion was all about purpose, KAF felt more like a work in progress that would never quite get to the end state. Aside from the astonishingly large number of REMFs for whom it was a permanent base, almost everyone else there was in transit – either on their way home or on their way to be deployed forward, whether to Kabul, Bastion, a FOB or a Patrol Base somewhere in Helmand Province.

On the plus side, it did have a decent gym we'd sometimes hang out at, there was the Green Bean Cafe, and then there was the boardwalk, the manufactured 'heart' of the base. Constructed of raw, unfinished timber, it played host to a range of takeaways and shops, such as Pizza Hut, Burger King, Subway and Tim Horton's – a Canadian coffee and doughnuts franchise. There were also shops selling local crafts, rugs and ice cream. You could almost forget you were in a war zone at the boardwalk – aside from the background noise of fighter jets screaming overhead, helicopters and transports taking off and the sound of sporadic gunfire. Oh, and the fact that every diner was armed.

Then there was the BX, a gargantuan US-run retail outlet. Rich and I would often look around there, if only to laugh at the bizarre assortment of goods that they sell and see if there was anything new on offer. There never was, of course. It was just the same strange assortment of big fuck-off knives, tactical vests and other gear for Special-Forces types and SF wannabes, near-beer, strangely flavoured 'potato chips' and Hershey Bars, that funny-tasting excuse for chocolate that Americans love. We could never work out who bought most of the stuff on offer. I mean, sure, buy all the 'gung-ho-look-at-me-I'm-Johnny-Rambo' stuff that some Americans on Det love to buy. Yeah, buy a flat screen 42" TV for your tent, and a PS3 and kit yourself up like Sergeant Rock, but what the fuck to do you do with it all at the end of your tour?

Everything about working and living alongside the Americans was bizarre. I know Winston Churchill said we're two nations divided by a common language, but nowhere is this more evident than on military ops. Our SOPs, working practices, autonomy on ops – everything is different. A couple of days later, Rich and I were crewing one of the task lines and we had a US AH-64 Apache flying with us.

We were just transiting out across the deconfliction line and they called us over the radio, 'Ah, Hardwood Thirteen, Destruction One Five. Be advised we are going to test fire the guns,' so we dropped back behind them expecting to see a bit of 30mm fire from their cannon. That's one aspect of US military culture I love – their call signs. Ours are all sober and dull – 'Hardwood' or 'Beefcake', for the Chinooks, 'Ugly' for the Apaches. But their Apaches have call signs like 'Destruction One Five' or 'Barbarian One Zero'. Legend!

Anyway, as expected, we saw a hail of 30mm cannon fire from the AH and we were about to move up again thinking they'd finished, when they radioed us to say, 'Yeah, test firing's good. Further test fire coming up. Standby . . .' and Rich and I looked at one another like, 'What the fuck?!' just as they fired rockets at the fucking desert floor! That one thing highlights the dichotomy between them and us from a military perspective – a lot of what they do is so much more laid-back than for us. I guess it's largely economy-driven; they have so much more money to spend on defence than us, and it shows in the way that they can afford to be so profligate with ordnance. On the other hand, they have very little autonomy in how they operate – micromanagement seems to be the order of the day, whereas in the Army or RAF we are generally given a task or objective and it's up to us as junior commanders as to how that is achieved.

They were great to work with though, because when we were down at low level, they'd be there with us. When we got down on the deck for the run in, whether that was at 50ft or even 10ft, they'd be right there in the dirt with us on our wing. British Apache crews tend to sit up at around 2,000ft and a couple of klicks back, which gives them a degree of protection while providing them with an overview of the battle area or HLS, but these two guys, wherever we were, they were on our wing all the way. They're good people – and they have a surprising number of female Apache pilots, something our own Forces could benefit from.

August 18th saw us back on the HRF/IRT cycle back at Bastion. It felt good to be back doing some proper work again. We all know that taskings are vital to the operation, but I think most of us felt more of a sense of achievement on the IRT because we could see first-hand that we were making a difference.

While we were on HRF, Sir Richard Dannatt, the then Chief of the General Staff (CGS), was undertaking a tour of Helmand Province. Now Dannatt was a really, really good bloke, a proper soldiers' soldier, and the lads really liked and respected him. He was like a breath of fresh air compared to most of the faceless generals who'd preceded him and he garnered a lot of respect from the rank and file when he wilfully stepped the wrong side of the political divide as far as the PM and his Cabinet were concerned, by refusing to back the Government line. Dannatt infuriated Gordon Brown who, as the media have widely reported, was never the military's greatest fan, by speaking out on everything from our strategy in Iraq and Afghanistan to soldiers' pay and conditions. He was refreshingly honest, spoke it as he saw it and was respected and well liked by all of us.

He was at Lashkar Gah, where I assumed he'd been taken the day before by one of the cabs on tasking. We were tasked to pick him up and take him to Shorabak, which was the base where all the ANA were trained. After dropping him there, we did some resupply taskings around the province until it was time to collect the CGS.

His easy manner and natural charm were evident the minute we picked him up; he spent a few minutes chatting with the crewmen and then came straight to the front and sat on the jump seat.

'Welcome aboard Eurotrash, sir,' I said. He laughed but, perhaps wisely, didn't ask any more. 'I assume you've been to the front several times now, but have you ever flown to KAF at low level?'

'No, I haven't.'

'Would you like to?'

'I'd love to,' he said. 'Assuming it doesn't impact your tasking.'

'It's the end of a long day; it'll keep me awake if anything, sir! What we'll do then is take you down south from Lashkar Gah where there are some brilliant valleys running west to east in the middle of the Red Desert. Fancy some of that?'

'Sounds great!'

So that's what we did. We were flying as a pair with Morris and JP; we dropped down to 50ft and flew across the Red Desert to KAF.

'So sir, what's going on with regard to new aircraft? Are we going to get Blackhawks or anything else decent?'

'In short, sadly not. I wanted Blackhawks – far superior aircraft and much more capable platform for what we need – but we got Merlin instead. If I had my choice, it would be Blackhawk and Chinook all the way, nothing else. No Sea King, no Merlin, no Pumas.'

It should be about the right tool for the job but, more often than not, it's about what is politically expedient and beneficial to those who make the decisions. It's realpolitik in action again but, as we're British, we take what we're given graciously, and somehow still more or less manage to do what is asked of us.

He was very gracious and appreciative when we arrived back at KAF and didn't rush off, but hung around to chat. He took a genuine interest on the flight back, asking lots of questions, listening and making notes. I found him to be a thoroughly nice chap, really easy to talk to, candid, open and with a manner and approachability that belied his rank as head of the Army. After saying goodbye, I felt genuinely enlightened about a lot of things that were happening in theatre – and in the Army itself. I think he's a great bloke, really interesting. His retirement from the military was the Army's – and the Government's – loss.

He'll be missed.

22

THE FOG OF WAR

In war, there's neither truth nor lies. It's not all packaged up and chronological, with answers and successful outcomes to nicely timelined battles. The understanding, order and control – that all comes later, when the exhibitions of photographers' despatches have taken place, the newspaper and magazine articles have been published and the books by those who were there have been researched, written and reviewed.

War is dynamic, disordered and chaotic. Information and intelligence is king, but they are scarce commodities at the time and valueless in the aftermath. War is confusion. You get snippets. Things get misinterpreted. Viewed through the lens of hindsight, some events appear ludicrous, but at the time they are impossible to interpret in any way other than how they appear. You can only act according to the information you have available at the time.

It took the best part of three years to make sense of the incident that took place in Helmand Province on the evening of Thursday August 23rd. After all the interviews, the investigations, the hearings and coroners' courts, what we know now is that three British soldiers – Privates Aaron McClure, Rob Foster and John Thrumble from 1st Battalion The Royal Anglian Regiment – were killed in a 'blue-on-blue' incident. It took place after their platoon came under heavy fire from a determined Taliban force during a fighting patrol to disrupt enemy activity north-west of Kajaki. During the ensuing firefight, air support was requested from two US F15 aircraft, but the 500lb bomb dropped to take out the enemy positions some 500 yards away struck the compound where the three soldiers and their section were located instead. Privates McClure, Foster and Thrumble were killed instantly and two others soldiers were injured in the incident. It later transpired that the platoon's forward air controller gave the Americans the correct eight-digit coordinate for the airstrike but, deafened by enemy mortars, he replied 'Roger' after they were incorrectly repeated back to him.

Rich and I were at Camp Bastion with Bob and Jim on IRT/HRF rotation that day. We'd been in the JOC when we became aware that something had happened – people were running backwards and forwards way more than usual. There were worried expressions and people went about their tasks with a noticeable sense of urgency. Information was scarce, and what there was was confused. All we knew at the time was that there'd been an 'incident' near Kajaki involving The Royal Anglians. We knew there were multiple casualties, but at that stage we didn't know the 'who, what, how or why'.

The JOC was right next to The Royal Anglians' control centre, so we could see how everything was ramping up, and one of the hardest things to witness was the sense of panic in the eyes of their officers. They knew at the time they were looking at three missing from 7 Platoon B (Suffolk) Company – a major loss by any yardstick.

They wanted to scramble us to take some troops up to the area to search for survivors and to recover the injured, but it was really difficult for them to get the order for us to lift because the command structure had just changed. Although we were based out of Bastion, the Chinooks and Apaches were a NATO/ISAF asset, and control had switched to HQ Regional Command South (RC South) under the command of a NATO 2-star General at KAF. Everything now had to be cleared by JHF (A) at Kandahar but they, in turn, had to go up the line to HQ RC South for that clearance before coming back to us. It was a crazy, convoluted and time-consuming chain of command.

We were really desperate to get going and JHF (A) at Bastion wanted us airborne, but it wasn't their call any longer, so it was hell waiting around to get authorisation to lift. The order had to be thought through and there was a process to follow. It's about assessing where the incident is – do they scramble an aircraft from Bastion or KAF? What else was going on? What were the risk factors to the aircraft and crew? For the commanders, it was all about balance.

The biggest frustration of coming under RC South and its much bigger command structure was that we couldn't just go. It was the worst feeling for us – we knew that our boys were bleeding somewhere on the ground; they were suffering and they needed us. We had aircraft and crews ready to go, and we knew that sometimes we were the thin line between living and dying. Every second counts – it's that simple, and when you're that close to it, you think, 'Fuck it, let's just go and get them.' If it was down to us, we'd lift every time as soon as the call came, so we couldn't always understand why it took the higher-ups so long to make a decision.

As if things weren't tense enough, suddenly we heard that The Royal Anglians' control centre had received an emergency signal from Private Rob Foster's Bowman radio. Private Foster was one of the three missing guys, so they're thinking that at least one of the guys was still alive; maybe he was alone and had the Taliban running after him? You can imagine the pandemonium. The wheel had come off and it was all hands to the pump.

While we were waiting, we noticed a Squadron Leader who we knew. He was working as Air Liaison officer to some of our forces in theatre who were mentoring the ANA.

While waiting for the order to lift, Rich and I had been looking at the plot ahead; we were quite close to the end of Det and had some concerns about being able to get a flight out of Bastion so we could get back to KAF and on to a TriStar home. The Squadron Leader overheard us talking and said to us, 'Listen boys, if you are worried about missing your transport back to KAF we might be able to help you out if our Herc is operating in the area and has the time to do a detour.'

I looked at Rich; Rich looked at me and we said, 'Er . . . thanks.' I was hoping we'd never have to call in this favour because

I knew there had to be a quid pro quo; the guy must have some kind of an agenda. We didn't have to wait long.

'Look, I've got a tasking for my boys in our Herc but it looks like we're not going to get supported by the Chinook force on this op. I need to insert 54 ANA soldiers to a location near Lashkar Gah.'

Rich and I had originally been tasked to help out on that mission, but events had since moved on and our priority had to be the rescue of Robert Foster. I didn't have a problem helping the Squadron Leader out and I didn't like the way the mission had been planned so that would have to be changed but – personal Herc to KAF or not – the missing soldier had to take precedence.

One of my concerns about the plan was that the Squadron Leader wanted to use two Chinooks to insert his 54 troops into Lash late at night but that was never going to happen – do two moves and you might tell the enemy you're coming. So I suggested that we move the whole lot in a single cab. He didn't think it was possible so I said we'd look at the figures. Rich and I worked the numbers and logistically, it was possible – we'd have to have some of them standing, but I felt more confident about it because we wouldn't be flying into fire. The lift was into a 'safe' HLS so I thought if we fuelled light – about 800kgs – it might be a goer.

The Squadron Leader's Herc was supposed to be flying down from Kabul to land on a dust strip alongside FOB Phoenix – an ANA base – pick up the troops and bring them to Bastion where we'd be waiting with our rotors turning ready to pick them up and fly them to Lash. 800kgs of fuel gave us enough for 15 minutes of loiter and the flight there and back so I went to work out how we could slot this in.

By now, the order to lift had been cleared by RC South and the plan was for us to fly to FOB Robinson at Sangin, collect two companies' worth of troops and drop them in Kajaki to look for Private Foster and return them all to Bastion. By the time we got back, the sun would be coming up so I told the Squadron Leader that we'd drop the troops at Kajaki and instead of waiting for them, we'd fly back to Bastion to refuel to 800kgs, do his job, refuel again at Bastion and then fly up to Kajaki for the extraction. It would be tight, but we'd get everything done.

The best laid plans of mice and men eh? As it was, there were so many people for us to move when we got to FOB Rob that the night flew past in a miasma of lifts: Bastion to Sangin to Kajaki to Sangin to Kajaki to Bastion to FOB Rob to Kajaki to FOB Rob to Kajaki and back to Bastion. In the end, we'd dropped over 200 troops at Kajaki, and they were fanning out in the search for Private Foster. Everything would be done to find and rescue him; no man left behind.

When I'm on HRF or IRT, I always make a point of briefing the engineers on what we've done – as well as keeping the guys enthused, it also boosts morale when they know that what they're doing is worthwhile. There's nothing worse than being in the dark and I think it's vital that whenever they take the ropes off an aircraft, or refuel it in double-quick time while the rotors are turning, they know that they're helping someone else to live because they're doing their job so quickly. We landed back at Bastion with about 5-600kgs of fuel left so I stressed to the engineers that I wanted 800kgs total – no more – and I did it three times because you tell one guy who tells someone else it's 800 and he tells someone else and suddenly, you've got 1,800kgs and that extra ton of fuel translates to 5% less power available.

Rich and I then strolled back to the tent to see what was going on and as we walked in I could see the Squadron Leader sat in a chair looking pretty gloomy. German and I walked past him and went to talk to one of the radio guys.

'Any news on the Herc for the next mission?' I asked him. 'Is it still on time?'

Then another guy walked past us and in a completely matter of fact tone, said, 'The Herc crashed' and carried on walking.

There was a moment where time sort of stopped. Rich and I were stood there trying to process this but it just wasn't computing – it's not exactly the sort of thing that happens every day.

'Come back here! What do you mean the fucking Herc crashed?' I said.

And he said, 'Yes sir, it crashed.'

We were firing questions at him like there was no tomorrow. 'Crashed? How? What, did it fall out of the sky, was it shot down, any casualties, what the fuck's going on?'

'There are no casualties sir,' he said. 'We think it landed a bit too heavily as they were going to pick up your passengers.'

'So the mission's off, then?' we said together.

Maybe it was the stress of the evening, the worry over Private Foster and the other missing lads but Rich and I had to walk outside the tent; after everything that had happened I think we both just needed a breath of fresh air. Those ten minutes outside made a world of difference though and we both felt better for the break.

We went back into the JOC. JP was talking about waking up the IRT crew if they found Private Foster, so I told him, 'Look, we're not that tired. I know we're going to push the limit, but if you wake up the IRT crew, you're starting their clock now which means they'll have to go into rest earlier and then you'll have to bring in another crew, which doesn't make sense. Just keep us on and we'll see it through. Hopefully they'll find him and then we can move all the troops back in.' As it was, we'd been on duty since 07:00 the previous morning, although we hadn't been called out – we'd spent most of the day lazing around, so we weren't inside-out with tiredness. JP considered it and agreed, so we stayed on.

Sadly, a short time later the news came in that everyone was dreading. They'd found Private Foster's body with those of his dead colleagues, Privates McClure and Thrumble, under the rubble of the building they'd been taking cover in when the JDAM hit. They wouldn't have known anything about it.

The worst twist of all was that the Bowman radio that Rob Foster had been carrying survived the blast intact and it's thought that a piece of rubble flicked the switch that sent out the emergency signal; he'd been dead all along. We were completely gutted by that and, as you might imagine, the mood in the JOC was very sombre. But there was work to be done – the bodies all needed recovering and the troops we'd moved up to search for Private Foster would all need moving back to their original positions.

The full details of what happened took almost three years to come out, so all that was known at the time was that the guys had been killed as the result of a JDAM dropped by a US fast jet. As you might imagine, emotions were running pretty high. Later that morning, we were joined in the JOC by the crew of a US Pave Hawk; they wanted to be part of any attempt to recover the bodies because they felt a sense of responsibility. Obviously, because of what had happened, you could have cut the atmosphere with a knife in the tent when they came in. There were a lot of heads down including, I'm ashamed to say, mine. It was difficult not to feel angry towards them at the time. Whenever there's a blue-on-blue, it always seems like it's the Americans dropping the bombs and our boys on the end of it, never the other way around.

All that said, I think it took a lot of guts on the part of that US crew to come in at that time. They must have known how we'd be feeling; it would have been easy for them to hide, but they faced up to it, and I think ultimately we respected them for that. We were all professionals and we had a job to do, so we brushed our feelings aside and soon there was the usual banter between aviators. It helped that the navigator was pretty fit too – blonde, female, really attractive, which always stands out, especially with so many alpha males floating around. She showed us some pretty cool kit that they have which we, of course, don't. Things like that really highlight the dichotomy between cultures in the US and UK – the US all Gucci kit, no expense spared; the UK more of a make-do, 'Heath Robinson' approach. She had a moving map on an iPad-like device and she said, 'We'll go this way, and this way,' and moved the map around, plotting the routes with her finger.

'That's a pretty impressive bit of kit,' I said.

'Really?' she asked. 'What sort of kit do you guys use?'

I unfolded a map from my pocket and waved it around and said, 'There you go. Mk.1 Human Eyeball and that's our moving map,' which really made her laugh, and that broke any remaining tension. The difference in the kit that we have access to compared to the

US is astounding. You make light of it at times like that, but you know the Americans are shaking their heads and thinking 'Oh my God, who are we working with?'

An hour or so later, we both flew up to Kajaki to recover the bodies. There'd been so much effort put into finding Rob Foster because we really believed he was out there, alive and alone. It was a crushing blow to us all to learn that he'd died. When they brought his body out, I felt awful. I had all sorts of thoughts in my head; all the stuff in life that this guy will never get to experience, all the lost opportunities. He was only nineteen, as was Private Aaron McClure. Private John Thrumble – the oldest – was just twenty-one.

I watched them bring Robert Foster's rifle and his kit out – they were all mangled up. It's funny how your mind works; I became so focused on that, and it got me thinking about the fragility of life. I don't know why it affected me so much – it's not like it was the first death we'd dealt with, but there was something really poignant, sad and hopeless about the futility of it all. I was feeling really melancholic and introspective.

I guess it might have been because this was the first Det I'd done since Guy was born. Being a father had given me a completely different perspective on it all. I felt a much greater insight into the family's loss and had a real empathy for the poor lad's parents – all the love, the experiences, the laughter and those rites of passage that everyone takes for granted that he'd never get to do. None of those poor soldiers would, not any more. Three young lives snuffed out, just like that. That was hard to bear.

Rich and I took off with the Pave Hawk and we ended up flying a complete reversal of what we'd done earlier that night, moving all the troops back to where we'd picked them up from. It was a long, very emotional and hard day's flying. After we'd shut down, I went to the showers and stripped off; I wanted to wash all the cares, the grit, the grime – all the thoughts of that long, hard night – off of me. It was pretty busy – at around 07:00, it was the time that everyone was getting ready for a new day in Helmand. I saw the OC Forward, Major Jules Face.

'Alright, mate. Here we are again. Start of another day in paradise, eh?' he said.

'Not for us, sir. It's the end of a very long one. You know how you saw us at the evening brief yesterday? We haven't stopped. That's a good twenty-four hours on duty. I think we must have moved somewhere in excess of 160 people; 160 people there, 160 people back again.'

I got that fuzzy feeling again, where every cell in my body seemed to be vibrating. I felt wired but drained; a paradox of emotions and feelings. It's hard to grasp how long we've been on duty. Days are measures of time divided by sleep, not by the cycle of night and day. So when you don't sleep the days become longer and 'yesterday' becomes a redundant concept.

I was dog tired. I could have slept for a week. But there was no chance of that because in a few hours we were up again for more of the same.

The end of Det couldn't come soon enough.

23

HISTORY REPEATING

I know one swallow doesn't make a summer, and I guess by the same token the difficulty I had getting home at the end of my Det in summer 2006 shouldn't have meant that history would repeat itself in 2007 – but it did!

Rich and I were positioned on the IRT/HRF for the last three days of our Det, and I still had concerns about making it back to KAF for the TriStar home – even more so now that the Squadron Leader's personal Herc wasn't an option. By September 3rd – our last day at Bastion – things were looking even bleaker for me.

We were handing over to 'A' Flight, 27 Sqn who were taking over from us to form 1310 Flight, but Squadron Leader John Murnane, their OC, had made it clear he wasn't prepared to take on any kind of tasking without one of us from 'C' Flight being on board the cab. JP tried to argue against it, but to no avail.

JP rang me that afternoon and the news wasn't good. 'Frenchie,' he said, 'I'm really sorry but you're going to have to stay an extra day.'

'Sir, you've got to be joking. We're supposed to be going tomorrow!'

'I'm so sorry, mate. Get your kit packed and take it on the cab with you. You can then bring it straight to KAF at the end of the sortie and still make the flight home. They want you on the jump seat with them tomorrow while they do a standard resupply tasking to Inkerman and back. You'll be there to give them some advice, so that they're entirely happy with what they're doing.'

They might have been happy but I wasn't, and sadly there was nothing I could do. The mission was for a pair of cabs escorted by one AH to take an underslung load from Bastion to FOB Inkerman at exactly the time of day when Inkerman gets hammered. You could set your watch by the Taliban; they were malleting the place every day from around 13:00, so that was a concern although, ironically, it turned out that they took that day off and the base wasn't hit. If it was a relief for us, it must have felt like Christmas come early for the poor guys at the FOB.

As we got close, the AH picked up some ICOM chatter about us coming in and orders for the Taliban to 'get the weapons ready', but we'd learned over time that it was more often than not just a load of hot air – it was probably some idiot in Gereshk watching us and making a radio call to his mate, knowing that we were listening.

As the lead cab went in, I could hear a buzzing noise above my head. I was distinctly uncomfortable with that, because sat in the jump seat you're directly under the forward gearbox. Noise from there never amounts to anything good, and there was a massive vibration emanating from it, which seemed to be getting worse. I got one of the crewmen to listen to it and he agreed, so I said to the guys in the front, 'Fellas, we've got some vibration from the forward gearbox,' and I thought they'd say that we'd drop the load and go straight home, except they didn't.

The captain came straight back with, 'Okay, but we're going to carry on with the mission as planned,' and I thought, 'You've got to be shitting me!'

By this point we were on the eastern side of Inkerman doing the run in, and as we were descending to low level the vibration was getting worse. It started to emit a regular pulsating noise and I was just about to say something to the pilot when there was an almighty bang right above my head. I scanned the instruments; as we were levelling off, the pilot was pulling power to arrest our descent. I looked at the captions on the caution advisory panel and it was displayed right there in front of me: No.1 Hydraulic Failure.

I thought, 'Okay, we're already at low level, we've got an underslung load, what would I do? Okay, two options: ditch the load at Inkerman and put down there, or ditch the load and fly straight back to Bastion. I don't care what he does, as long as he makes a decision and makes it now.'

He did. But it wasn't what I expected.

'Okay, we're going to drop the load at Inkerman,' he said (*Good decision!* I thought) And then the flight commander, who was in the left-hand seat said, 'Okay then we'll carry on as we briefed – we'll go south of the wadi at Sangin and we'll just hold there and wait to regroup with the other cab.'

By this point, I'd had enough.

I switched my intercom to live and told him, 'Right, this is what you're going to do. We're going to fly straight to Bastion right now. We're not going to wait for mutual support from any other aircraft; you have got to land as soon as possible. We have an emergency, so secure the hydraulics and we'll crack on. If we have to crash-land, we'll do so in the desert and we'll have somebody pick us up within five minutes, but we are not holding over Sangin to await the others. We're going.'

Fortunately common sense prevailed and that's exactly what happened. We got back without incident and after the aircraft was shut down, he asked me if I had any comments, so I said, 'Yes. Know your SOPs. Land as soon as possible. Do not fuck around waiting for anybody else so you can go back as part of a formation. If you're going to smack into the ground, do it in the desert half-way to Bastion, not in the wrong side of the Green Zone!'

In fairness, these guys had just touched down in Afghanistan from the UK; it highlighted the difference in thinking. You just arrive in theatre and your head's in a different place. I'm at the end of a two-month tour, we've taken fire, we're attuned to the differences of operating in a war zone and they're second nature to us. I guess it proved the value in having an experienced captain from the outgoing Flight on board. That said though, it was the last thing I wanted on my last day in theatre!

After saying my farewells, I managed to get straight on to a Herc to KAF – JP was as good as his word. He'd sorted my main kit and put it on the wagon with the rest of the Flight's and I joined them all at the Dutch cafe on the boardwalk. We were sat by the bar, which had wi-fi, and I was drinking a good cup of coffee so it even felt half-civilised – well, as far as it can be at KAF! Iain Cuthbertson walked over to me and said, 'Hey Frenchie, your son is walking mate!'

'What do you mean?'

'I was just on the phone talking to my missus and Ali was with Guy at our house and he took his first steps!' I couldn't believe it – he could have waited! It's like ten hours before I get home and I've missed it!

The flight home from Afghanistan was unremarkable other than for the fact it left on time, and when I got back to RAF Odiham Ali was there to meet me with Guy. She was holding him upright and he took two or three steps straight into me. Boof! The perfect welcome home.

It didn't take long for the magic to evaporate though. It's always the same when you get back – your head is in a different space. Nothing's the same for you; you're back and the contrast with what you've left is immense. We have to readjust; but for Ali, and I guess all the WAGs, it's just another day. Their lives have adapted to us not being there and they have a routine, and suddenly there's this big, hairy man invading and upending everything they've taken for granted.

You can just imagine – Ali's cleaned the house, dressed up, made an effort and I come back and dump my filthy kit in the hall. She's got her arms around me, she's kissing me, but you can bet your life she's got one eye open, looking over my shoulder, and she's not thinking, 'I love him so much, I'm so glad he's home.' No, she's thinking: 'For fuck's sake, there's a trail of his filthy kit all along the hallway and I've just cleaned it!'

In fairness, I think she lasted a week before she said, 'Move this dirty, stinking bag and get your kit out of the way!' She was pretty fucking threaders with me then!

I was left in no doubt the honeymoon was over.

PART THREE
INTO THE LION'S DEN

24

BACK IN THE BLACK

There was something different about my deployment to Helmand in Summer 2008 that became apparent even before I arrived in theatre. I felt more apprehensive than I'd done for my previous Dets, but perhaps that was down to my son Guy, who was approaching his second birthday. He was walking and talking and there was real interaction between us, so I knew that leaving him and Ali for two-and-a-bit months was going to be a wrench.

The landscape on the ground in Afghanistan was greatly different, too. We'd be supporting 16 Air Assault Brigade again, although it had a new CO in the form of Brigadier Mark Carleton-Smith, who'd replaced Brigadier John Lorimer. 3 Para had a different personality following the appointment of its new Commanding Officer, Lieutenant Colonel Huw Williams. His predecessor, Lt Col Stuart Tootal OBE, DSO had resigned his commission in protest at what he regarded as the appalling treatment and conditions of British soldiers.

In terms of the ground picture in Helmand, a de facto border now existed east of Garmsir along the banks of the Helmand River, dividing British-held from Taliban-held territory in what was essentially a stalemate. Despite us having over 8,000 troops in theatre at this stage, only a hardcore of around 1,500 were front line infantry units, the rest being support arms to enable them to fight. Consequently, we were outnumbered by a Taliban force which was receiving reinforcements from outside Afghanistan. Our arrival in theatre was to coincide with US Marine reinforcements, who assisted 16 Air Assault Brigade in an attack to break the stalemate at Garmsir.

The Taliban might be a ragtag enemy in flip-flops and pyjamas, but they're a formidable foe – they are tactically astute, display astonishing tenacity and are unquestionably courageous, given their propensity to fight regardless of the rate of attrition they suffer.

The war in Afghanistan is often described as asymmetric – basically the concept of conflict between the powerful and the weak – but I sometimes wonder if it is us who are the weak partner. Sure, we have superior weapons, tactics and equipment. We have body armour, fast jets, heavy artillery and armoured vehicles. We have vastly greater numbers of troops, who are considerably more experienced and capable than those we face. But we're not fighting on a level field. We are constrained by a moral and ethical code, and the binds and rules of an army of lawyers and theorists who abide by the tenets of the Geneva Conventions. We fight an enemy with no uniform; an enemy that is indistinguishable from the civilian population we seek to protect. It's a David vs. Goliath conflict, and we all know who won that particular fight. The outcome of the war in Afghanistan is by no means certain.

None of that detracted from our preparations before deployment – or our stomach for the fight ahead. Being a summer deployment it's hotter, so the physical toil is harder but that's not the issue – mid-May tends to be when everything kicks off because it's when the Taliban finish the poppy harvest, so we knew we'd be busy. The tempo was ramping up, so I think we knew it was going to be tough, although I don't think any of us realised just how tough.

On the plus side, I don't think we could have been more ready. JP had worked us exceptionally hard in the run-up, with by far the best pre-Det training (PDT) I'd ever done. We'd been based out of RAF Leuchars in Scotland and were using RAF Boulmer and RAF Spadeadam as radar units.

RAF Spadeadam isn't a conventional RAF Base, but a unique facility spanning almost 10,000 acres of forest and mire on the border of Cumbria and Northumberland. It's the only facility in Europe where aircrew can practise manoeuvres and tactics against the variety of threats and targets we face in contemporary warfare, and it attracts aircraft from the RAF, Army, Navy and NATO Forces. The survival of aircrews over Afghanistan, as well as the soldiers on the ground who depend on the air support they provide, all benefit from the training provided by RAF Spadeadam.

The training was just so realistic. We'd take off, speak to Boulmer – they'd been given a script by the training staff on what to say and, depending on what sortie we were doing and what mission number we'd give them, they would read a different script which might be them calling 'Troops in contact' or 'Weapons systems in place'. It was brilliantly well organised – we even had a Hawk fast jet to work with us to provide emergency close air support.

Afterwards, we felt completely ready – I think once you get to this point, you want to get away, get the Det done and come home. It's like a boxer coming up to a fight – he gears himself up and works harder and harder to peak at just the right time. That was us – we were really ramped up at that point. The difficulty is though, we don't just need to peak on one night; we need that peak to last for two months. That's a big ask! We worked very hard on the PDT, but not too hard, as we'd have ended up too tired. It left us on a high and at just the right level.

We marked our departure differently, too. We had a night out as a Flight at a local pub – it's a place that 27 Squadron frequents a lot and they know that when we book a room there it's time to run for cover! We play this game called Tequila Darts – the object is to throw the lowest number on the dartboard. If you do this you come out of the round. If you score the highest number, you drink a shot of tequila. If you score a 7 (as in 7 Squadron) you drink a shot of tequila; if you score 18 (18 Squadron) you drink a shot of tequila; if you score a triple 9 (i.e. 27) everybody else drinks a shot of tequila! So that's the game.

As it progresses, everyone is more drunk, new rules appear and it's a bit of a mess. You have ten seconds to make your way up to the dartboard, but after a while people are talking and don't make it, so they have to drink a shot of tequila. People are counting you down '7, 8, 9 . . . 10!' and somebody grabs the dart and throws it at the board, people are falling over . . . It's absolute carnage.

I'd phoned Alison to come and pick up German, Paul Farmer (otherwise known as 'Piggy') and me, but as soon as I put the phone down, I forgot I rang her and the three of us started walking. She eventually found us zigzagging our way up this unlit, winding country road. She stopped the car and was met with what constituted a train wreck; I tried to sit on her lap, German fell in a ditch, and Piggy just carried on walking. When we got back to the Mess I had to carry German up to his room – he was useless. To be fair, I wasn't much better. I lost my balance in the toilets and did a straight body flop onto my back, taking a framed picture of an old F4 Phantom on the way down with me. I woke up with a cracked head, lying on my back staring up at the ceiling!

Hannah fell asleep in the Ladies and locked herself in; she told her boyfriend she'd be sober by the time he came to get her but she was absolutely wankered! It was a great night – lots of shared memories, bonding as a Flight. This was about a week before we deployed. We went straight off on leave that night and didn't see each other again until the morning we flew out to KAF.

Alison dropped me off for this Det but we treated it as if I was just going off to work for the day – neither of us wanted to prolong the goodbye, so it was just a quick kiss, 'See you in a couple of months; look after yourself.' She drove away and as soon as I turned around, there were all my mates, all of us with our detachment haircuts – short and easy maintenance! All our kit went into a four-tonner, we got on the coach and off we went to Brize Norton. Next stop – Kandahar.

I don't quite know what I was expecting, but it surprised me when I arrived at KAF and found that nothing had really changed. It was the same old dusty hole except on a larger scale, with a far greater number of REMFs and senior officers stronzing – that's a metaphor we used for people who were strutting and bronzing at the same time – around. The base was now home to as many as 14,000 multinational personnel commanded by an RAF officer, Air

Commodore Bob Judson. We were taking over from 'B' Flight, 18 Squadron, so after the usual clusterfuck of admin – filling in forms, reclaiming weapons etc. – they helped us load our kit into the same old dusty vehicles and drove us to our accommodation. We roomed as formed crews and the lads we were taking over from had all moved into other rooms, so ours were clean and ready for us. I'd be flying for the first part of the Det alongside Pete Winn, with Mick Fry and Barry Fulton in the rear. Mick's a great bloke – a very experienced flight sergeant with a wickedly dry sense of humour who was a qualified crewman instructor at the OCF. Barry, known by everyone as 'Jay', was a brand new crewman.

We ramped up quickly, so after the usual drawing of morphine, zeroing weapons, and a couple of days of lectures about how life on the ground had changed, I did my TQ – with my good mate Aaron 'Tourette's' Stewart again. Then we hit the ground running, crewing the IRT.

Things were fairly quiet initially; we picked up a British soldier classified as a T1 who was suffering from heat stress. There were a lot of heat stress casualties around at that time because the winter temperatures can be quite harsh in Helmand – below zero at night – and the rise in summer is both brutal and sudden, so there's little time for them to acclimatise. We lifted a couple of civilian T1s from Lashkar Gah too and took them to the local hospital in Lash, and I even managed to get Pete Winn TQ'd so that was him all ticked up to handle the aircraft.

April 13th saw me flying as Hannah's wingman for a day's tasking, which ended up with us back at KAF. We'd just made radio contact with the tower for permission to land, when Hannah noticed a couple of RAF Regiment vehicles carrying out a stop-and-search on a vehicle and its occupants a few miles outside the perimeter fence. She'd made contact with them and offered to provide overwatch, so we flew an orbit above them with the rear crewmen watching events down the barrel of the Miniguns. Eventually, the patrol waved us off and we rejoined the circuit to land on at KAF.

An hour or so later, we were in the JHF (A) ops room

debriefing when information started coming in about a major incident involving KAF's resident RAF Regiment Squadron, just outside of the base. Information was sketchy at first; all we knew was that there'd been an explosion, there were several casualties and we were on standby to lift.

The RAF Regiment is the Royal Air Force's own infantry corps, responsible for force protection, airfield defence, forward air control and parachute capability. 3 Sqn RAF Regt was the resident unit at KAF. Their 420km² Area of Operation began outside the perimeter fence and stretched up to ten miles from the airfield, including Three Mile Mountain – the most prominent feature in an otherwise rugged and barren landscape.

As more information started coming in, we were able to put a picture together of what happened. Basically, a soft-skinned Land Rover Wolf – that's the British Army's primary utility vehicle – had been blown up while crossing a wadi on a routine patrol, just a few klicks outside of KAF. Two of its crew – SAC Gary Thompson ('Tommo'), who was a reservist, and SAC Graham Livingstone ('Livvy') – had died, and there were two survivors – Flt Lt Andy Costin, who was the Flight Commander, and Stu Smalley, the driver.

In the event, we weren't scrambled because the incident happened so close to KAF and the guys on the ground decided to drive one of the casualties straight there. They got there far quicker than we would have done, but sadly it was too late for both Tommo and Livvy. Although severely injured, Andy Costin showed remarkable determination to regain fitness and was sitting up and talking just three days later. I was intrigued by the story, so I sought him out later in the tour and this is what he told me:

'We were on an early evening patrol to the west of Kandahar to ensure the ground was free of Taliban insurgents who might threaten any aircraft due to land. A normal patrol consists of a flight – usually six vehicles and twenty-four men. We patrol in WIMIKs, which are the platform for the heavy weapons like the .50 calibre; Vectors, which are normally used as a command vehicle; and Snatches, old Land Rovers which were used extensively in Northern Ireland.

'We'd completed the first element of the patrol without incident and it was dusk – about 18:30 – when we heard that the next aircraft we had to protect had changed its course and was due in from the east. I diverted the patrol and, by about 18:45, we reached a river we needed to cross. The two vehicles at the head of the patrol crossed safely; I was in the third. We never made it.

'As we drove down the near bank to cross the water, we ran over a mine, which detonated at the rear left-hand side of the vehicle with astonishing force. Tommo was thrown approximately 25m from the vehicle to the far side of the stream. I never actually heard a bang. One minute we were just about to go through the river and the next thing I remember is water across my face. I thought at first that Stu had gone through too quickly. But then I realised I was on all fours with my rifle in my hands, in the stream with my eyes open – I was actually in the water. My rifle had to be destroyed because I'd bent it with the force of landing on it!

'As I was lifting my head clear of the water, I looked left and right of me. To the right was our mangled Land Rover. Livvy was hanging out of the back of the vehicle facing towards me; then I looked to my left and saw Stu – both he and I had been blown out of the vehicle. Looking back on it now, it was actually quite funny because he looked like Eric Morecambe with his glasses at an angle. At that point, it was quite dark because the explosion had just happened and all of the dust and muck and everything was just coming back down again. There seemed to be an extraordinary tranquillity and silence but I guess that was more my hearing being affected by the force of the explosion.

'My Land Rover was the main comms vehicle, so we'd lost most of our means of communication. The vehicle was a wreck – it's hard to believe we got out of it alive. The rear looked as though it was a tin can that had been crushed. It was literally bent in half and the driver's seat was rammed forward, so how Stu got out I'm not quite sure. My side of the vehicle was a mess – the roof canopy had been shredded and the metal frame was twisted beyond recognition.

'My immediate concern was for Livvy – to get him out of the vehicle – which two of the guys did. They put the fire out in the back of the Land Rover and cut him free, brought him round the back of me and started administering first aid. Oz – one of my corporals – was one of our team of medics along with Owen Hughes. We also had SAC Caterill ('Cat') who was one of the drivers; he was assisting too. Both Owen and Oz worked tirelessly on Livvy. He had no broken bones but the force of the explosion had mortally wounded him. They brought him back to life three times with CPR and mouth-to-mouth.

'With Livvy being taken care of, I needed to locate Tommo because, at that stage, we couldn't immediately see where he'd been thrown. I shouted across to the guys who were crewing the two vehicles that had crossed the stream ahead of us – a WIMIK led by Corporal Wood, and another Land Rover Wolf commanded by Corporal Hodginson – and they set about searching for him. They found Tommo on the other side of the stream using one of the big Dragon Eye torches that we carry; he'd been thrown almost 30m by the force of the explosion. John Toghill, one of our battlefield medics, got to work on him the minute they found him. He was in a bad way.

'We established that it would take at least fifty minutes before you could scramble from Bastion and land on to casevac us. The patrol was split by the river, and the two vehicles that had crossed ahead of mine were only 1km away from KAF's western gate, so I made the decision to put Tommo in the back of one of those and take him straight to the hospital. Once I'd made the decision, he was at the Role Three hospital in KAF within fifteen minutes. Sadly, both Livvy's and Tommo's injuries were too severe and despite the very best efforts of everyone who'd fought so hard to save them, they died. The full force of the explosion was taken by the rear left of the vehicle, which was where Tommo was sitting – they found what was left of the wheel the next day some 200m away from our vehicle.

'Obviously, the usual thing in an incident like this is for your next of kin to get the knock – you know, the full Monty; uniformed officers turning up at the house – but I couldn't let that happen to my wife Yvonne. People always assume the worst, don't they? I knew that she'd open the door, see them standing there and that'd be it. Why go through that when there's no need? So I fought to do it my way and rang her from hospital a couple of days after the incident. Hannah, our five-year-old, was the only one who wasn't told what had really happened. Yvonne just said that Daddy had fallen out of the Land Rover and Hannah's response was, "Well, Daddy should've had his seatbelt on, shouldn't he?"

'I was initially immobile and somewhat banged up. I'm deaf on my left side as a result of the blast; I injured my right shoulder and back, literally from the lower back to my neck, just from the force of the explosion and landing on all fours wearing the Osprey armour, my webbing, rifle, plus a full load of kit and the radio as well. I remember lying in the hospital when I first got there, and everything had been completely cut off me – that was quite entertaining. I couldn't move because of my back.

'I felt so frustrated immediately afterwards because the only place for a commander is on the ground leading, but I couldn't get back out with my troops. Within forty-eight hours of the incident, they were back out patrolling, and that's where I should've been – with my guys out on the ground.

'The squadron had a ceremony for Livvy and Tommo at Bridge Lines, our base at KAF, twenty-four hours after the event and I was adamant that I was going to be there for it. I was aided and abetted, so to speak, by a couple of the nurses, and brought there in a wheel-chair. I was assisted in standing up towards the end, and once the dedication ceremony was finished I was sat back in my wheelchair again, whisked away by the nurses and injected with some more morphine. But almost two weeks after the event, I felt I couldn't do anything else out here and I needed to go home to Yvonne because, as you can imagine, she was beside herself.

'I was able to go to the boys' funerals too, and pay my respects – that was obviously very important to me. Yvonne was an absolute brick because she came up to Scotland with me – she was my chauf-feur as well. The funerals were back-to-back. And then I spent another four weeks at home. I found both of the funerals really upset-ting because I felt very close to the guys; we were a close-knit team. And I remember saying to Yvonne before I deployed that my main objective was to come out here with twenty-four guys and to bring them all home again – every one of them – and looking back on that,

I feel that I've failed in that respect. That is by far the hardest thing for me. You always think, *what if?*

'Hindsight is absolutely brilliant, isn't it? But I always think to myself, would we have done anything differently? Well no, probably not. There was a strike op happening to the north, and my main objective was to move across to the east of the airfield to actually get out into where we were required. Ultimately it was my decision that we went the way we did, so obviously the responsibility rests with me.

'I found talking to the Padre out here really helped and I also think – in true regiment style – there's a lot of black humour that would be lost on a lot of people. We talk of it after the event but obviously no disrespect is meant. I've earned the nickname of Panther now, which is quite bizarre because the Italians built a new vehicle a few years ago called a Panther and it can survive the blast of a TC/6, which is the mine that did for our vehicle. It's that sort of humour that actually brings you through it and helps you deal with it.

'I was offered counselling but I turned it down and chose to speak with the Padres instead, although I wouldn't say I was a religious person. I still found it beneficial to talk to them though. Padre Peter, or 'the mad Scotsman' as we call him, was great. We'd sit down, have a cup of tea – several actually – myself and Stu Smalley, and we'd just talk. I suppose in some respects Stu and I now have a bond that transcends rank and any other consideration. I know the road ahead isn't going to be easy, but I'm determined to get to the end, regardless of what it takes. My aim is to redeploy out here again as soon as I'm fit.'

25

LIGHTING THE WAY

Our first couple of weeks in theatre didn't really produce any surprises; we flew a steady routine of taskings and rotations on the IRT/HRF down at Bastion. It was a good way to acclimatise. Although we flew a couple of minor pre-planned ops, nothing happened to get the hairs on the back of my neck standing up, and I was even beginning to believe that the whole Det might prove uneventful.

Towards the end of April, I was involved in an operation called 'Jnu Brishna' or 'Sudden Thunder', which I was quite excited about because it meant us providing support to Easy Company of the 101st Airborne. On our downtime in theatre, one of the most popular DVD box sets was *Band of Brothers*. In the crew tent, killing time waiting for a shout on the IRT, it was back-to-back *Band of Brothers* as we followed Major Dick Winters and his men through France, Belgium and into the Berchtesgaden in Germany. Now we were tasked to fly their latter-day successors into battle; what a privilege.

I expected the mission to be quite straightforward; it was to be a simple movement of troops from one point to another, in the area south-west of Qalat, to enable them to take over a couple of villages. I wasn't really expecting much in the way of enemy activity there; the Americans on the other hand, were.

To be perfectly honest, the thing that worried me more than Taliban activity was flying in a massive package of US Army helicopters. It would be the first time I'd operated as part of such a large gaggle; all my previous experience being with just my own cab and one other – a Black Hawk, Pave Hawk or Apache, or even another Chinook. This, though, would involve something like six US Chinooks and two of ours, plus several Apaches and Black Hawks . . . ten aircraft just to move the troops.

I mentioned previously that the Americans have a different way of doing things, but this operation really opened my eyes to just how different we are. Before we undertake any operation, we do what we call RoC (Rehearsal of Concept) drills; they are something we learn at basic Officer Training and are common throughout the British Military but essentially do exactly what the name suggests. For us, it means rehearsing the operation by making a rough representation of the battlefield using mud, sand or whatever, and then using objects such as rocks, twigs and sticks to represent soldiers, compounds, vehicles etc. We'll walk around talking about what we'd do here if this happened, or what we'd do there if that happened. It's a really useful and effective way to iron out all the ifs and buts and make sure everybody knows what they're doing.

For the Americans, the principle is the same, except it allows no room for invention or 'on the fly' planning. It's rigid, overblown and unnecessarily complicated. The American method requires one standard-size aircraft hangar (empty); everyone involved in the op; and finally, a full script. Their rehearsal means everyone going through every single aspect, including all the radio calls, as if we were actually flying – the fucking rehearsal takes longer than the actual mission! It's unbelievable – there is no latitude for independent thinking. What alarmed me most was when this question came up: 'How are we going to hold if there's a contact and the area is hot?'

Their holding plan was appalling, and I said to Pete, 'If that happens, we're buggering off about three miles down that way and we're staying well away from them.'

I'll tell you why I was worried – the Lt Col who was their commanding officer said to them: 'If you come to a halt with an underslung load, you'll have to come down to minimum power speed.'

I looked at Pete and said, 'Can you believe these guys have to be reminded when to come back to minimum power speed?' That in itself spoke volumes. It's Helicopter 101 and they have to be reminded of the basic techniques. That really had the hairs on the back of my neck waking up!

In the event, we flew two loads of troops and, logistically, it was well organised. It ran on rails, nobody came under contact and we all shut down back at KAF at the end of the day, satisfied with a job well done. They don't often end that way.

We had a change of crew at the end of the month and for the rest of the Det, I was flying with Alex Townsend, Bob Ruffles and Neil 'Coops' Cooper. Both Bob and Coops are ex-7 Squadron, and you couldn't ask for a more experienced rear crew.

We flew some interesting sorties to kick off with. There was one we flew with German as my wingman in a two-ship where we were delivering multiple HICHS (Helicopter Internal Cargo Handling System) loads. Basically, the cabin floor is fitted with rollers and all the loads are secured to special pallets, so they just roll straight off the ramp when it's lowered. We flew all over the north-east of Kandahar Province to myriad bases, but the icing on the cake was taking one of the drops to a mountain peak where a US sniper team was located. It was a prime location, giving them commanding views down the valley, but it meant there was nowhere for the helicopter to land. So German did the only thing you can do at a time like that – he landed the rear wheels onto the ridge.

It's a tough manoeuvre because you have one rotor head that's on the ground and the other rotor head is still trying to fly – we're entirely reliant on the rear to keep us informed, flying that particular manoeuvre. Bear in mind we're sixty feet or so forward of the ramp and below us, through the clear glass under our feet, all we can see is a 3,000 ft drop. The back wheels are on the ridgeline, so the loadmaster is in the back hanging off the ramp and screaming in our ear to keep the wheels down, 'Nag, nag, nag!' It's the longest thirty seconds you can spend at the controls. German's rear crew threw the load out on what looked like an empty ridge line and then suddenly, all these superbly well-camouflaged snipers appeared from out of nowhere. It was incredible to see – one minute I could have sworn there was nobody on the ridge, and then these guys just stood up and there they were. That was pretty awesome – not just the snipers, but watching German hovering on the edge of that peak. It's one thing flying the actual manoeuvre, but it was the first time I'd actually watched another cab doing it.

We also had a run of non-standard underslung loads to deal with. Properly set up, underslung loads present no problem to any Chinook crew – they're the bread and butter of what we do, after all. But all it takes is for someone to get their figures wrong, or for us to pick up a load at the extreme end of the weight parameters, and suddenly life gets very interesting. Sweating the metal was never fun.

A run that really stands out came about when we had to take a Warrior engine pack to FOB Edinburgh. I hated doing that because the underslung load weighs four tonnes and it bends the cab. You've got no speed, it takes forever and a day to get anywhere and twice as long to slow down – you have to start slowing almost before you've taken off! Basically, the Warrior engine pack acted as a pendulum suspended from the belly of the cab and took on a momentum of its own. The load pulled on the aircraft and caused a phugoid motion, where the aircraft started to oscillate, intermittently diving and climbing. It gained speed during the dive portion until the added speed caused it to climb, and then lost speed until the cycle was repeated. It made me feel nauseous, and it was a complete pain in the ass. We also have the rotor blades spinning round at 225rpm, so we had all these gyros going around. Putting a load underneath it meant we had the aircraft gyroscoping around the weight. It was no fun at all, so we were all pleased when we finally dropped that load.

By then the light was fading so I thought it would be a good opportunity to finish off Alex's TQ with some night flying. When we fly at night, conditions are green, red or black illume. Green is normal – that is, there is sufficient ambient light for the NVGs to deliver a good picture. Red illume is the opposite – on a night with full cloud cover, no moon and no cultural or reflected light, you're as good as blind, even with the NVGs, because they have no light to amplify. Flying under those conditions is nigh on impossible because you have no references; it's frightening, dangerous and extraordinarily draining. Consequently, the only flying we usually do under red illume is on the IRT and training sorties – you have to know what to expect.

When it starts to get dark, we'll put down what we call a desert box to practise night landings – four cyalume light sticks are placed on the ground to form a rectangle big enough to land a Chinook in. The aim is to land on with the cockpit by the rearmost two cyalumes so that when you run on, you stop by the two at the front of the box. That way, you have markers in view throughout. People often make the mistake of landing in the middle of the box, but if you do that, the two markers at the back are about as useful as tits on a fish! What you want is to see the rear cyalumes at your 11 o'clock and 2 o'clock when your wheels touch ground, so that by the time you get engulfed in dust, with a bit of run on, you'll move forward, the dust will clear and the front two should now be in your 11 and 2 o'clock.

I found us a nice empty patch of desert just as the light was going down and landed on.

'Okay Bob, can you do us a box outside please?'

'No worries Frenchie, one box coming up,' Bob said and got busy doing the necessary. He took four one-litre bottles of water from the cool box, broke four cyalume sticks to activate them and placed one in each bottle of water before resealing the bottles. The benefits are twofold; the weight of the water anchors the bottle and the water magnifies the glow from the sticks. Like all the best ideas, it's simple and effective. Job done, he ran off the ramp, placed the bottles then jumped back in.

'All done, Frenchie. Clear above and behind,' he said, so I pulled power and pulled back on the stick, doing a nice aggressive J-turn, or over-the-shoulder departure, to take us out into the empty desert. There was no reason for it; I just felt like it.

Bear in mind it was very dark now and there was no moon. Although it was a cloudless night, there's very little cultural lighting in Afghanistan, even in populated areas. Over the desert, it's non-existent, so we were in red illume conditions.

'Okay Alex, you just follow me through on the controls with this one. I'll do a demo and then you have a go,' I told him and he came back with an 'Okay.'

I flew around the corner and turned back to make my approach, but as I became visual with the cyalumes, I noticed there was something wrong with the box.

'Bob, that is the shittiest box I've ever seen, mate! It's like a fucking triangle. What did you do?!' I asked.

'Frenchie,' he said, 'I know the difference between a box and a fucking triangle, and I made a box! Maybe one of them blew away when you lifted?'

It might sound like I was giving him a hard time, but it was just the normal sort of banter and piss-taking that characterises every sortie. Well, there was little we could do about it now so I told him, 'Don't worry, mate. I'll just work with what we've got.'

I looked ahead and we were downwind so I did the pre-landing checks – all good. I came around the corner again crosswind and then Bob came over the radio again, 'For fuck's sake, what's going on? You saw it – it was a box – then we had a triangle and now the fucking thing has changed shape.'

And as we watched, one of the other cyalumes started moving. I thought, 'What the fuck is going on?' and then the moving cyalume disappeared. We were trying to take it in when a third one disappeared. And then I got it.

'I bet some fucker down on the ground is nicking them!' As I said it, I hit the IR lights on the underside of the cab. Caught full-on in its glare was an Afghan male doing the rabbit-caught-in-headlights dance. He'd seen Bob putting the box out and after we took off, ran out from his compound about 200 metres away and started nicking them!

I flew over him at about 50ft and I could see him looking up at me; because I had the IR on, it was reflecting off the back of his retinas – through the NVGs he looked like a cat or dog when the light catches its eyes. He stood resolutely on the spot, frozen in time. I was coming in low with all the dirt, grit, corruption and destruction that the downforce gives birth to and he just stood there with our four cyalumes, ready to take them home. Fuck knows what he was doing with them – they're no use to man or beast – but there you go.

'Bet he goes to market tomorrow,' said Alex.

'Yeah,' said Bob. 'He'll be going round saying, "Look everyone, I got magic light stick, I got magic light stick! I sell to you for good price!"'

'Yeah,' I said. 'But imagine his surprise when they burn out and suddenly stop working! Someone's going to come looking for him wanting their money back!'

So much for Alex's TQ.

26

STANDING MY GROUND

The beginning of May saw Alex, Bob, Coops and I down at Bastion on the HRF. First thing in the morning, some troops on a patrol out of Kajaki found a huge IED, so we were tasked with flying the EOD (bomb disposal) team up from Bastion to deal with it. Those guys have got guts; that's real bravery to me, and all the money in the world wouldn't convince me to do what they do. They're seriously impressive – they went straight to the site of the IED, defused it, job done. That was a nice result.

When we returned to Bastion that afternoon, we swapped cabs and took over the IRT with the call sign Lobster Three One. All our kit stays on board the aircraft, whether we're doing HRF or IRT. Weapons will be slung on to the seats, my water will be on the right and I always leave my flying helmet on a seat at the back right of the aircraft because that way if I'm late because I've been planning, the aircraft is turning and burning and I can just put it on as I run up the ramp. Then I'll pull on my Mk61 and secure it, eject the clip from the 9mm on my chest, check it, holster my pistol, and finally jump into my seat, plug in and brief the boys.

The IRT is just a cab with the MERT on board and all their equipment in the back – oxygen, saline drips, drug packs, tubes, scalpels, defibrillators – basically everything they might possibly need to perform life-saving surgical interventions on the badly wounded and dying. It's axiomatic that the victim's chances of survival are greatest if they receive care within a very short period of time after a severe injury. The whole focus, the very *raison d'être* of the MERT, is to get the doctor and the med team there as soon as is humanly possible, and we shave off every minute, every second, we can. A minute saved at our end means a greater chance of survival for whoever we're being scrambled to scoop and run. The injured will feel the touch of a doctor within an hour whether they are in camp or on the ground. There's also a 'Platinum 10 Minutes' which is the preserve of the medics with the soldiers. They accompany them on patrol and live with them in the FOBs or PBs so British casualties will be seen by one of them within ten minutes and treated. That preliminary treatment really makes a difference.

Sometimes, the combat medics who patrol with the soldiers are so efficient there's little for the MERT team to do once the casualties are loaded on. Take someone with a traumatic injury – they'll apply a 'cat' (a combat tourniquet) and a first field dressing and they'll have completely stopped any exsanguination (bleeding out). That's something that guys were dying from just twelve months ago. The MERT team say casualties are coming on with beautifully applied first field dressings, and they are seeing patients who are already cannulated so they can take on fluids. While there's always something for the MERT to do, often the hardest and most important bits have been done on the ground. That's a massive improvement on last year and shows how the standard of medicine – and the overall awareness of the guys on the ground of basic first aid – has evolved.

When we switch from HRF, we can't just say, 'Right, we're now IRT on this cab' – we have to change cabs. So every two days we move all our kit across – weapons, bits of uniform, helmets, personal go kits etc. It takes about half an hour, which is a bit of a nightmare if a call comes in while we're mid-transfer. So we make sure we're on the radio at all times and if a shout comes in, one of the crew will go to get the details and the non-IRT crew will pull out all the stops to help the MERT team get their kit on board.

That day, pretty soon after we'd swapped, we got a shout to pick up a T1 from a spot just north-west of FOB Edinburgh – a British soldier suffering from heat stress. There was a convoy running between Now Zad and Musa Qala and when we came in all the guys were waving at us. I think they were enjoying the downtime to be honest – they were all logistics guys and these resupply convoys that have to go by road are massive undertakings with loads of vehicles involved, so it must get a bit tedious. They can only travel slowly and have to stop repeatedly to check for IEDs.

I landed on and the QRF guys ran out to defend us, although they were rather surplus to requirements given the firepower that ranged around us in the convoy. Basically, whenever our convoys leave the base, they always travel with their own force protection – an infantry unit travelling in a mix of relatively fast, armoured vehicles with heavy firepower. Also, most of the trucks in the convoy have guys on top cover manning .50 calibre machine-guns.

Anyway, we got the guy on board and I took off over the convoy and turned sharp left back to Bastion. It was 11:40 when I landed, so I did a quick debrief and we were back in the tent for 12:10. We just had time for a bit of lunch at the DFAC and then went back to the tent to chill out watching TV for bit.

At 13:30 the phone rings – we've got a shout. I pull myself out of the chair and put my boots on, grab my notebook and run for the JOC. Bob drives Coops and Alex to the cab and while they're getting her going, he races back to find me in the JOC, where I'm taking down the details from the nine-liner. There's not much; there's been an IED strike at a grid east of where we'd picked up the T1 from the convoy a couple of hours earlier. We have five casualties to pick up – two T1s, two T2s and a T3. Bob drives us the short distance to the cab and parks the vehicle at the edge of the pan and we sprint for the ramp. I grab my helmet from its perch at the rear, put my vest on and check my pistol, and then I jump into my seat. Alex has got us turning and burning, so I plug in and brief the crew as we complete our last few checks.

Our Apache escort is already airborne as Alex says, 'Pre-take offs good; ready to lift.'

'Clear above and behind,' says Bob.

'Lifting,' I say, pulling power, and the two Lycoming Turbo-shafts make light work of lifting us into the blindingly bright Afghanistan sky. I drop the dark visor on my helmet and immediately the picture improves. We're airborne by 13:40.

As we're running in, my mind starts to work over the detail. We're flying to an area very close to where we'd lifted the guy with heat stress earlier that morning. There are no FOBs or PBs at or near the grid we've been given, so it has to be the convoy: one of the vehicles must have run over an IED.

Sadly, my fears are confirmed almost immediately as I look ahead. There on the nose in my 12 o'clock, I can see the same convoy that we visited earlier snaking away into the distance. At its head is a thick pall of black smoke drifting lazily into the windless Afghan sky, like a dirty smear on the windscreen of the cab. My heart sinks; it's funny how little it takes for something to become personal, but this one most definitely is. We'd been to these guys already; we were their focus of interest for a while and they ours.

When we landed alongside them earlier, some of their guys came aboard to give us bottles of ice-cold water. We had a drink with them and Bob and Coops enjoyed a bit of banter with a couple of the guys. There was a connection. Now we're back again in circumstances much less happy. We're sat on the aircraft as the doctor heads off to meet the ground team bringing the casualties, dealing with the knowledge that, once again, the lives of several of our boys, who had been at the peak of physical fitness and in prime health, have changed forever. They got up that morning as they always did – just another day, doing what they've done so many times before. Some with thoughts of loved ones back home, others daydreaming about girls they've met on Facebook; probably wondering about stuff as mundane as what they'd be eating later. An ordinary day like any other suddenly turned into a personal hell for all those involved, courtesy of that most cowardly and indiscriminate of weapons: an IED.

The Taliban's increased use of IEDs evidenced a sea change in tactics; no fighting force can suffer the rate of attrition that the

Taliban did throughout 2006 and 2007 without feeling it. So they went the only way they could. IEDs require one man to manufacture, one or two men to plant. No maintenance required. No risk to their fighters. Forty-seven ISAF troops died as a result of IEDs in 2006; but in twelve months to December 2008, that figure had more than trebled to 152. Everything changes in a nanosecond; life really does turn on a sixpence.

It's one of the vehicles that had been providing force protection for the convoy that has been blown up. The MERT is off and on again in quick order, bringing with them five casualties. One is beyond help, having died on the ground – Fijian Trooper Ratu Babakobau, twenty-nine, of the Household Cavalry. Princes William and Harry will both later pay tribute to him. Poor guy, he'd been in theatre less than a month and it was his first deployment overseas. He was married, and the father of two young boys aged four and one who will now have to grow up without him. It's heartbreaking. Another of the casualties is in a bad way, with traumatic injuries to his legs and arms – it looks like he and Ratu took the brunt of the blast. Two others have burns of varying degrees – one is another soldier from the Household Cavalry, the other an Afghan national who had been working with the team as a translator. Finally, there is one T3, another soldier of the Household Cavalry who is walking wounded.

We race back to Bastion as quickly as we can and are on the ground at Nightingale by 14:20, so it's a quick mission. Fortunately, the four casualties survived.

There's to be no rest for us, however. Ten minutes after shutting down and arriving back at the IRT tent, I'm sat back in the same chair with my boots off, cooling down with an ice-cold Coke from the fridge and a nice cool Mars Bar. Chocolate is a rare commodity here for obvious reasons. There's no chance for me to enjoy this one though. Just as I take my second bite, the phone rings again; we've got another shout. I throw the Mars Bar on the sofa and swallow the last of my Coke as I lace up my boots and run once again for the JOC. Here we go again.

This time, we're being scrambled for a baby girl at FOB

Gibraltar. She's a T1, suffering from meningitis. This job could really get to you if you let it, and somehow it's even harder when you're dealing with kids. We land on at Gibraltar without incident and the baby girl is brought on almost as soon as the ramp comes down. She's in a bad way. I've no idea who her parents are, but my heart goes out to them.

As soon as I'm away from Gibraltar, the MERT surgeon talks to me on the radio. 'Guys, we have to take this one to Lashkar Gah,' he says.

'Negative.' I tell him, we're taking her to Bastion.

'No,' says the surgeon. 'We have been told by our ops that Afghan civilians have to go to the Afghan hospital at Lashkar Gah. If she goes to Bastion she's going to take a bed that might be needed for a British soldier.'

I can tell from the timbre of his voice that he's unhappy about this. He's speaking the words but there's no heart behind what he's saying. However, the standing orders are explicit: if we are picking up an Afghan civilian, they have to be taken to an Afghan hospital.

'Okay,' I say to the doctor. 'Straight down the line; I want you to tell me honestly. Don't colour your response with your own thoughts or feelings – has Lashkar Gah got the facilities to deal with a case of meningitis?'

'I don't think they do.'

I didn't have to think for very long. 'Right, then I've made my decision,' I say. 'My responsibility as aircraft captain is to ensure the safety of all the passengers on this aircraft and to make decisions to ensure they remain safe. Taking this girl to Lashkar Gah will not ensure her safety so we are flying straight to Bastion.'

When I called the tower at Bastion to advise them of our impending arrival, they tried to direct us to Lashkar Gah, but I was having none of it.

'Bastion Tower, Lobster Three One, negative. We are en route to Bastion with one casualty.'

'Lobster Three One, Tower, do you require Nightingale?' At last. They got the message.

'Tower, Lobster 31, affirmative.'

'Roger, cleared to land, Nightingale.'

The ambulance is waiting as we land and there's a quick hand-over from the MERT. The girl is whisked off to all the expertise and know-how that British medicine and clinical care can offer. At least this way she has a chance.

As soon as I'm back at the JOC, I tell JP exactly what I've done.

'Don't worry mate, that's fine, I'll sort it out,' he says. That's one of the things that make him such a great leader. Do the right thing and even if it goes against SOP, he'll support you to the hilt. I don't know what he did or said, or to whom, but I know it caused a stir.

The reasons for my actions were simple: there was no point in risking the aircraft and crew only to take a casualty to a place where she was not going to survive. We may as well have saved ourselves the bother and stayed at home. Taking her to Lash would've been tantamount to signing her death warrant and I wasn't prepared to do that.

If the situation arose again I'd make the same decision.

27

APACHE DOWN

Something unusual to break the monotony of day-to-day taskings is always welcome in Helmand Province but, perhaps surprisingly for a war zone, unusual happenings are in short supply. I guess it's all a matter of perspective, but it's amazing what you get used to. By now, with several Dets under our belts, most of us were well used to the daily litany of resupply runs, underslung loads, troop insertions and extractions, and yes – to a degree – even coming under fire.

There are some things that we really enjoy doing, and generally they are the things that we know are going to have the biggest impact on the guys at the front. For all that we as aircrew gripe about the conditions at KAF, and Bastion to a degree, we're just sounding off – we know we have it good by comparison. It's in the nature of the beast to complain; all military people do it, it's in our DNA. But the guys at the FOBs and PBs, not only are they living in spartan, primitive conditions – in some cases without running water or proper toilets, living off basic rations – on top of all that, they get malleted by the Taliban when they're inside, and attacked when they venture out on patrol. So anything we can do to improve morale is good from our perspective and we'll go out of our way to do it.

The thing that takes up the most room in the cabs is mail and it's the one thing we never turn down because we know how important it is. So much of it comes through – what with the letters, welfare shoeboxes and the guys going mental on Amazon and Play.com – we get it by the four-tonne load! The guys really appreciate the welfare boxes. We get quite a few that come to us at Bastion and KAF but we take them all to the troops at the FOBs and hand them out there because it lifts their morale so much. We've been known to literally stack the aircraft floor to ceiling. The guys are used to it now and prioritise handwritten mail and then squeeze in whatever else they can.

We flew a fair bit of mail on May 10th, which started out as a fairly routine day, but finished anything but. We were operating out of KAF on the task line with the call sign Daybreaker Two One, flying with Hannah who was in Daybreaker Two Zero. It had been a long day that saw us flying all over the province with supplies, post and other assorted items. Towards the end of the day, we were en route to FOB Inkerman and FOB Robinson. Hannah was leading the formation and I was her wingman.

Robinson and Inkerman are near Sangin, and the two bases are very close together. Instead of us each having two loads – one each for Robinson and Inkerman – Hannah takes my load for Inkerman and I take hers for Robinson. That means we won't be risking two cabs by us both dropping a load at each base. Hannah has completed her drop at Inkerman and I am at Robinson; I've got my passengers off and am waiting for the pax that I have to pick up. Bob Ruffles is getting excited – he gets impatient after about two minutes on the ground; although in fairness, I do too.

'Wankers!' he says. 'If they can't get their fucking act together, we should just fuck off and leave them. It's not fucking difficult, is it? Maybe they'll be ready next time then!' Fuck me, his Det Tourette's is getting worse by the day!

'Got the painters in, Bob?' asks Coops.

'Ha fucking ha.'

'Must admit, I'm a bit fucked off myself,' I say. But I have a well-tested plan to calm the tensions in the air.

I dig out a dog-eared copy of *FHM's 100 High Street Honeys* that Alison gave me before I left for this Det. It's well thumbed and quite knackered, bearing the battle scars of a hundred pairs of mitts pawing over its pages.

'Okay boys, pick a number between one and a hundred,' I say.

'Five!' from Bob.

'Fifty-six!' – Coops.

'Twenty-two!' from Alex.

'Okay, and I'll go with ninety-five,' I say, writing them all down on my kneeboard. Now for the hard part.

I flick through and see who has picked the fittest girl of the lot. It's a bit like playing Top Trumps for High Street Honeys, except we make up the scores and rip the piss out of each other – and I'm judge, jury and executioner!

Bob and Coops lean in to the cockpit through the gangway as I turn to each girl in the magazine.

'Fucking hell! You fancy her?' says Bob as I turn to No.56. Her name is Kayleigh and she's the girl who corresponds to the number Coops picked at random. 'She looks like the Loch Ness Munter!'

I turn to Alex's 'choice' – Donna, No.2. 'Hmm,' we all say. 'Not ba—'

The radio bursts into life and we freeze as we hear the words that all aircrew dread, signalling that an aircraft is in grave and imminent danger and requires immediate assistance.

'Mayday! Mayday! Mayday! Ugly Five One Mayday!'

Alex and I look at one another and almost simultaneously, we both say, 'What the fuck?!'

'Daybreaker Two One, Ugly Five One, we have an engine on fire. We are going to land at Robinson.'

'Ugly Five One, Daybreaker Two Zero, stay where you are. We'll intercept your location for a visual inspection,' cuts in Hannah.

The Apache is in a slow orbit at about 2,000ft, so Hannah quickly pulls in the power and climbs straight up so that she's visual with the AH. It might sound daft, but aircraft warning systems aren't immune from the odd gremlin, so it's possible that it's just the Apache's fire-warning circuit that's gone nuclear rather than its engine.

It takes Hannah about two seconds to confirm the crew's worst fears.

'Ugly, Daybreaker Two Zero, confirm smoke from your engine,' she says.

'Daybreaker Two One, Ugly Five One, we are landing where you are now, repeat, we are landing now at your location.'

Bear in mind we're sat forward in the cockpit some 60ft ahead of the ramp and in my mind, all this is going on above and behind us. I wouldn't say I was panicking . . . but I can visualise the Apache literally directly above us, with one engine out and he's coming down fast. The laws of physics don't allow for two solid objects to occupy the same space and he's landing right where we are. We need to get the hell out of there . . . and fast!

'Bob, get everyone off or everyone on, or fuck them, just get the fucking ramp up. We're going NOW!' I scream. Maybe not the most eloquent or articulate I've ever been, but I think it conveyed the urgency of our situation clearly enough.

He sprints for the ramp and, literally within a second, I hear him on the radio with a reply.

He doesn't even finish his sentence. I hear the words 'Clear above and . . .' and I'm pulling the collective, demanding every inch of power the two engines can spare. The gearboxes whine in protest and the blades fight a battle that the air can't win. I push the cyclic hard forward to get the nose down and hear the engine note rise as we lift and propel forward, gaining speed.

'. . . behind' comes the rest of Bob's sentence, as I shout over the radio, 'Daybreaker Two Zero is clear of the area.'

Arse. My voice isn't usually that high. I'm going to pay for that later.

Despite me pulling full power it feels like we're travelling at half-speed, but I guess that's as good an example as I'll find of perception distortion. It's quite common when you're stressed or under threat, and that's exactly how we feel. I am literally waiting for the AH to attempt to perform an unnatural coupling with our Chinook, an unnatural coupling which is only going to end one way . . . badly!

I'm bracing myself for impact but it doesn't come. I pull a sharp left and look . . . which is when I see that the Apache is still at about 1,500ft!

It must have seemed bizarre to everyone but us – the urgency in my voice, the panicked lift off with the ramp barely up, the hardcore nose-down turn. We were lifting up and away like the ground was opening up beneath us, and all the while the AH is almost leisurely descending from altitude. Hannah's up there with a bird's-eye view of the whole thing from 2,000ft and she's doubtless thinking, 'What the fuck is up with Frenchie? He seems a little stressed!'

I had to pull something out of the hat, so I got on the radio and said, 'Ugly Five One, Daybreaker Two One, I'll position behind you and shepherd you in. If you have any problems, we'll be right there to lift you.'

It's unlikely, but there's still a possibility of the AH landing badly and slamming into the HLS. An AH is like a flying tank. They're armoured, literally bullet-proof, and carry enough arma-ment and firepower to prosecute a small war on their own; but all that comes at a cost – weight. With one engine out, they wouldn't have enough power to hover and there would be no opportunity to go around or run on if they get the landing wrong. It has to be right first time or not at all. And if the worst happens, I want us in a position where we could be on the ground within seconds to pull them from the wreckage and extract them if need be. I want them to know we've got their backs.

'Daybreaker Two One, Ugly Five One thank you.'

And with that, the pilot brings the aircraft down in a textbook one-engine landing; it's perfection. She settles on to the ground, her pilot shuts the remaining engine down and that's it – job done!

It's such a difficult thing to do, because with only one engine, when you start pulling power, there's only so much it can give to the NR. The impulse then is to increase the pitch to get more lift, but the engine is already maxed out and has no more to give so the NR will actually slow down. When the rotor slows down, lift decreases, and that means you accelerate towards the ground faster.

When you're in that position, normally, the collective will be up somewhere near your armpit and with the NR dropping, you have to lower the lever, which is completely counter-intuitive – it's utterly alien to every pilot. But the AH pilot does it beautifully. The Apache just wafts down to the ground and it's almost graceful.

I think the pilot got a Green Endorsement for that, and quite right too, because he only had a small area to get down onto and he popped it bang in the middle. Also, the aircraft was fine – the engineers performed an engine change in situ and it was eventually flown out.

All's well that ends well, then.

28

MILLION DOLLAR BILL

A couple of days later, we flew a routine tasking out of KAF that saw me undertake a technique I'd never tried before, with the Chinook operating right on the very edge of its capabilities.

The airflow over a Chinook is at its most efficient when it's off the 10 o'clock. This doesn't mean that we fly sideways to achieve best-efficiency of the rotors, and anyway, the difference is so slight as to only really matter in extreme circumstances. I considered the circumstances extreme enough on this sortie, though, that I needed every bit of help I could get.

Alex and I were flying as No.2 to Hannah on a routine tasking day out of KAF. The bulk of the day was pretty uneventful – a series of routine admin and mail runs to various locations in the Upper Gereshk Valley. Our final sortie late in the evening saw us at Bastion where we lifted two cabs full of troops en route to Kajaki, where they were destined to relieve two units there that had experienced quite an intense period on the front line.

We flew the route from Bastion at high altitude as the ridges surrounding Kajaki Dam go up to 6,000ft plus. Hannah was ahead as lead and our Apache escort called the Widow call sign at Kajaki to obtain clearance. Hannah was cleared in straight away, while Alex and I went to hold further up the lake.

If I'm honest, we were more or less doing a bit of war tourism, so I wasn't complaining. There are worse places to fly a holding pattern than over the forbiddingly beautiful lake and surrounding topography at Kajaki – it's not like you could ever grow bored of the view. We ended up holding for some twenty minutes, a lot longer than expected, before Hannah advised us that she was lifting. I repositioned the aircraft at low level over the lake pointing to the south-west, in order to see her as she came out flying over the dam.

There are two ways in and out of Kajaki. You fly over the dam to get in, but as the landing site is so low in the valley, you need to watch your speed as you cross it and ensure it remains above 60kts or you end up flirting with Vortex Ring, a phenomenon in which the rotors lose lift at speeds below 30kts and a rate of descent above 500ft per minute.

There is however a sluice gate further to the east-north-east of the dam which is literally a cut in the mountain. You fly through it at 50ft with the sides of the mountain close on each side, pressing in on you and making you feel small even though you're in 99ft of aircraft. You end up following the Helmand River as it winds down the valley, which increases the distance to the landing site and allows you to carry more speed on the approach. This is what I opted to do for my run in.

Everything has limits and that includes the Chinook's capabilities. Regardless of what it can do in ideal conditions – cold and as close to sea level as possible – the higher and hotter you go, the greater the impact on what you can lift. So Afghanistan in summer – very hot and very high – is not exactly ideal. For this sortie, we were tasked and limited to picking up twenty-one soldiers.

As soon as I landed on, Bob came over the intercom. 'Er, two minutes, Frenchie mate, we've got somebody approaching and he wants a chat. It looks like we've got at least thirty blokes here. I'm going off-intercom.'

Five minutes later, he's back.

'Okay Frenchie, this is the deal. We have twenty-one guys as flagged on the task sheet to go back to Bastion. We also have twelve guys with their kit for R&R. They didn't get on a Chinook yesterday, as it broke down, so they missed their TriStar home.

The dickhead in the tasking cell obviously didn't think of putting them on another cab so they're trying to hitch a ride.'

Shit. I don't want to leave them here, but how the fuck am I going to get airborne with that many bodies?

'Okay, let me think about it for a minute,' I say.

The clock for R&R starts as soon as front line troops leave their units, so if they stay fourteen days at Kajaki, or their aircraft goes tech and they spend nine days waiting for a replacement, it makes no difference. Regardless of if or when they get home, as far as their parent unit is concerned they've had their fourteen days R&R. It sucks, but that's how it is.

I want to take them but I have a problem: the aircraft's available power. What we have in hand is enough for us to lift one-and-a-half tonnes above the limit given to me by the taskers and, if I'm honest, I'm not sure my trusty Chinook can even achieve that.

Things are compounded by our location; the only way out is up and over the dam. However the dam rises high ahead, with steep sides left and right and some wires strung across the wall and mountain sides. Then I recall a technique that I learned way back in my early days at RAF Odiham from Bill Thompson, my first instructor on the Chinook. He was old even then, but God that man knew how to fly. What he didn't know was not worth knowing and he had probably forgotten more than I'll ever learn.

We were on an instructional sortie and he showed me how to accelerate using the minimum of power by using the air cushion that builds up under the aircraft. Doing this, you build up enough speed to climb and you use the Chinook's unique aerodynamic effect; the airflow from the 10 o'clock.

I look at Alex with this 'trust me' look in my eyes and say, 'Okay Bob, we'll take them and we'll have a shot at clearing the dam. If we can't make it, then we'll come back here and I'm afraid they'll have to wait for the next cab. But guys, as you know, R&R time is running out for them so we have to give it a go.'

As expected, the guys agree immediately. Now for the hard part. Bob gets them all on board. Thirty-three people and their kit instead of the twenty-one we were expecting. I'm not even sure this will work.

'CAP, Ts and Ps, brakes off, clear lift?' I check.

'Clear above and behind,' says Coops.

'Lifting,' I say, heaving on the collective. I can feel the aircraft is heavier immediately; the engine notes rise in pitch as both strain to deliver everything they have, and the lever in my hand is almost in my armpit. We are well into the ten-minute power band and only just in the hover.

'Okay chaps, I'll go down the river towards Kajaki town – not too far though, because we all know what a shithole it is. We'll use that as the run-up and I'll bias myself on the left-hand side of the dam. In the event that we run out of power and climb, I'll be able to see clearly from the right-hand seat into a right-hand turn back to the landing site. Any questions?'

There are none. Good, as I'm not sure I've got any answers. This is unknown territory. I slowly hover-taxi down the river and turn the aircraft through 180° to face the dam. It looks intimidating ahead of us and as I look at it, I could swear that somebody has just built an extra 10ft on top. It looks like it's daring me. *Come and have a go if you think you're hard enough.* I hold us in the hover with nothing in reserve. Well, I can't look at it forever so fuck it! I go for it.

I gently trickle the aircraft forward using the ground cushion; it's a balancing act. I can't dip the nose too hard or we'll descend and I don't have the power available to arrest the descent. If that happens, we'll hit the river and I don't even want to think about that.

Alex is calling the power settings to ensure that I use everything available. The speed is building. 'Come on Frenchie,' I think. 'For once in your life be smooth.' The speed continues to build . . . 60kts, and half the distance covered. I know that in about 10–15kts I'll be at what we call minimum power speed; this is the speed at which most power is available, where the aircraft is at its most efficient. 65kts; 70kts. 'Come on!' 75kts; 80kts.

I take a quick look and notice that I've actually lowered the lever to maintain my low altitude; I have spare power, but is it enough? The dam rises before us; it's dead ahead. I pull the lever and take everything the engines have got, every last ounce of power. We climb, but it's not enough. We'll never make it.

'You need to increase your rate of climb, matey,' says Alex, a note of concern in his voice.

'I know mate, but have a look at this,' I say, with more confidence than I feel. It's all or nothing now. I carefully apply some right pedal, tipping the aircraft 20° out of balance and therefore putting the airflow in the 10 o'clock of the disc, while still flying on the same track. Suddenly the cab's rate of climb increases. Just like Old Bill Thompson – Million Dollar Bill – showed me.

We clear the dam by the barest of margins, but it doesn't matter – a win's a win – and as I resume straight flight, I've got enough power in hand to climb above the mountains around the lake. I can hear the cheers from the guys in the back even over the sound of the rotors and the whine of the engines. That's twelve very happy souls back there.

'Fuck me, Frenchie, that was close, but pretty impressive,' says Alex.

'Cheers mate.' I feel a lift in myself that more than matches what the cab has given us. It's been a long day; lots of flying hours and sectors ending with this. It's thirty to forty-five minutes back to KAF, so I decide to keep the crew occupied on the way there. And there's nothing like a game of Fuck, Marry, Kill to keep them on the ball . . .

'Mélissa Theuriau, Lorraine Kelly, Kelly Brook,' I say.

'Oh for fuck's sake, Frenchie,' says Bob and I think for a moment that I've misjudged the mood. 'You and that bloody Mélissa! Why can't we play Fuck, Marry, Kill with girls that everyone knows?'

'I don't know, Bob,' says Alex. 'I've seen a picture of that Mélissa. Christ, the *Daily Express* called her the world's most beautiful news reporter.'

'How'd you know all this?' Coops asks.

'I looked her up on Google after Frenchie mentioned her on our last Det,' says Alex. 'She is one seriously fit woman. You don't make it easy, do you Frenchie?'

'You think thats tough try this,' says Coops. 'Ann Widdecombe, Margaret Thatcher, Harriet Harman!'

I shake my head. 'You bastard!'

'I feel sick!' says Alex. 'Seriously, Coops . . . that's a perfect definition of being between a rock and a hard place!'

Anything that involves the whole crew is good and Fuck, Marry, Kill is a perennial favourite when we're held off or on those long transits back to KAF or Bastion at height. Funnily enough, we find crews are much more likely to catch something happening on the aircraft when we're doing this than if they are doing nothing. Anything that gets your brain ticking over is good.

The guys are happy, I'm happy, and we've got thirty-three happy soldiers in the back. Once again the Chinook has delivered more than expected and because of that, we've now got twelve troops who are going to be on a TriStar back home tonight.

'Things on a Det don't get any better than this,' I think.

I have no idea how right I am.

29

FROM RUSSIA WITH LOVE

Hindsight is a wonderful thing, isn't it? Looking back, it's so easy to see that the week or so following May 15th was unusual in the extreme but, at the time, there just seemed to be a marked increase in activity on the Taliban's part. As it turned out, the series of seemingly unrelated events we experienced over that ten-day period were all part of a concerted effort by the Taliban to achieve a series of spectaculars; it was only down to an extraordinary degree of luck, daring, and some spectacular flying by the Chinook Force that they failed.

Over eight days, several cabs took rounds and an assassination attempt was made against Gulab Mangal, governor of Helmand Province, while I was flying him to Musa Qala. Also, the Taliban used a suicide bomber in a crowded market in a cynical attempt to lure a Chinook into a position where they could try and shoot it down.

Morris Oxford was the first to experience the Taliban's renewed sense of purpose when he was diverted in the middle of a normal tasking day. He was flying with Greg Lloyd Davies as 'Black Cat Two One'. They had just loaded some Canadian troops, along with some freight, when he was called by Bastion Ops over the radio. To many of us in the Chinook Force, his actions in the sortie that followed warranted a gallantry award and it's inexplicable why he never received recognition. This is his account:

'We were told by Bastion Ops to offload all our pax and await further tasking. It'd taken us the best part of twenty minutes to get them all loaded and then we kicked them all off again. That was not something we'd experienced before, so we were sat there thinking, "What the hell?"

'We were told to get airborne, head north of the field and make contact with another call sign – Wildman One Zero, a Russian Mil Mi-8 (or "Hip") twin-turbine transport helicopter that's used by Afghan forces. We were then told to fly to an area just north of Sangin where we'd be performing an emergency extraction of some British troops on the ground there. They'd been inserted earlier that morning by the Wildman call sign and his wingman but they'd come under intense fire from the Taliban almost immediately, and had been involved in a rolling contact ever since – some eight hours by this stage.

'An Apache had been tasked to support us and had gone ahead to provide air support for the troops on the ground, and us once we arrived on station. We held off to the west while we waited for a pair of RAF Harrier GR-9s to fly in and strafe the area. They stormed in and worked their magic, releasing a salvo of CRV7 rockets to take out some of the Taliban in the area, which can't have been very pleasant for those on the receiving end – they travel at Mach 3 and make quite a mess on impact! After that, we were called in.

'The HLS had been chosen by the ground call sign; it was a reasonably large open area in the middle of a village. Wildman One Zero decided he'd go in first, extract his troops and then we'd go in and extract those remaining. The guys on the ground were desperate – they'd been in a contact for eight hours plus, they were running low on ammunition and things were deteriorating rapidly. Despite the rocket attack by the Harriers, they had to fire and manoeuvre to get away. I don't think they'd expected the weight of response that met them when they were first landed.

'We got overhead so we were visual with the LS and stayed at height while the Hip made its approach. As it did so, it came under a barrage of heavy small arms fire. Just as it was about to land on, several RPGs were fired at it, missing by mere feet. It was awful to watch – to me, from height, they looked like fireworks, but a strike by any one of those warheads would have splintered the Hip into a million pieces. The pilot managed to overshoot at the very last second and come back up to height with us so we could carry out a visual inspection of his aircraft. I've no idea how, but he got away unscathed – given the weight of fire that was ranged at it, that was just astonishing. There was no way we'd be able to get into that HLS – it was just too hot. We had a quick discussion with the Hip, the Apache and the ground call sign and worked out an alternate plan to lift the troops from another LS.

'We were trying to get them to move east about 500m away from the village and towards the desert area. They said it'd take them about thirty minutes. By this stage, we were almost bingo fuel, so we flew back to Bastion with the Hip to refuel; it was about fifteen minutes flying time there, fifteen on the ground for a hot refuel and fifteen minutes back – forty-five minutes in all. Luckily, the Apache had enough fuel to stay on station and provide support until we got back. That support must have been hell for both the Taliban and friendly forces because a lot of it was Danger Close. Being in the immediate vicinity of an Apache's flechette rocket attack or 30mm cannon fire – even under cover – isn't an experience I'd like to try. Despite the overwhelming suppressing fire, the Taliban fought on, and the ground troops barely had the breathing space to fire-and-manoeuvre their way to the new HLS. It must have been hell for them.

'When we arrived back, the troops on the ground were surrounded and taking fire from 360°, so we knew if we didn't get them out we'd be leaving them to die. It was like the Alamo – there's no way they could have withstood the weight of fire ranged against them for much longer. To make matters worse, the Apache was almost out of ordnance and close to bingo fuel – he reckoned he only had enough for another ten minutes on scene.

'The Apache crew were awesome. Even while laying down suppressing fire, they'd scoped out a routing that would provide us with maximum cover on our run in – a wadi running towards the village. The HLS was an L-shaped compound at the end of the wadi on the right. So, as before, the Hip went in first and we stayed at height orbiting while the Apache led him in. That was impressive and way beyond the AH crew's call of duty – Apaches almost always stay at height. Not this one – it dropped down to low level and led the Hip right in to the HLS, then overshot to act as a bullet magnet, flying a low orbit to draw Taliban fire. Despite that, the Taliban still opened up on the Hip as it made its descent – small arms fire, RPGs and about three or four mortar rounds too. Luckily they all fell short, landing just outside the compound. If it was hell for the Hip crew, it was no picnic for us either, knowing that we were next up to be the Taliban's target practice.

'The Hip was only on the ground for about a minute but as he climbed out, he routed to the south – and took yet more fire as he overflew another enemy position. By now, we were making our run in. The Apache called us and said, "We'll lead you in," and I dropped us down into the wadi at 150kts flying 20 on the light, 10 on the noise – as low and as fast as I dared.

'I left it right to the last minute to scrub off my speed, standing the aircraft on its tail. Booting it left and right, I flared on the approach into the compound; we were coming in along the upright of the "L" with the horizontal bit out to the right. As I came in, there were some trees about 25ft high, so I had to get us over those and then drop down. The compound had recently been dug out and I thought for a moment our blades would hit the walls and that'd be it for us, but as our wheels settled on, the blades ended up sitting just above the walls on either side! That in itself was pretty scary!

'I've never seen British troops move so fast! They were on the cab within thirty seconds, which really highlights the benefits of the Chinook's ramp against the Hip's side-opening door. Quite a few of the soldiers had taken rounds, which indicated the ferocity of the firefights. It was bullets to their legs mostly, although they weren't "through-and-throughs" – they were mostly grazes. That said though, the guys were pumped up on adrenaline and running as fast and hard as the rest of them! Three stayed on the ramp with Daz Beattie, one of the crewmen, and he said over the intercom, "Morris, if they open fire, I'm going to open fire as well!"

'The lads we'd loaded on said they'd seen us taking rounds on the approach, but as it was daylight and noisy as hell, we hadn't seen or heard anything. They said they couldn't believe the weight of fire and we'd got pretty much the same as the Hip when it came in. I was amazed – one, that we hadn't noticed; but two, that we hadn't been hit. After watching the Hip taking fire, I'd been worried about following him in, but once I started the run I was so focused on the flying that I didn't have any spare capacity to feel scared.

'We were so lucky not to lose any vital systems and I can't believe they missed us! I'd been worried that the mortars we'd seen landing short while the Hip was on the ground had been zeroed in and would be raining down exactly where we were sat, but they all missed us too. There was a kind of irony in that the walls around the compound afforded us protection from small arms fire once we were on the ground, but by being where we were, the blast from any mortar rounds that might have landed inside the walls would have been amplified.

'I was away as soon as the ramp was up. I lifted to the hover, and as soon as I'd cleared the walls I turned hard right and pulled power, the nose hard down. I flew north to avoid the enemy position to the south – no point giving them another bite at the cherry! The cab was squealing like a stuck pig. The NR dipped a bit at one stage because I was asking it for more than it had to give, in an effort to get us away as quickly as possible. I flew fast and low to the east of the village and once I was convinced we'd reached a safe area, I pulled power and climbed to altitude where I met up with the Hip for the transit back to Bastion.

'Once we reached the Bastion perimeter, we were directed to a specific pan to offload our troops and then Bastion Ops came over the radio and said, "Yeah, Black Cat Two One, pick up the program at Serial 14," and that was it, back to "normality". We carried on with the program as if nothing had happened.

'It took us a while to come down after the high of that extraction. The adrenaline had been running and I remember thinking as the Hip went in and started taking rounds that first time, "I didn't ring my family yesterday because Op Minimise was on." I did wonder then whether I'd ever get to speak to them again, although I quickly pushed that thought away – it's not helpful to anyone to think like that, least of all yourself. I think it's worse looking back though, and I still can't believe that with the amount of ordnance being thrown at us, we didn't take a single round.'

I didn't know it at the time, but Morris' experience signalled the start of a week I'd never forget.

30

ASSASSIN'S CREED

May 17th started out so simply: a routine three-ship tasking made up of JP flying as captain in the No.2 cab, with Alex and myself in the No.3 and German in the No.1 as lead. JP and I were based out of Bastion, while German was operating from Kandahar. It was a straightforward mission involving my cab and JP's meeting up with German's over Lashkar Gah, picking up some pax and freight, and the three of us then doing a couple of runs to Musa Qala, then back to Bastion for us, and KAF for German. Easy as . . .

We launched early in the morning; it would have been around 09:00, just as the sun was arcing its way to its high point, so the temperature – although well on its way to the top – was still manageable. An Apache took off with us from Bastion and we flew up to Lash where we met up with Rich as planned. Each of us then landed on and picked up a load, together with some VIP passengers for Rich's cab. Once we were loaded up, we launched and off we went as a three-ship.

We flew over Gereshk and out into the desert, but as we got there – I think we were probably about five miles north of Bastion – German's aircraft had a Defensive Aids Suite problem. There are a lot of faults that we'll carry on with, but a DAS problem isn't one of them. With that out of action, you're effectively flying naked and exposed to any ordnance that Terry Taliban has pointed towards you. So German peeled off towards Bastion, the nearest base to his position, and Alex and I carried on towards Musa Qala with JP as formation leader.

On the run in to Musa Qala, the Apache said there had been a ten-fold increase in ICOM chatter, but I didn't think too much of it. The Taliban knew we could intercept their radio traffic – it's not like it's encrypted or anything – so they weren't averse to trying to give us false intel. I registered it, but it was just there at the back of my mind and I wasn't unduly concerned. We flew to Musa Qala without incident, landed on with JP and, after we'd offloaded our pax, lifted off again. On the way back, JP called me over the radio and said, 'Look, Rich's VIPs are stuck at Bastion so I think we'll be a bit pro-active. We're gonna do the tasking for his aircraft and take his passengers to Musa Qala.'

First though, we both needed refuelling so we stopped off at Gereshk, which was our nearest refuelling base at the time. It's pretty straightforward normally, but as our tanks were filling, JP's aircraft had a massive fuel leak – and I mean massive. I've never seen anything like it. The Chinook has tanks on each side and they've got these vents that allow the air in and out to prevent the tanks collapsing as fuel is used, and to prevent them exploding under pressure when refuelling. There's a shut-off valve on each tank that's supposed to activate when it's full – it's a similar sort of principle to what happens when you fill up your car really; when the tank's full, the nozzle cuts off. Except the valve on one of JP's cabs failed and didn't shut, so the fuel continued to pour in. With the tank full, it followed the only path available, which was out of the vent.

Now, Chinooks take a lot of fuel and it tends to flow at high pressure, so it was literally jetting out of the vent where it atomised in the air, just by the engine. It could have ignited at any time and we were right behind JP's cab, still attached and taking on fuel ourselves.

We couldn't move and we couldn't call JP over the radio because of the risk of an electrical discharge from the aerials. If that happened, we'd do the Taliban's job for them . . . boom, two Chinooks and their crews out of the game for good. Alex and I were both close to panic, sat immobile in the cockpit, and JP's crewman was just stood by the cab refuelling and chatting away to his mate without a care in the world, a veritable Niagara Falls of fuel cascading out behind him. Eventually he turned around and saw it. His mouth formed a perfect 'O' as he realised what was happening, but fortunately he immediately shut off the fuel and we narrowly averted what could have been a major disaster.

It did mean that JP would be going nowhere though. The fuel pouring out of the vent had cascaded over the flares that the Defensive Aids Suite fire to create a white-hot target, thus deflecting heat-seeking missiles from the Chinook's engines. Soaked in fuel, they were now useless. This was rapidly turning into a farce – what had started out a few hours earlier as a routine, run-of-the-mill three-ship tasking suddenly had just my aircraft on it. After the fuel fountain abated, I called JP over the radio.

'Black Cat Two Three, Black Cat Two Two. Seeing as you're stuck here, we'll fly on to Bastion with the Apache and take over Rich's tasking. We'll get the VIPs on board and I'll speak to Bastion Ops to arrange for an armourer to come to my cab. I'll drop him off here, en route to Musa Qala with Rich's pax, so he can change your flares over.'

'Black Cat Two Two, thanks for that, copied. We'll stay here and await the armourer.'

Pre-flight checks done, Coops calls me from the rear to confirm we're clear above and behind and I pull power, lifting off en route for Bastion. So the VIPs Rich picked up from Lash have now been waiting at Bastion for at least an hour. They were then going to be JP's pax, but he's stuck at Gereshk and going nowhere so they're now ours. Rich's cab is fucked, JP's cab is fucked. Can the day get any worse?

I see Bastion on the nose from miles away; it's huge, you can't miss it. Twenty miles of desert and nothingness and then suddenly the base appears out of nowhere and dominates the landscape, its 8,000ft concrete runway like a black scar along the belly of a sleeping giant.

'Bastion Tower, Black Cat Two Two, request clearance to land.'

'Black Cat Two Two, do you require Nightingale?'

'Tower, Black Cat Two Two, negative, normal spots.'

'Black Cat Two Two, cleared to land, spots.'

'Tower, roger that. Cleared to land, spots,' I say as I cross the perimeter fence, fly to the landing spots and turn the aircraft through 180° to land on. The wheels compress as the ground comes up to meet us and I call Bastion Ops to request the armourer, then sit back and wait. This could take a while – nothing happens quickly at Bastion as messages are passed up the chain of command and on to the right person.

Coops goes off to locate Rich's VIPs and returns a short time later, a line of well-dressed passengers following him like he's the Pied Piper of Hamelin. We wait. And wait.

The heat is stifling, the dashboard too hot to touch. A bead of sweat draws a path from under my helmet down my forehead and I can feel it heading inexorably for my eyes – my gloved hand swipes it away. The rotors turn, fuel burns, but we're going nowhere. Where the fuck is the armourer?

I check my watch; we've been sitting 'turning and burning' for fifty minutes now.

'Bastion Ops, Black Cat Two Two, where's the armourer?' I ask.

'Black Cat Two Two, Bastion Ops, should be with you now.'

I twist and look over my left shoulder and see him walking up the ramp. I motion for him to sit on the jump seat. Bob Ruffles assists the armourer and plugs his helmet into the comms.

'Okay, this is what we've got,' I tell him. 'We landed at Gereshk to refuel with our formation leader and his cab had a massive fuel leak. It's completely soaked his Defensive Aids Suite, so his flares are now bathed in it. We'll fly you to Gereshk so you can replace them. We'll be back for you after our next sortie – it shouldn't be more than about forty-five minutes.'

I look past him to the full load of VIPs. I don't know who they are except they're very formally dressed so they look a bit out of place. Their questioning glares and furrowed brows tell me they're an unhappy group of suits. I'm pissed off and I've only been wait-ing for an hour; they've been sat in the cab almost as long as I have, and they were waiting in the heat for over an hour before boarding. No wonder they're not smiling.

It's time to get moving. But while we've been waiting, things have gone from bad to worse as yet another cab has developed a fault. Bastion Ops advises me that the Apache that has been with us all morning has also gone tits up. What the hell is going on today? Another AH is scrambled; it flies on ahead to take up station and await our arrival into Musa Qala.

'Bastion Tower, Black Cat Two Two is ready for departure.'

'Black Cat Two Two, you're cleared for take-off and cross as required. Visibility is 5km, wind two-five-zero at 10kts.'

'Pre-take-offs good, ready to lift,' says Alex.

'Clear above and behind,' says Coops at the ramp. Bob mans the port Minigun as we lift.

'Take off, Black Cat Two Two.'

I pull pitch and lift into the afternoon sky and turn towards Gereshk, just off to our east. We're in the air no more than five minutes before I land us on and drop off the armourer. Thirty seconds on the ground, no more. Coops gives the all clear again and I lift us once more into the crystal-clear azure sky and turn due north for Musa Qala.

Ten more minutes and we're about six miles from the target. I radio ahead to the Apache: 'Ugly Five Zero, Black Cat Two Two. Inbound. Next location in figures five.'

'Black Cat Two Two, Ugly Five Zero, visual. Be aware, enemy forces moving weapons along your route. Hold, we're checking it out.'

We don't have long to wait.

'Black Cat Two Two, Ugly Five Zero. Enemy forces moving weapons to the south-west – suggest you try alternative routing. Guys, the ICOM chatter has got ten times worse. They're up to something.'

That's the second time they've told us that today. Maybe something is going on after all. I feel the hairs on the back of my neck stand up. I click the PTT button on the end of the cyclic to confirm I've received the message.

What I don't know is that the Taliban has brought in an assassination team especially to take out our cab – and with it our VIPs, who include Gulab Mangal, the governor of Helmand Province and a crucial figure in Britain's long-term plan to stabilise the region. Mangal's support for UK Forces in Helmand has been instrumental in securing approval for foreign troops among the Afghan population, but that and his hardline stance against corruption and the poppy trade have made the governor a prized scalp for the Taliban. Also aboard are his bodyguards and the Foreign & Commonwealth Office's entire Provincial Reconstruction Team.

'Okay guys, I'm not going to abort the mission for this, but we have to be a bit careful, so keep your eyes peeled.'

'Agreed,' says Alex. 'Call it a sixth sense, but I'm feeling distinctly edgy. C'mon, let's crack on.'

I decide to fly a feint to confuse anyone on the ground that might have something nefarious in mind. I share my thoughts with the crew.

'I'm going to shoot an approach into FOB Edinburgh and pretend we're unloading there.'

FOB Edinburgh is a couple of miles away from Musa Qala, but it's on higher ground. If the Taliban are dicking us, they'll think that's our intended destination and stand down any weapons they've got at Musa Qala. It's dusty there though – really dusty – and the dust cloud tends to completely fill the cabin on landing.

'These VIPs are very well dressed, mate, and they look even more pissed off than when we took off,' says Bob in the back. 'I'm not sure that half a tonne of sand is going to improve their mood much.'

'Yeah, fair point.'

I make a decision. 'I'll just do a low-level orbit over Edinburgh and use terrain masking so they won't see us at Musa Qala.'

Obviously, FOBs and PBs are fixed sites and we're into the same LSs every time; you can change your routes, your angles but there are only so many ways into the same destination. The Taliban know this so they'll sit and wait. When we landed at Musa Qala earlier that day, I'd flown in from the south-west and JP had come in from the west. So this time, I decide to come in from the north-west and make a totally different approach.

I brief Alex. 'Okay, I want you to put us four miles north of Edinburgh. There's a deep wadi there and I want to be flying low through it at max speed on the approach. Bug the RadAlt down to 10ft; I'm gonna put the light on at 20 and we're going to go in fast and low.'

'Bob, get on the starboard Minigun. Standard Rules of Engagement; you have my authority to engage without reference to me if we come under fire. Clear?'

'Absolutely, Frenchie.'

I want him on the right because, looking at the topography of the area, that's where we'd most likely take fire from. He can scan his arcs, I've got the front and right, and Alex and Coops have the left. We're as well prepared as we can be, even if it does feel like we're flying into the lion's den.

Alex gets us into the perfect position and I drop down low into the wadi as I fly us towards FOB Edinburgh at 160 knots. Trees are rushing past the cockpit windows on either side, but I'm totally focused on the job at hand so they barely register. We're so low, I'm climbing to avoid tall blades of grass as we scream along the wadi, and I'm working the collective up and down like a whore's knickers, throwing the aircraft around. Anyone trying to get a bead on us is going to have a fucking hard time.

It's about twenty seconds later when I see the Toyota Hilux with a man standing in the back. It's alongside the wadi in our 1 o'clock position and about half a mile ahead. It's redolent of one of the Technicals – the flat-bed pick-up trucks with a machine-gun or recoilless rifle in the back that caused so much mayhem in *Black Hawk Down*. They're popular with the Taliban too. Suddenly, alarm bells are ringing in my head. They're so loud, I'm sure the others can hear.

'Threat right,' I shout as both Alex and I look at the guy in the truck.

My response is automatic. I act even before the thought has formed and throw the cyclic hard left to jink the cab away from danger. Except the threat isn't right; the truck is nothing to do with the Taliban.

The threat lies unseen on our left, on the far bank of the wadi. The team brought in specifically to take us out is waiting there and they have a view of the whole vista below them, including us. I've just flown us right into the jaws of the trap they've laid just for us and Gulab Mangal, the VIP that the Taliban is so desperate to take out.

BANG, BANG, BANG, BANG, BANG!

The Defensive Aids Suite explodes into life and fires off flares to draw the threat away from us; too late though. Everything happens in a nanosecond, but perception distortion has me in its grip, so it seems like an age.

I feel the airframe shudder violently as we simultaneously lurch upwards and to the right. I know what's happened even as Coops shouts over the comms: 'We've been hit, we've been hit!'

There's no time for Bob to react on the gun. The aircraft has just done the polar opposite of what I've asked of it. And for any pilot, that's the worst thing imaginable – loss of control.

'RPG!' shouts Coops. 'We've lost a huge piece of the blade!'

The Master Caution goes off and I'm thrust into a world of *son et lumière*. Warning lights are flashing and the RadAlt alarm is sounding through my helmet speakers.

'Mayday! Mayday! Mayday! Black Cat Two Two, Mayday. We've been hit!' says Alex over the radio. Then, 'Frenchie, we've lost the No.2 hydraulic system and the AFCS, both secured.'

'It could be worse,' I think. The AFCS is an auto-stabiliser that helps keep the aircraft straight and level, but I can fly without it. The No.2 hydraulic system is more of a concern, but it's not life-and-death. The real concern is the blade; I've no idea how badly damaged it is, or how long it will last.

I push the cyclic forward and left again and amazingly the cab responds. Something is seriously wrong though; it's woolly and there's a lag to my input. The aircraft is shaking like a bastard; the pedals are shaking, the cyclic is vibrating in my hand. The aircraft feels completely wrong as I'm trying to fly her; the rear is skidding

– a sign of a big imbalance there. It's the rotor head telling me that it's missing a piece.

I manage to fly a wing over to get us out of the wadi. Suddenly, Roshan Tower looms large through the cockpit window and zooms past.

'Fuck, where did that come from?!' I ask. Somehow, I've been able to turn inside it.

The mast sits on the site of an old Afghan fort and stands 260ft over the Musa Qala district, providing mobile phone coverage to the whole of that part of Helmand province, so it's of key strategic importance. The Taliban are forever launching rocket attacks against it – twenty-seven in the past three months at that point – so it's well defended by us. I've almost brought it down single-handedly!

'C'mon, think!' I tell myself. I consider putting the aircraft straight down and immediately dismiss the thought. It's not feasible – I have sixteen civilians in the back, we have four rifles between us to defend them with, and we can't be any more than 400 metres from the firing point – we'd have no chance.

I'm really worried about losing the blade completely – if that happens we're fucked. I set myself small targets – you know, 'I just want to make it to that tree over there.' My aim is just to put some distance between the cab and the kill zone. At the back of my mind I know I have the option of putting the aircraft down, just throwing it in. I need to gain a bit of height, but will keep us low. 'Rebug the RadAlt to 40ft your side, Alex,' I say as I reset the bug for the light to 50.

'RPG!' shouts Bob as another one streaks past us, fire streaming from its tail. It misses us by a matter of feet. I can almost feel its heat.

The whole cockpit is shaking like a food processor on its fastest setting.

'How're the Ts and Ps?' Bob asks, but I barely register the question; it's taking everything I have to fly the aircraft and I have no spare capacity. Alex, though, is doing a brilliant job of handling everything else.

'Yep, they're fine,' he tells Bob.

'Guys, I think we're going to be alright. She's a bitch to fly but she's hanging in,' I tell the crew, sounding more confident than I feel.

'Coops is securing our pax, mate. They're obviously a bit shaken up,' says Bob.

I see FOB Edinburgh on the nose and for the first time since we got hit, I start to believe that we might actually make it.

'I'm going to go for a baby basic dust landing at the LS,' I say. 'It's dusty as fuck at Edinburgh, so I'm not going to fuck around and try to put it anywhere specific – just right in the middle.'

I need to minimise my input on the controls; I don't want to damage the blade further. We'll try for a zero-speed landing.

I call the Forward Air Controller at Edinburgh to let him know we're inbound.

'Widow Seven Five, this is Black Cat Two Two. We are inbound, your location in figures two.'

'Black Cat Two Two, you're cleared straight in. Site is clear and secure.' I thank him and mouth a silent apology for the fact that we're just about to block his HLS.

'Okay, pre-landing checks please Alex,' I say.

'Holds out, CAP shows No.2 hydraulics and AFCS secured, otherwise clear; Ts and Ps are good, brakes are off, swivel switch is locked. Bug at 40ft on my side.'

I flare us for the descent, scrubbing off speed. '50ft and 22kts, you're in the gate,' says Alex. '40; 16.'

Simultaneously, the RadAlt warning sounds.

'Cancel, continuing,' I say, killing the alarm.

Bob and Coops start calling my height: '30 . . . 20 . . . dust cloud forming . . . 15 . . . at the ramp . . . 10, 8 . . . centre . . . 6 . . . at the door; with you . . .'

I see the dust cloud enveloping the nose.

'4 . . . 3 . . . 2 . . . 1, two wheels on,' says Bob as the rear wheels touch. I lower the collective to get the nose down. 'Six wheels on,' he continues, as a huge, swirling cloud of grit and fine, powdery sand envelops the cab, coating everyone in it. We're down.

'Fuck me, Frenchie, that was an awesome bit of flying mate,' says Alex.

'Guys, I think we can all give ourselves a good old pat on the back,' I tell the crew. 'That was a real team effort. Well done!'

Coops shepherds our pax to safety. Then a thought occurs to me: 'Guys, we can't shut down here, it'll block the FOB and nobody will be able to get in. We may need the space to land another aircraft full of engineers and spares to repair her. The cab's got us this far, so I don't think it's going to give up on us now.'

'Passengers are all off,' says Coops raising the ramp. 'Clear above and behind.'

I pull power and lift us no more than 2ft off the ground, push the cyclic right and forward, and we crab to the far corner of the base where I land on again.

'Stabs are secured, brakes are on, EAPS off, clear APU,' says Alex as we start to shut down the cab.

I reach up to the overhead panel and flick the switch to engage the Auxiliary Power Unit. The APU supplies power to the cab with the engines off. I move my hand to the twin engine control levers (ECLs) – and pull them out of the 'Flight' position and into the gate marked 'Stop'. With the power cut, the blades immediately begin to slow.

'DAS and nav kit off,' says Alex.

'Engaging rotor brake,' I say as I pull on the huge handle that stops the rotors spinning. As they come to a halt, I switch off the APU and silence descends.

I unbuckle my chin strap and remove my flying helmet, placing it on the centre console. I run my hand through my matted hair. All I can hear is the ticking sound of the engines cooling.

It's over.

31

NINE LIVES DOWN

Alex and I look at one another across the cockpit. 'Mate, you look fucked!' he tells me. I smile. I don't care how I look – I'm alive!

'You're not exactly going to make the cover of *Vogue* yourself mate!' I retort. 'How fucking lucky were we, though? Two RPGs nearly hit us! I guess we were lucky that we were only hit by small arms, although I reckon it must have been a .50 cal to take out the blade like that.'

The two of us unstrap ourselves from the machine that almost took us to our deaths, and walk through the cab and down the ramp. Coops and Bob are standing there looking at the aft disc.

'Fucking hell, Frenchie, look at the twist on that blade,' says Coops and I look up to see a massive chunk of it missing. The whole outer end of one of the blades has ceased to exist.

'How the fuck could a .50 cal do that?' I ask.

'That was no .50 cal,' says Coops. 'We've been hit by an RPG!'

I look at Alex and all the colour has drained from his face. He looks like he's in shock. Bob's laughing, but then Bob's always laughing. I think it's nervous laughter now though.

I look at the aft pylon and there are huge football-sized, RPG-shaped holes through both sides of it, and that's when my blood runs cold; it feels like it's turned to ice in my veins.

'We've been hit by a fucking RPG,' I think. But it's too big – I can't get my mind around it. The thought repeats like a mantra, over and over. My brain's working overtime, trying to figure it out. It can't have armed – if it had, it would have taken the cab out in a huge fireball and there'd be nothing left. It's hit the aft head in an upward trajectory, passed clean through both sides of the aft pylon and travelled up and through the blades.

I walk around the cab and when I take in the extent of the damage, I can't conceive of how we stayed aloft after the incident. We've been hit by three separate weapons systems: as well as the RPG passing through the pylon and taking out part of the aft rotor, we've taken a significant degree of shrapnel damage, seven or eight rounds of .50 cal and some 7.62mm. In total there are thirty-four holes in the aircraft.

The thoughts are coming thick and fast as I play it back in my mind. I saw a Toyota Hilux and jinked the aircraft left suddenly, a second before we were hit . . . I shiver as I realise that that probably saved our lives, because the RPG would have hit us square on otherwise. The angle at which it hit means it didn't arm; it struck us more of a glancing blow.

We learn much later that the RPG was identified as being first generation – investigators were able to tell via cut marks on the rotor that showed the round as having four fins. One of the problems of the first-generation RPG is that it needs to hit a target square-on. If it doesn't, the fuse fails to detonate and it remains inert. That's the only reason it didn't explode when it hit us.

The head of the RPG went through the pylon, then it deviated into the blade, which disintegrated under the force. Boeing, the Chinook's manufacturers, told us that the blade whipped it back round, so we were effectively hit a second time by the RPG; some of the shrapnel damage we took was caused by its outer casing coming in. It was that which nicked a hydraulic pipe – just the tiniest bit. But the hydraulic system is pressurised to 3,000psi, so we lost the lot within a second; there you are, no hydraulics, just to make life a bit more interesting. One of the .50 cal rounds hit the gearbox, but it struck a big round nut and didn't go in – it just bounced off and disappeared. If it had hit straight on, it would have jammed the gearbox and destroyed it.

Fuck me; are life and death really so finely balanced on a knife's edge?

As we're standing by the cab, a Mastiff AFV drives up and some

Scots Guards soldiers get out to look at the cab. One of the sergeants comes over to Alex and me.

'Fuck me, sirs. I was listening to the ICOM – I can't believe you guys carried on!' he says. I wonder then just what the ICOM was saying. 'I can't believe how lucky you are!' He looks at the airframe and laughs. There seems to be a lot of nervous laughter around today.

I mull over the irony of our call sign, Black Cat Two Two. To take an RPG and have it punch a hole through your rotor – that's got to be all nine lives lost in one go.

A Squadron Leader approaches us and shakes my hand. 'Bloody hell, guys. Well done!' he says. 'That was almost a strategic victory for the Taliban – that's how close it was.' And I guess it would have been. When you bear in mind that as well as Gulab Mangal, we had his whole team in the back and the FCO Provincial Reconstruction Team, and then there was the aircraft itself – it wouldn't just have represented a major tactical and PR victory for the Taliban, but it would arguably have meant a strategic disaster for ISAF that could have changed the course of events in Helmand Province. That's how serious it was.

Widow Seven Five comes over and introduces himself and he's hospitality itself. He wakes up the chef, gets him to knock something up for us. We're humbled and touched beyond belief because these guys have nothing and they're sharing what little they've got with us.

We spent over six hours at FOB Edinburgh in the end, while waiting for a lift back to Camp Bastion, and it was a real eye-opener. It's the first time I'd ever seen life in a FOB first-hand and, if I'm honest, it shocked me just how spartan it was. They didn't even have any running water there. A couple of hours after we touched down, my digestive system woke up and had an argument with my guts, which is when I got to use the Vietnam-style toilet – a plank of wood with a hole in, laid over a ten-gallon oil drum. Gulab Mangal came over to say thanks a short time later and he shook my hand – fortunately I'd washed them at that point!

Being at Edinburgh all that time made me realise just how different the war can be for those of us out there; this was illustrated in vivid, colourful fashion. Although FOBs are our bread and butter – and we're flying in to as many as ten, maybe more, each day – all we ever really see is the HLS. We get a brief overview of the camp as we come in, we're on the ground for a minute or so, and then we're off again. Here, we actually got a taste of how the guys lived because we were up close and personal.

We saw their accommodation, got a good look at their faces – drawn, tired, unshaven, unkempt. No running water, no electricity, primitive toilets. They lived in shelters built out of two blocks of Hesco with a sheet of black fabric over the top to create an air gap (and hopefully provide some rudimentary cooling) and they slept on cots with mozzie nets over them. That was quite literally it – this is how they live for their six-month tours. Spartan doesn't even come close. We were left with an even deeper respect for the guys that we serve.

What we experienced at the FOB made us feel embarrassed by the relative opulence of KAF – its shops and restaurants on the boardwalk, the air-conditioned, brick-built accommodation and flushing toilets, proper showers, wi-fi – the whole nine yards. The contrast is immense between the guys on the ground and the guys driving desks, and somehow it all seems upside down and back to front.

For us, it meant that every opportunity we got subsequently, we'd make a personal effort to get stuff to the FOBs, anything to make the guys' lives easier. We'd buy crates of Coke – as many as we could afford – and kick them out to the guys whenever we could.

I think all of us found it pretty hard in the aftermath, while we sat around waiting to be lifted, because suddenly we had nothing to do and all the adrenaline was wearing off. Once the initial elation of having survived waned, we were all left alone with our thoughts, each of us reliving what had happened, what might have been.

One of the PRT's close protection officers sought us out later and told us he'd seen the firing point – it was about 300m away in our 10 o'clock as we flew along the wadi – and he saw how many guys there were. He said he saw the RPG being fired at us, and even noticed the puff of dust from the back-blast. He'd seen other guys around the trigger man armed with heavy machine-guns and AK-47s; they'd been hiding behind a compound, which was why neither Alex nor I had seen them on our run in. It was complete luck – the bodyguard happened to look out of the window at precisely the time we were engaged. On such matters of chance, life is built.

Eventually we got back to Bastion and JP met us off the cab with Woodsy, who'd been my flight commander on my first Det in 2006. Typical JP – he's straight down the line and brutally honest.

'Are you going to be alright fellas? Do you want to stand down or crack on?'

'Don't worry Frenchie,' added Woodsy, 'lightning never strikes twice.'

I glanced at the other guys and they all nodded. I looked JP in the eye and said, 'I think it's best to get straight back into that saddle and not think about it.'

I've mulled over what happened extensively; all of us have. You try and look for explanations; but even now, I still can't believe we survived after that RPG hit us. You don't even want to think about the fallout if we'd gone down: the PR cost to the Government or the tactical impact on the guys in theatre. We only had eight Chinooks in Afghanistan then and they were being flown relent-lessly – losing one would have been an absolute nightmare.

The only way I can rationalise it is that it was down to my train-ing: had I not flown the way I did, had I not been trained the way I was, we'd have been killed – full stop. I made the firer's job so much harder by flying fast and low. Had I been higher, he could have put two RPGs in the aircraft. It was partially to do with luck – but it was mostly about professionalism and training.

32

TAKING THE BAIT

True to his word, JP had us flying again the following morning; although he kept it simple, so there was nothing too taxing about the day's taskings. Perhaps more importantly, one of them allowed me to do something I'd been planning since the previous evening: thank Widow Seven Five at Edinburgh for everything he'd done for us.

I guess things were a little awkward for Alex, Coops, Bob and I at first. The day started just like every other day in theatre, except the last time we'd gone through the machinations before taking off, we'd ended the day having been shot down. I guess things were just a little bit harder than we expected and the entire crew was very, very nervous, so we just took everything very slowly. We had a resupply to do first thing into a grid just west of Gereshk, followed by a tasking into FOB Edinburgh.

We went in at high level this time so we could see exactly where we'd been hit. It was all a bit difficult to get our heads around, I guess. I wasn't sure how I'd feel landing at Edinburgh, but I soon found out. Landing next to ZD575 – our cab – now that was weird. There's nothing like a bit of psychological hangover to start your day.

Before we'd left that morning, we'd filled the cab with crates of Coca Cola and porn from our own budget, so we could give it all to Widow Seven Five by way of a thank you. I said to Alex as we were flying in, 'I know it's going against protocol, but I'm going to unstrap myself and walk off the aircraft when we get there because I want to look that bloke in the eye and shake his hand,' and that's exactly what happened. I gathered everything up and went and found him and I said, 'Cheers mate.'

He was so modest. 'You must be joking; you gave us all sorts of stuff yesterday.'

I was like, 'Forget it mate, you have nothing here. We want you to have this.' After we'd been shot down, it was him I spoke to on the radio, he'd cleared us in, guided us, met us off the aircraft, sorted food and everything else for us while we were kicking around. His humility really touched us all. What a top bloke.

However, if we thought the Chinook Force's run of bad luck was out of the way, we were very much mistaken. It would be German's cab that was next in the Taliban's firing line.

It's thought that the Taliban had brought in various teams of shooters for the assassination attempt on Gulab Mangal and, with that attempt made, the teams were about to leave Helmand. They were determined to down a Chinook (ours!) and they'd failed, so they engineered a situation to get the IRT cab into a certain place, at a time of their choosing. And how best to scramble the IRT and get it where you want it? Kill a load of civilians, of course. So that's what the Taliban did.

Late that evening, a suicide bomber drove a vehicle packed with explosives into a crowded market square in Musa Qala and detonated himself. The ensuing carnage left mass casualties and the British Army's first-aid post in the DC was soon over-whelmed. I was in the JOC when the first reports started coming in and a debate started about whether or not to scramble the IRT. The consensus of opinion was that the suicide bombing was a 'come on' designed to lure the helicopter in, but there were a lot of casualties and, regardless of the risk, they all needed treating. There's no ambulance service in Afghanistan and almost no medical care as we know it, so either we reacted or the casualties would die.

I suggested that instead of risking the IRT, they consider picking the casualties up using Mastiffs which, at the time, offered protection against mines and IEDs. If we'd done that and driven them to Edinburgh, we could have sent a cab in there to scoop them up and run, but the thinking was that it would take three to four hours, which was simply too long for many of the casualties.

There's an irony there, because by the time they'd worked through all the iterations of the numerous plans and decided on which HLS they were going to use, it was three or four hours before an aircraft got in anyway. German went in and did really well. He came in from the west at low level, which was the right way to do it, and once the casualties were on board, flew away as fast as he could. Unfortunately he'd been lured into a trap, and he flew right over the compound where the Taliban team was based. They opened up and several rounds found their mark, hitting the cab when the MERT were busy treating the six severely wounded casualties they'd picked up. Among them was Rahima, a five-year-old Afghani who had suffered a traumatic amputation of her left hand and shrapnel to the stomach in the explosion, and was in critical condition.

I later learned that Flt Lt Vanessa Miles, an emergency nurse on the MERT, was on her very first mission in Afghanistan; a quite literal baptism of fire! Through it all she remained completely composed and focused, working tirelessly with her colleagues to keep every one of those casualties alive. To me, that speaks volumes about the skill, bravery and dedication of the MERT crews working in Helmand.

And Vanessa wasn't the only hero that day. Pete Winn was Rich's co-pilot and Mark 'Gammo' Gamson was the No.2 crewman that night. Gammo got a line on the firing point for three separate weapons. Showing great initiative, he didn't wait to get authorisation – he took it upon himself to open up on them, rather than describe the target and miss the window of opportunity. This was Gammo's first Det and he'd only been in theatre a month, but he had the balls and the intelligence to do what had to be done without being told. He fired into the compound and suppressed all three firing points, enabling German to get them out of the danger zone. Top man!

Before Gammo took the shooters out, several rounds hit the right-hand side of the cab, although thankfully none hit vital systems. In fact, the Chinook survived its enemy encounter well and lived up to its reputation: it'll take a tremendous amount of punishment and still get you back to base!

33

THE WELL OF COURAGE

There's nowhere quite like Afghanistan to disabuse you of quaint, idealistic notions about fear. I thought I knew what fear was after being shot down on May 17th, but an operation less than a week later showed me that I knew nothing.

JP had outlined the operation to me and said he wanted me on it. He asked me if I felt happy to fly the mission and I told him I did. The operation was Oqab Sturga (Eagle's Eye), a helicopter raid involving four Chinooks with Apaches providing support, planned for the night of May 23rd. The objective was to move hundreds of troops to disrupt the Taliban south of Musa Qala.

The mission profile was for two pairs, separated by five minutes, to fly from Bastion to FOB Gibraltar to collect 'C' Company, 2 Para. Five minutes later, both two-ships would fly to FOB Inkerman to pick up 'B' Company, and the plan then was for us to insert the troops at a grid between Sangin and Musa Qala for an assault to clear the Taliban from two nearby villages.

The first two-ship would be led by JP, flying alongside Ian 'Chomper' Fortune, with Hannah Brown and Debbers as his wingman. I was leading the second formation, flying with Alex as my co-pilot and German and Stu Hague as my wingman. It was all worked out; JP and Hannah would be four minutes on the ground; we would land one minute later.

We couldn't have been more sorted on the planning. JP is a brilliant boss and tactician, as I've said, and on the afternoon before the op we'd done our RoC drills outside the tent and then went into crew rest, so the lead-up was perfection. We slept until about

22:00 and got up ready for departure at 01:00. We had the pre-brief, double-checked the weather, and then went into the JOC for the intelligence brief. Then, as had become our custom, all the captains walked out together down to the line. I happened to walk with Hannah that night. We were all wearing red head torches to preserve our night vision and they were giving off an eerie glow.

The enormity of what had happened to us near Musa Qala a week earlier was really playing on my mind, so I wasn't exactly brimming with confidence as we walked out. I'd always had the same attitude as most aircrew: 'It'll never happen to me.' It's how you cope – aviation is a relatively dangerous business; military aviation more so. Flying on the front line? Dodgy as hell. Sadly, I couldn't think like that any more because events had proven that it could, and did, happen to me. We were so close to going home at the end of tour by then too, so I was more than a little worried; in fact, if I'm being honest, I was shit-scared.

'Mate, I've not got a lot left in the tank . . . I'm scraping the bottom of my well of courage,' I said to Hannah.

'Come on mate, dig deep. One more mission; that's it.'

'Hannah, I've got nothing left.'

'Come on, Frenchie; it'll be okay.'

And with that, we walked in silence to the line.

When we reached the pan, we peeled off one by one to our respective cabs, but things started to go wrong from the off. JP lifted five minutes early and even though he had ten minutes to do the pick-up, his troops were slow in loading so we had to hold off. Then we had problems getting ours on too, so we were eight minutes behind the timeline lifting off.

Suddenly, during the transit to the first target area, I heard the radio crackling with shouts of contacts. Hannah saw tracer and it was coming up thick and fast towards both her and JP's cabs.

I heard her call 'Tracer, tracer, tracer!' swiftly followed by 'Contact!' and then it all became a bit *Star Wars*. There seemed to be fire coming from everywhere. She and JP were both flying really aggressively to try to get in and somehow they managed to land and get their troops off. Then RPGs started flying across the sky as the Taliban tried to take out their cabs. Bob Ruffles, who was now her No.2 crewman, and Dan Temple both opened up with the Miniguns, returning fire on two separate locations. Then a heavy machine-gun opened up and it was absolute carnage. But somehow they flew evasive manoeuvres and escaped the kill zone.

Alex and I, and Stu and German are both eight minutes back, but we can hear Hannah calling 'Contact!' and see the weight of fire that is ranged up at them. It looks like the night sky over Berlin during World War II, as the Lancasters dropped their bombs. We have a choice. There's a secondary HLS picked for precisely this reason – so that we'd have an alternative if the primary became too hot.

'Why not use the secondary HLS?' asks Alex, echoing my thoughts. His comment makes me realise that I'm not the only one fighting my nerves.

The problem is that the Paras are already engaged in heavy combat against the enemy and if I use the alternate, it will take the troops I have onboard at least fifteen minutes to reach the engagement zone and support their mates.

I'm dying inside, gripped by a fear I can't show because *this* is what leadership is. This is where I earn my money. This is what comes with rank. I want to put the aircraft somewhere else; anywhere else, but I have to fly into the fight. Every cell in my body is trying to run in the opposite direction – to safety and away from danger. Running into danger is counter-intuitive, but it's what we have to do. The Paras in my cab are needed to support those that JP and Hannah had on board, for the fight on the ground.

Whatever lies inside me stays inside me, and I win the struggle between my face and my feelings because I'm the captain of this aircraft, and I have to lead my crew and another aircraft into the fight.

'C'mon guys,' I say. 'It probably looks worse than it is.'

We have eight minutes to think on what awaits us at the LS and it's the longest eight minutes of my life, a million times worse than when I nursed 575 down at Edinburgh. That was sudden, reactive. It wasn't brave; it wasn't courageous – I just flew my aircraft and my training kicked in. This? This is a world apart from that. It's fear on another level.

'Right Frenchie, you should be visual with the landing site. 12 o'clock, where all that tracer fire is. That's it. Nav complete,' says Alex, smiling.

I laugh and the feeling lifts me just enough. There's nothing for me to hold on to going in, but I'm smiling and – outside at least – I'm strong. 'Stay cool, stay composed, appear ready to confront what's ahead and the crew will follow,' I keep telling myself.

'Right guys, this is what they pay us for. Andy, I want you on the starboard Minigun for the approach and Griz, make ready on the M60,' I tell the guys in the back.

We're about two minutes out now. More tracer starts coming up but I'm focused on flying the aircraft and nothing else matters. As Alex gives me the pre-landing checks and I find the gate, suddenly it all stops. What the fuck? Griz and Andy take over with the height calls, and I settle the rear wheels on before lowering the collective to get the nose down. Six on, and we're down. The ramp goes down, the troops rush off and Andy's on the intercom saying, 'Clear above and behind.' I pull power and we're away. Just a trip to Inkerman now, lift the troops, insert them at the second village and we can all get the fuck out of Dodge.

I transition and start to fly over a wadi at around 100ft when my peripheral vision catches a massive flash to the left, and the fabric of time stretches and becomes elastic. It's 'bullet time' and everything slows.

'R . . . P . . . G!' I shout, but the words seem to take forever. It's flying straight for us and I watch its fiery tail describe a lazy line behind it. I'm transfixed as I watch it s . . . l . . . o . . . w . . . l . . . y and inexorably head for the cockpit.

I look down and see it through the glass panels below my pedals as it flies under my feet. It's so close, I feel I could put my hand out and grab it. The tail crackles and sparkles as it passes

Soldiers serving with Somme Company, 1st Battalion The Duke of Lancaster's Regiment, waiting to be extracted after a firefight with Taliban forces near Sayedebad in southern Afghanistan.

Territorial Army (TA) medics from 212 Field Hospital, receive a casualty from the MERT as we land at Nightingale, Camp Bastion's £10m state-of-the-art hospital.

Flying over Three Mile Mountain enroute to join the circuit and land on at KAF. Three Mile Mountain dominates the landscape around KAF.

With my crew shortly after nursing 575 down at FOB Edinburgh following an assassination attempt by the Taliban, 17 May 2008. I'm second from right, with Master Aircrewman Bob Ruffles (left), my co-pilot Flt Lt Alex Townsend, and Flt Sgt Neil 'Coops' Cooper (far right).

Helmand Governor Gulab Mangal greets ISAF troops. Mangal's support for UK forces in Helmand has been instrumental in securing acceptance of foreign troops among the Afghan population, but that, and his hardline stance against corruption and the opium trade, have made him a prized scalp for the Taliban.

A graphic demonstration of the difficulties we face when landing in the dusty landscape that delineates so much of Helmand Province. The dust cloud here completely obscures the underslung load.

JP says hello in his own inimitable style as he flies past the control tower at Camp Bastion, 2008 Det.

Troops from 5 Scots, 16 Air Assault Brigade, shield themselves from the downdraft as we depart Nadi Alie following their insertion, 15 November 2010.

A soldier from 3 Para chats to young Afghan children in the town of Naquilabad Kalay while on a patrol to find up to 40 suitable local people to volunteer for training at the Helmand Police Training Centre in Lashkar Gah, before returning to their community and joining the police force.

A soldier from 3 Company, 1st Battalion the Coldstream Guards on patrol in a poppy field near Babaji. The opium that poppies yield is Afghanistan's only major export and the primary source of funding for Taliban forces in the south. Poppies are a mainstay for many farmers who are reluctant to sacrifice its high-yield crop for lower-paying legal crops such as wheat.

Fusiliers Mark Goodie (left) and Louie Kimroy (right) of 6 Platoon, B Coy, 1st Battalion the Royal Welsh, returning fire against insurgents in the Green Zone. Our whole purpose in theatre is to support the troops: moving them, extracting them, rescuing them when wounded and flying in vital supplies. It's a role that all of us on the Chinook force are proud to undertake.

Local girls gather for the ribbon cutting of Laki Girls School, in Garmsir district, Helmand province, while coalition forces provide security. The Taliban banned girls' education when they were in power between 1996 and 2001. Following their overthrow, the Karzai administration received substantial international aid to restore the education system. According to UNICEF, there were 2.5 million girls in school in 2010, up from 839,000 in 2002.

Much of Afghanistan is biblical in appearance with no modern technology for even the simplest of tasks. Here, a farmer carries his crop from the fields on his back at a strip village near PB Luke, Kandahar.

A Hercules C130J touches down at Camp Bastion. The Herc is the RAF's workhorse, flying troops and cargo all over the country and providing the vital airbridge between Bastion and KAF. KAF handles 10,000 movements a month, some 50 per cent of Gatwick Airport's traffic and is one of the busiest single-runway airports in the world.

The faces of these Parachute Regiment soldiers bear the strain of the intense fighting they experience on a daily basis at their FOB near Kajaki Dam. These soldiers are part of a squad being airlifted by Chinook for R&R.

A proud day. With Alison at Buckingham Palace to receive the DFC from HM the Queen on 15 July 2009.

underneath me, jetting purple and yellow fire that is close enough for the reflection to dance across the instruments in the control panel. My NVGs show it in green, but it's close enough that I can see it through the gap where the tubes meet my eyes.

Instinctively, I lift my feet off the controls as though by leaving them there they'll burn in the rocket's tail.

Then German calls 'Contact!' as he sees an explosion to the right of our aircraft and another RPG flies harmlessly behind us, where it hits the ground beneath and explodes.

'The Taliban have got two firing points,' says Alex and I'm thinking, 'For fuck's sake, not again. Surely not again?'

Almost unbelievably, we're away and time reverts to normal speed again. The danger is behind us – for now.

Suddenly, the radio comes to life and I hear Stu Hague call, 'Contact, 3 o'clock!'

I look right, and I see tracer arcing towards the sky. I've never seen anything like this. There's so much tracer and rocket fire coming up you could have walked across it to Sangin. It's like an unholy union between the opening scenes to *Saving Private Ryan* and the lobby shootout in *The Matrix*. Hannah and JP are ahead of us, and again we will have to follow them in.

I guess Hannah and JP's location as I can see more tracer flying upwards south of our position. During the planning phase I wasn't happy with JP's planned routing away from the target. It's the only time I've ever disagreed with his plan. I'd explained my thinking and my intention of routing a different way, one that I considered presented less danger, and now I'm pleased I'd done so because I can see the guns on their aircraft putting rounds down all the way down the valley from Inkerman to Sangin.

I swiftly depart FOB Inkerman to fly the approach to the second village, which goes without a hitch. We're clear in, the troops are off in double-quick time and I get the 'Clear above and behind' from Andy. I pull pitch, while going backwards initially, and once I get a bit of speed I simultaneously apply bank and a lot of pedal to whip the aircraft round, almost around my own shoulder. Must be careful with the rate of yaw though – too much and the aircraft will lose some of its inertia, making it uncomfortable for the guys in the back. For once it's nicely done!

We're now away from the target. So far, so good; no contact. Suddenly, I hear Stu over the radio calling 'Contact!' Oh crap! That's what I get for being smug!

An RPG just misses him as he's transitioning. He's doing 40kts; he's at about 50ft so he's both low and slow. He's in 99ft of Chinook and vulnerable as hell . . . and it flies right by! How the fuck have they missed?

I don't know how we escape, but we do. It shouldn't be possible. All that fire, a sky full of lead and explosives, and not one round shares the same space and time as us at any stage. Nothing hits the cab.

We're not going back to Bastion though; not yet. We have another mission to fly as a four-ship, extracting some other British soldiers from a grid in the desert. As dust landings go, it's horrible – one of the worst I've experienced before or since. A complete dustbowl full of aerials, tents, troops, without any visual references at all, so having faced a barrage of fire, we have to keep our nerve and execute perfect landings.

There's nowhere to run on. The landing site is surrounded ahead and on both sides by tents and soldiers. JP and Hannah have already been and gone and in doing so, they've left a soft dust cloud behind them for us to contend with. As I fly the approach, Stu Hague is tight on my left so I have to fly smoothly to make his life as simple as possible and help him get in. It's not going to be easy. You might think, 'Yeah, so what? You're helicopter pilots; it's what you do,' but there's difficult and then there's nigh-on impossible, and you don't get to cry off the really hard ones. This is real life, not a PS3 game – we're playing without extra lives and we only get one chance.

Twice I tried and twice I had to overshoot as the ground wasn't visible, even from 40ft. I repositioned for a standard 100ft, 30kts gate in order to trim the aircraft five degrees 'nose up' for the descent. Using this technique the aircraft literally flies itself to the ground, ensuring you make all the other gates on the way down.

The landing is so heavy it knocks the air out of my lungs and I'm thrown forward so far that I'm only held in by my straps. We made it. The aircraft is in one piece.

As difficult as my landing may have been though, it couldn't have been harder than Stu's, as he had to contend with my dust too. Yet he executed a perfect 'controlled crash' and landed exactly in the right position next to me. It's called a controlled crash when you lose all your references at 20ft and rely on your technique and trimming of the aircraft. And that's exactly what he did. There aren't many others who would have got that aircraft in. We quickly got the troops on and lifted off.

Then JP calls me on the radio. A point about JP – he never does that. Ever.

'Black Cat Two Two, Black Cat Two Three, are you ok?'

I look at Alex and he says, 'What the fuck?'

'He must be shit-scared for us. It's not like him at all.'

'Yeah, Black Cat Two Three, shaken not stirred!' I reply, and with that we begin the forty-minute transit back to Bastion.

Now's the time the banter starts. It's one of our ways of reconnecting with reality. It's usually intensely personal stuff, which is cool because we all know each other, but predictably I'm an easy target because of my French heritage. The guys have had a field day since we got shot down.

'I'm surprised they managed to hit the world's only fighting Frenchman.'

'What's the difference between a Frenchman and a piece of toast? You can make soldiers out of a piece of toast . . .'

The feeling when we land on at Bastion and shut the aircraft down is electric. I feel so alive! We all do a walk-around to inspect the cabs on landing, see if we'd picked up any holes. It's amazing – you come through a shitstorm like that with so much lead flying around, and you can't conceive that you haven't taken some rounds – it's like walking through a rainstorm without getting wet. But that's exactly what all of us did. What are the chances?

We walk back to the line to sign the aircraft over to the engineers the same way we walked out, four captains. All four of us walking in and looking at each other and we're all but speech-less. I mean, what can you say, really? Words somehow don't seem enough; you don't know how to articulate it. I think all of us are surfing a wave of elation; we're hyped up with all sorts of emotions still surging through our bodies and none of us can stop smiling. It's the strangest feeling. We embrace in a huge group hug in the hangar and, finally, I'm spent – utterly done in. I think the adrenaline has worn off. It's a funny hormone that one – when it runs out, it's like it's replaced with an all-consuming fatigue. I'm empty.

The sun's coming up as we go into the JOC to report and deliver an unprecedented four accounts of coming under fire. Strange . . . tired as I am, I can't imagine sleeping.

I mull over the past few days and I am convinced there's nothing I or anyone else did that any of us wouldn't have done again. We just did what we had to do, and then got on with the next mission. A lot is said and written about courage, but I'm still not sure what it is. I've heard it described like a bank balance – that each of us has a finite store to dip into before it runs out – but I don't think it's like that. I think it's sanity that runs out. Courage is either there or it's not, but it's stock doesn't run down if you have it. Too much combat, on the other hand, will drive you insane.

34

95% BOREDOM, 5% FEAR

A police officer friend of mine memorably described police work as nine hours of boredom interspersed with ten minutes of adrenaline. What lifts it above the mundane and leaves you drained at the end of every shift is that you never know when those ten minutes are going to come, so you're permanently on edge, ready to react.

My numerous Dets in theatre have shown me that being a Chinook pilot isn't that different – it's 95% boredom and 5% fear, except you don't know when that 5% is going to swamp you. The only thing I knew for sure by this point was that I'd had more than my share of adrenaline and kinetic ops.

Obviously at this stage of any Det it gets harder to keep your eye on the ball, but you can't slacken off simply because you'll be going home soon – that's the quickest way to die. Tiredness becomes your constant companion simply because of the tempo of ops and the shortage of cabs and crew in theatre, but there's nothing you can do about that except man up and get on with it.

Even though the sun was up long before we got to bed after Oqab Sturga, we were back out on ops and airborne by 15:00 the following day, flying Des Browne, the then Secretary of State with dual responsibilities for Scotland and Defence. As has been widely reported, Gordon Brown was never popular with the military, given his bizarre decision to make the Cabinet post of defence part-time. The fact that we were committed in both Afghanistan and Iraq at that time made it all the more inexplicable.

We were flying mail and supplies around theatre; at one point the crewmen had Des Browne helping to unload the mail, which we joked was about the only good thing he ever did while in office. We dropped him off at Gereshk and then returned later to pick him up and bring him back to Bastion. Now, some people might have considered just landing in the Green Zone and going: 'Okay Mr Browne, we've arrived at Bastion. Best of luck. Bye!' then putting the ramp up and flying away. Me? I couldn't possibly comment.

Later that evening we were on the IRT again. We were scrambled to FOB Inkerman to collect a T2 – a British soldier had taken a round through his leg. The flying was an absolute nightmare; it was red illume, as dark as a witch's tit over Helmand, and it took me forever to get down because I couldn't see the ground and we had no horizon, even through the NVGs.

We started our descent from 3,500ft, over an area hemmed in by three mountains, so there was no way I was going to rocket down like I normally would. All I could rely on was a map and our GPS, so I was hoping that both my map-reading skills and GPS were accurate! I could only muster the courage to descend at 250–500ft per minute in the total blackness. You do the maths, but it felt ten times longer knowing the mountains were there, with us in the middle of them, and no way of seeing where we were in relation. Far away, the lights of the town and the fires in the desert merged with the stars so we didn't know which way was up and which way was down.

I had to use white light as well my NVGs to carry out the approach but even then I had to overshoot once, as at 30ft I lost all sight of the ground and the cyalume box used as a landing aid. The second attempt wasn't much better, but this time I trusted my trimming and the aircraft flew itself to a 'positive' landing. We got in – just – and got the casualty back to Bastion.

We were also scrambled to take a 'Compassionate A' case from Kajaki to KAF – a British soldier whose mother had suddenly taken a turn for the worse and was dying. That's one of the great things about the Armed Forces: if someone close to you is ill or dying, they'll move mountains to get you home yesterday, regardless of rank or where in the world you are. They'll even divert a

TriStar full of troops just to get that one person to where they need to be. We scooped this guy up, landed on at KAF, where we taxied to the end of the runway and stopped next to a C-17 waiting with its ramp down. He was straight off the cab, onto the waiting C-17 and they were away, straight back to England. After that, we flew back to Bastion and shut down. We weren't called out again that night.

If I thought Op Oqab Sturga was behind us, I was wrong. The following morning, May 25th, illustrated that fact all too vividly. Sadly it meant the death of one young soldier, and life-changing injuries for two others.

While we'd been flying the Paras in on the night of the 23rd, Royal Marines travelling in armoured vehicles had provided reinforcement and support on the ground and were only now returning to their bases. As they did so, they were engaged about halfway up the valley, between FOB Inkerman and Sangin, in a rolling contact that lasted about four hours. They were driving, stopping, fighting; driving, stopping, fighting; and they were harassed all the way down the valley as they tried to return to their FOB at Sangin.

Sadly, the Taliban had managed to plant a massive IED right in the middle of the wadi, within about 500m of the main gate to the FOB, and it sat there waiting for them, inert and silent, until the lead BvS10 Viking – driven by Marine Dale Gostick of 3 Troop Armoured Support Company – rolled over it.

The phone rings back at the IRT tent and I run to the JOC with Andy Rutter to get the grid and the details while Alex and Griz head for the aircraft. The nine-liner shows we have three T1 casualties; the grid is the Sangin crossing of the Helmand River. Andy races us across Bastion to the pan where Alex is spinning up the cab. As ever, the MERT and QRF teams are ready and waiting in the back. The Apache is already on station because it has been supporting the Marines during their contact.

As soon as we get authorisation (and for once, it isn't long in coming) it's pull pitch, nose down and we crack on as fast as we can. I call the Apache to tell them we're inbound.

'Ugly Five Two, Black Cat Two Two, inbound your location in figures twenty.'

The AH pilot keys the mike and, against a background track of 30mm cannon fire, he says, 'Yeah, Black Cat Two Two, you'll need to hold. We're still in contact and the HLS is hot. Repeat, HLS is hot.'

I acknowledge and fly us along the river to a point about eight miles west of the target and set up in a figure-of-eight orbit there. As I'm flying, I see a young Afghan male of fighting age, sitting on top of a hill in that classic stance that Afghans seem to adopt – sitting on their haunches – and he's just gazing out over the land, a mobile phone to his ear.

'Clock him,' I say to Alex. 'What's the betting he's dicking us?'

'Yeah, the fucker's probably passing intel up the chain to another motherfucker with an RPG who's waiting to shoot at us,' says Alex. 'Here we go again.'

I take us down and fly close enough to him that, had it been me down there, I'd have ducked, but we may as well be silent and invisible for all the fucking difference it makes. He continues talking on his phone, almost oblivious to our proximity. Now look, I'm sorry, but if you've got a fuck-off great noisy Chinook flying within a few feet of your head, you're going to move, aren't you? Not this guy. I know there are cultural differences, but there are limits. The whole thing has me worried, so I say, 'Okay Andy, get on the port Minigun. I want you to put some rounds down on the next hill, see if that gives him the incentive to move away.'

'No problem, Frenchie. I'm ready on your order.'

'Hold one; I'm just going to have a quick sweep around. I want to make sure that if we have any stray rounds they're not going to hit anybody.'

It's as well I do; just as I clear the hill, I see a flock of goats at the bottom. I look back at the guy on the hill, who I thought had been dicking us, and suddenly the threat evaporates. I see him for what he is – a young goat-herder, his gaze on his flock while he sits talking on his phone to a mate in the next valley, perhaps. Then again, he could be all that and still be dicking us. That's what I hate about this fucking country; nothing is what it seems.

Suddenly, the man stands up, ends his phone conversation and sets off down the hill towards his flock. 'Okay Andy, you can stand down mate,' I say. I let out a sigh of relief and curse my heart, which I realise is beating faster than it should be. I wipe away a bead of sweat that's running down my face.

Thirty minutes later nothing's changed; we're still holding. I need to think about the mission.

'Right guys, time's running out and I'm not prepared to go back and refuel.'

Returning to Bastion for more fuel would be tantamount to signing a death sentence on the casualties – time is something they don't have. I need to conserve the fuel we have, so if we can't go forward and we can't go back, I've got one option: down. I'll land in the wadi below us and we can wait on the ground until we're called in for the extraction.

I pick the wadi because it looks almost impossible to access and its banks are too steep to climb. A scan of the area reveals nobody within two miles of the spot I've chosen and time-wise, it'll take them longer to get to us than we'll be there for. Of course, it's sod's law that as soon as I apply the brakes and complete the after-landing checks, the Apache will clear us in, isn't it? And that's exactly what happens . . .

'Okay Alex, rebug your RadAlt to 10, I've got 20 on the light,' I say. 'I'm going to fly us in low and dirty.'

My head is full of memories of the 17th, when I'd been flying at 20ft and 160kts and we'd still been hit, so I'm determined to fly even lower this time. I'll stick rigidly to 10ft. For this mission, as well as the MERT, I also have an ITV camera crew onboard who are filming for the third episode of *Doctors and Nurses at War*.

I pull power and lift us above the wadi and, completely

oblivious to the fact that they are recording the audio from the intercom, I jokingly say to Andy and Griz, 'Right, Rules of Engagement are easy – if it's bearded and looks at us, kill it.' Of course, my comment makes the final cut and is played to a primetime audience on ITV seven months later when the programme is broadcast. It's not like I was ever going to be able to deny it was me – I mean, how many Chinook pilots does the RAF have who speak with a French accent?

I'm at 10ft now as we're running in, and the needle on the airspeed indicator is at 150. I'm wringing all the power she's got out of the collective. I'm flying so low insects on the ground are running for cover, and I'm moving the cyclic like I'm whipping egg whites as I throw the aircraft around. If anyone's trying to get a bead on us, I'm going to make their job as near fucking impossible as I can.

We are well shielded by the wadi from Sangin town, so anyone having a go from the right would have to be within spitting distance of us, and that is never going to happen. The only real threat is going to come from the left where there is a network of old Russian trenches and tunnels – prime Taliban territory.

We have about six miles to run when the JTAC at Sangin calls us over the radio to advise, 'Black Cat Two Two, I've got reports of rounds being fired at you from the west. You are under contact. Repeat: you are under contact.'

I can appreciate why the JTAC is telling us, but it doesn't exactly help – there's nothing I can do anyway. What we're doing is like walking down a crowded high street with a sign on your back saying 'Spit here!' and expecting to get to your destination dry.

I'm focused on flying though and I don't have a lot of spare capacity because of our altitude and speed, which mean the constant dinking of the airframe, left, right, up, down. I'm scanning the front obsessively – panel, horizon, panel, horizon – right the way to the grid; my focus at a point just in front of the cab; my only thoughts where we're going and what's ahead.

Suddenly, with two miles still to run, I notice a huge pall of black smoke and a massive fire in the distance; it's obviously where the IED has taken out the Viking.

It's funny how your thought process works; I know a Viking has driven over an IED so I'm looking for a Viking, albeit mangled. Yet I can't see one. Something's burning, but it isn't anything that was once recognisably a vehicle. I'm seeing but not computing; it just doesn't accord with what's in my head.

We get closer; a mile, 600 yards to go . . . we're still under threat, but I'm manoeuvring hard, there are no impacts on the aircraft that we're aware of. Then suddenly, the Defensive Aids Suite explodes into life and we're firing off flares like it's 4th July in Times Square.

'BANG, BANG, BANG, BANG!'

There's a flurry of them every second, along with a warning signal in our headphones, an alternating two-tone alarm that coincides with the flares launching. It must be terrible for the MERT team in the back – they're not on the intercom but they can see and hear the flares going off. Each one is like a small sun, creating a blinding white light that eclipses daylight. They have no idea what's going on. Are they RPGs? Are we hit? They don't know – all they're aware of is that the aircraft is moving all over the sky and suddenly there's a series of small explosions around us.

I don't think we've been engaged with a Surface-to-Air Missile (SAM) and I haven't seen an RPG blast or felt one strike the aircraft, so the DAS must have picked up the heat signature from the fire below and interpreted it as a missile launch. It's done its job – it's not sentient, just a highly complex computer that uses a series of algorithms to determine whether the heat and light sources it detects are potentially harmful to the aircraft. Either way, the threat has passed and we're on the target.

I'm still carrying 150kts, so I flare abruptly to shave off some speed. I feel the aircraft slow, so I bank right and apply some pedal. More bank, more pedal; more bank, more pedal . . . the nose starts to drop exactly the way I want it to and I assist it with a bit of forward cyclic. The windscreen's now full of Afghan wadi with the blades uncomfortably close to the ground – we're nose down at a massively steep angle. I pivot the cab through 270° to scrub off more speed and place us where we want to be. In the cockpit, it feels like we're not far off the vertical, so I know that the effect is amplified several times over for the guys in the back. Done right, the crewmen shouldn't feel more than 1g all the way round, but the more aggressively you do it, the more g-force they experience. It isn't pretty but it's effective.

As I look down, I see the burning wreckage clearly through the screen. The IED must have been huge – the Viking's tracks have been blown at least 150 metres away and the cab and the main body of the vehicle have literally ceased to exist. All that's left is a solid, mangled square mass of burning metal about two foot high; everything that was above that level has disappeared into the ether. How anyone can have survived is beyond belief, but we're here to pick up the three Marines who were its crew, so they obviously have.

As the aircraft pivots round to the right heading and the speed reduces to the correct approach speed, I finally bring the nose up, levelling the cab at the attitude I want for landing into the wind – the smoke from the fire tells me the direction it's coming from. I can see our makeshift HLS perfectly below us. The Marines have fanned out into a defensive circle with a clear area in the middle for us to put down in.

The dust is building; it's at the ramp, 10ft, 7, 6, 5, 4, 3 . . . two wheels on . . . six wheels on, we're down. It's not the prettiest text-book landing – we roll forward about three or four metres – but I was coming in so fast in order to keep us safe, there was no way we were going to scrub all the speed off before we slammed into the ground. Kinetic force just doesn't work that way. The important thing is we've arrived, we're all safe and nothing's damaged.

The ramp goes down. The dust clears and I can see a Royal Marine in my 1 o'clock. Alex has got someone in his 11 o'clock and I'm thinking, 'I don't know why but something's not right here.' And it takes me about four seconds before it hits me: his SA80 is on the ground next to him, but he's stood up and firing with his 9mm pistol, which is attached to his leg via a lanyard that connects to the grip. The firefight has been so intense he's run out of ammunition and has resorted to his last line of defence. Things must be desperate – you've more chance of missing your target than hitting it with a pistol, even at close quarters. Then I notice the puffs of dust around us and the guys that are defending us, and I realise that they're impacts from incoming rounds.

The synapses in my brain are decoding all the information and giving me a word that sums the whole thing up: 'Fuck!' Alex and I shrink ourselves into balls in our seats. I'm making all sorts of silent promises to myself, commitments to give up certain vices if only the rounds keep hitting the ground. We're trapped and immobile in our seats – perfect illustrations of the term 'sitting target'.

Griz gives us a commentary from the rear: 'One casualty on board . . . okay, two casualties on board . . .'

'Where's the third casualty?' I ask. 'We have three guys to take.'

'No idea,' comes the reply. 'Wait one.'

All of this is taking time and the longer we sit here, the greater the risk. Luck, providence, fortune, call it what you will, but with this many rounds coming in, with all this lead in the air, every second increases the likelihood of it running out.

Griz is back. 'The surgeon said not to worry about the third casualty; we'll get him later. His injuries are incompatible with life.'

My heart sinks as it always does when I realise we're too late. Could we have saved him if we'd got in sooner? What if we hadn't held off for thirty minutes? Whatever rationale you employ, it's still a nightmare. Part of you regrets playing it safe; the other part of you chides yourself for even thinking about exposing a 99ft flying leviathan to enemy fire. It's a constant balancing act: the risk to one vitally needed helicopter with its crew and the combat-experienced soldiers that compose the QRF and the MERT on one hand; one or more dying British soldiers on the other. Where's the line? How much risk is too much?

'Ramp up, clear above and behind,' says Griz, so I pull in maximum pitch, nose down and we disappear, leaving the Marines to it. The two we've got on board are in a bad way, but both will go on to survive; one has extensive burns, the other has had a traumatic amputation of his lower leg. Their dead colleague was the Viking's driver, Marine Dale Gostick.

However, we still need to get them back to the safety and assistance of the hospital at Camp Bastion, which means flying along the Sangin Valley again. We've been lucky once; can we ride our luck a second time? Speed and low altitude are our best defences, so I wring all available power from the cab as I route us over the Russian trenches on the west side of the wadi – not only is it the most direct track back to Bastion, but it also has the benefit of being the most difficult point for the enemy to get a bearing on us from.

As soon as we're over open desert, I ask the medics if they're happy for me to climb, and get the reassuring message that both casualties are stable and time isn't an issue. I pull in the power and the cab responds to my input on the collective, taking us up to altitude. We arrive back at the sanctuary of Nightingale HLS at Bastion without incident.

As it transpires, Dale Gostick and the other two Royal Marines we lifted were returning to base on the last operational day of their tour. Six months of fighting, six months of risk and fear and depravation, six months of worry for their families, and on the last day one dies and two incur life-changing injuries. It makes no sense, but the thought comes anyway: *so near and yet so far.*

I can't help thinking about the impact these injuries have on the guys that are out on the front line, fighting on our behalf. Imagine you're a Royal Marine. You're fitter than a butcher's dog, at the absolute peak of human endurance and fitness. These guys can run up mountains without breaking a sweat, they undertake triathlons for fun, and their bodies are testament to all that man is capable of. They're like machines; the complete antithesis of the average aircrew with our soft bodies, pampered existence at KAF and two-month tours.

The guys at the front take their fitness for granted. Just like the two in the back of my cab who got up this morning and probably went through the same routine that they've done every morning in theatre. Suddenly, in less time than it takes to read this sentence, their lives are ripped apart and changed forever. Having to learn to walk on one, maybe two, prosthetic legs; the long road back to fitness after months in Selly Oak and Headley Court; wasted muscle, torn bodies, all the upheaval and heartbreak. How do you come back from that? Your athlete's body is now broken and wracked with pain. And then there's the guilt of surviving when your best mate and oppo has died.

It's funny how some things strike you more than others, but all of us were particularly concerned about the two Marines, so I wandered over to the hospital after dinner to seek an update on their condition. What really lifted me was the knowledge that both patients were as high as kites on morphine, and not only conscious, but had spent most of the evening flirting with the nurses and taking the piss out of one another's injuries. I felt buoyed up on the walk back to the IRT tent.

That sortie marked my last kinetic op on the Det, although it was also the third op since I was shot down that involved my aircraft taking fire. After that, my nickname of Frenchie was temporarily replaced by the equally apposite 'Bullet Magnet.'

35

SERENDIPITY

My feet rested on my body armour as I sat opposite JP in the crew tent. We'd been chatting for some time, but to be honest, I didn't hear much after he said what basically amounted to, 'Ah, Mr Duncan; for you, the war is over.' On the conclusion of our last sortie on that day, May 28th, my crew and I would fly back to KAF to await our flight home. But before we left, he had one more surprise up his sleeve: our final mission would be an air test.

Air tests are a routine part of life when you're at KAF – we take airframes that have had major work done on them and fly them out over the Red Desert to give them a full work up, basically ensuring that all major systems are functioning as they should and that there are no minor gripes that could impact on a sortie once the aircraft is signed back in to fly the line.

Of course when I signed for the airframe that we were to test, I was more than a little surprised to discover that it was ZD575, the one we'd been shot down in, on its first test before return to service. After I'd unceremoniously landed her at FOB Edinburgh, a few engineers had flown forward from KAF to perform emergency repairs on her in situ. Once they ensured she was safe to fly, the aircraft was flown back to KAF for the major work and repairs to be undertaken. I'd been given the honour of taking her up and signing her off.

As expected, the sortie went without a hitch – the airframe

looked as good as new, the hydraulics were faultless and she handled sublimely. Responsive as ever, she flew as smooth as a baby's bottom and performed with alacrity. After completing the various tests so that I could sign her off with confidence, I said to the crew, 'Right, that's the air test finished. Let's go and have some fun!'

I flew a couple of wing overs and then a thought occurred to me: *I want to take some of Afghanistan home with me; let's land in the Red Desert.*

'Let's go and see what these dunes are really like,' I said over the intercom, and I picked out a particularly big one and landed right on top of it. Griz filled a couple of empty water bottles with its fine-grain, iron-rich sand and, with that, we were away. Some of that sand now sits proudly on the mantelpiece at home (now in a fine glass container rather than a grotty old plastic water bottle!)

There seemed to be some serendipity at work with my starting and finishing the Det in ZD575; in a way, things had come full-circle for me. I must admit, when I shut her down on the deck at FOB Edinburgh – after limping home with a chunk of the rotor missing and the hydraulic system out of action – I wondered when I might see her again. The opportunity of nursing her back into service, fully functional and good as new after her spell with the engineers, was a nice end note to my time in theatre and a safe, non-kinetic mission to wind down with.

A few minutes before I left the departure lounge at KAF to board the aircraft home the following night, our Squadron boss at 27 Sqn walked in. Wing Commander (now Group Captain) Dom Toriati came over to see me, having just arrived in theatre. After seeking out JP, he walked over to me and reached out to shake my hand. As he did so, he looked me in the eye and said, 'You lucky, lucky bastard, Frenchie!' I'm sure what he was actually thinking was: 'Thank fuck you didn't lose the squadron an aircraft, because the paperwork would have been a nightmare!'

Either way, it was a nice moment because I felt a genuine sense of relief on his part, a touching concern that we had all got away unharmed from the attempt to shoot us down. I daresay he had a sleepless night when news of what had happened filtered through to him back at RAF Odiham in the immediate aftermath of the event. All joking aside, the paperwork and headaches that the loss of an aircraft generates would have been astronomical, and however much it shouldn't, something like that follows you around your whole career. Obviously, because of his role as Squadron boss, Toriati is quite remote from the minutiae of day-to-day life, but it was nice that he showed such concern. I wished him the best of luck as he started his four-month staff tour in theatre, and with that we were on our way home.

It's a minor perk (and one of the few divides in theatre between officers and enlisted personnel) but as officers, we board the TriStar first and get the pick of the seats. It's rather academic to a degree; there are no business-class recliners at the front, just more of the same layout that you find throughout the cabin. I chose to sit at the front and luckily, as it wasn't a busy flight, I got a row of three seats to myself.

Perhaps unsurprisingly, the sense of relief I felt as the TriStar departed Kandahar was almost palpable. I don't think I'd appreciated how tightly I'd been wound. As the wheels came up and the aircraft gained altitude, I sat back in my seat and let out a huge but silent sigh as I felt the weight on my shoulders lift and the worry start to fall further and further behind. It was over; we'd done it and we'd all got out. I felt a mass of conflicting emotions; relief principally, but also apprehension – the experience had changed me, but how? How would Ali feel when she saw me? What about Guy? A tiny part of me had got used to the existence in Helmand as it always did, and despite my happiness at leaving it behind me, I was going to miss it. She's a cruel mistress, Helmand; a complete head fuck.

As soon as we reached altitude and began the long journey home, I gave up on analysing what had gone on – there'd be plenty of time for the reckoning in the months to come. Now, all I wanted was to sleep. I pulled my green maggot from the overhead compartment and snuggled inside, inflating my pillow and pulling a mask over my eyes. I wondered how I'd feel when I got home, but I never got to think it through because it was my last conscious notion as sleep claimed me. I didn't wake up again until the thump of the undercarriage descending ready for landing at Brize roused me about five minutes out. We were back.

This close to home, I was thinking that my days of trouble at the end of a Det were behind me. After all, I hadn't had any problems getting out; the flight had even been on time. In actual fact, because of the intensity of the ops and the attempt to blast us from the sky on the 17th, JP had thoughtfully sent us home a few days early. However, I hadn't reckoned on the complexity of the female mind!

Alison had known about the incident on the 17th almost immediately after it happened because of her job and her connections. In fact, she found a cable with all the details, sent over by a mutual friend at the Foreign & Commonwealth Office, in her office when she got into work the day afterwards. When I eventually rang her, she already had some idea of what had happened and knew I was okay. We'd spoken several times since, but not after JP had told me I'd be coming back three days early, so she didn't know. I considered ringing her as I was heading from Brize to RAF Odiham. She wasn't expecting me, so I was sure she'd be delighted. In the end, I decided against it. She'd see me soon enough.

Unfortunately for me, circumstance and fate intervened. When I got home, my parents were there, having flown over from Paris to await my return, but Ali wasn't – she was out walking our dog with Paul Farmer's wife Becs. Paul had come home earlier and had told his wife that we would be home early too. Becs mentioned it to Ali while they were out with the dogs.

'How much are you looking forward to seeing Alex later, then?' she asked.

Ali played it cool. 'Ah, it'll be great to have him back. I can't wait. But I want to surprise him, so I'm getting my hair done tomorrow and I'm going to dress up and really give him something to remember!'

'Well you're leaving it a bit late, aren't you?'

'Late?' Ali asked. 'I know us girls are known for the time it takes us to get ready, but two days is hardly a rush, is it?'

'Two days? They're on their way home now. I thought you knew!'

Apparently Ali's face was a picture. She dialled my number and when I saw her name flashing on the screen I thought, 'Shall I answer?' But then it dawned on me – she'd know I was back from the way it rang. I hit Answer.

'Hi babe,' I said.

'Hi. When'd you get back?'

I told her I'd been at the house for about five minutes.

'Fine. See you later,' she said coldly and hung up.

Every man will know what I'm talking about when I say that I didn't really get why she was so irked. And I guess every woman will sympathise with Ali and intrinsically understand her mood.

She'd had it all mapped out; what she was going to wear, her make-up, her hair. The champagne was on ice, the house was clean and tidy – she'd even arranged for my parents to be out with Guy when I got back so we got an hour or two on our own. She'd planned on looking like a million dollars, and instead I'd caught her unawares. Her hair was unwashed and unkempt, she had no make-up on and she'd been out in the forest walking the dogs. But she always looks gorgeous to me, so I didn't get what all the fuss was about.

It wasn't the welcome that I expected. And it wasn't five minutes of the cold shoulder either; let's just say it was a good few hours before I managed to break the ice!

36

PRE-EMPTIVE STRIKE

After my post-detachment leave, which Ali and I spent in the South of France (the perfect antidote to the rigours of life on Det in Afghanistan), I left 27 Squadron and returned to RAF Shawbury to train as a Qualified Helicopter Instructor.

JP had asked me where I wanted to go earlier in the year and I'd asked him to look into my obtaining a 'fixed-wing crossover', allowing me to move to the multi-engine fleet, but it simply wasn't an option.

I guess it was because there was a desperate need for Chinook pilots in Afghanistan. Also the recession was beginning to bite, so the airlines weren't recruiting; this meant there wasn't the usual exodus of fixed-wing pilots from the RAF into civil aviation that normally creates demand in the service to replace them. So he said, 'If you're sure you don't want promotion at the moment – although I'm certain you'll change your mind at some stage – the obvious route for you is to become a QHI.'

The only reason I didn't want to take promotion then was because I joined the RAF to fly and it's something I love; for me, aviation is not so much a profession as it is a disease with no cure. The only thing that alleviates the symptoms is flying and, no matter how hard you try, it's inevitable that with every step up the promotion ladder you do less and less of that.

But the offer of QHI was on the table so I took it. It made sense, and at least I would know where I was going. It offered a degree of consistency and stability and it would mean, perhaps more importantly for me at that stage, no more tours of Afghanistan.

I think it's fair to say that at the time, with all that had happened on my last Det, I was ready for a break from combat ops.

It was a hard course, there's no question. I'd come from the Chinook where I'd been a training captain, a big fish in a small pond, and suddenly I was back, initially at least, in a Squirrel. I was used to flying this huge, powerful helicopter with its twin rotors and suddenly I was in this tiny little Squirrel, which has the shape of a sperm, is made of plastic, and gets upset in five knots of wind. That element was a complete nightmare; it was just so difficult making the backwards transition. It's demoralising too, because you know you can fly – you've flown countless missions under fire, you're combat experienced, you've performed some really aggressive manoeuvres that come naturally to you – and all of a sudden you're back to basics in a helicopter that's the aviation equivalent of a Fisher Price toy and you're thinking, 'Fuck, I can't fly anymore, let alone teach!' That was a bit of a shock.

But everyone got through the training and I actually enjoyed it in the end. It was a tri-service course, so it brought Army, Navy and RAF together. We've all got the same ethos, and it was great socially too.

I began my work in December 2008, and by the end of January 2009 I was back at RAF Odiham as a QHI on 'C' Flight, 18 Sqn – the Chinook OCF.

Monday March 2nd looked like being a pretty crap day. I was at my desk in the OCF preparing for the day ahead and I was pretty pissed off because aside from it being a Monday, I'd been given a really shitty job to do. The Flight had gone to RAF Leeming and I'd been told I had to stay behind and sort out some statistics that were going to take me hours. I was not a happy bunny, although – as I was to learn – there was an agenda at work behind my being kept at Odiham. My mood wasn't improved when Squadron Leader Geary, the Squadron 2i/c, came to see me and said, 'Frenchie, you need to go and see OC 27 Sqn at 11:00hrs.'

'Er . . . okay. What have I done now?' I ask, laughing.

'Dunno,' says Geary, 'but he wants to see you. 11:00hrs sharp. Be there!' and with that he was gone. As he shuts the door my brain goes into overdrive trying to work out what on earth the OC could want with me. I'd officially left 27 Sqn on July 14th 2008 when I went off to Shawbury to do the QHI course, and although Dom Toriati was still in charge of the Squadron, he wasn't my boss anymore. Whatever it was, it didn't look good. I wrack my brain, and slowly a thought comes to mind that makes my heart sink.

Three days previously, on the Friday night, there'd been a 'dining-in' night at the Mess. It was a big one and I'd got properly shit-faced. I still had some issues surrounding what had happened in theatre on my last Det at the time – I was quick to anger and was also having trouble sleeping. I'd sleep, but it felt like I wasn't resting, so whether I slept ten hours through or one hour I'd still feel like I hadn't been to bed at all. It was really starting to get me down. I was tired and irritable and probably drinking more than was good for me. So now I'm sat there thinking, *What did I say? Did I tell anyone a few home truths?*

All these things are racing around in my mind and I put two and two together and make four. Obviously I've offended someone, it's gone right to the top and I'm in for the mother of all bollockings. I have no idea what I've done – how could I? I can barely remember going to bed that night. 'Oh God, I've probably been rude to Dom Toriati or one of his guests and I'm about to get my ass chewed,' I decide.

So, 10:50 comes, and by 10:55 I'm standing outside his office – five minutes early so I can prepare myself for the gathering storm. Also I won't be out of breath, sweating or otherwise uncomfortable as I stand before the boss. I check my watch and at 10:59 and 55 seconds, I knock smartly on his door.

'Come in,' he says, the sound muffled through the barrier between us. I open the door and march through. He's on the phone and he looks serious. I'm thinking, 'Oh shit the bed! This isn't good.'

I have a lot of respect for Dom; he's a great bloke and he'd been a really good boss when I served under him, but my God he could deliver a bollocking! I'm looking at him and I can see he's winding the phone call up and as he bids farewell to the person on the other end of the line, he begins to stand. That's when I decide the best form of defence is attack and launch my pre-emptive strike.

'Sir, if it's about Friday night, I must say that I have no recollection whatsoever of what I said or did after 23:00hrs, so if I've been rude, I am really sorry. I probably said a lot of things that I shouldn't have said. It's no excuse, and anything I say now is going to sound like I'm trying to justify it, so all I'm going to say is sorry.'

The words are pouring out like water from a dam; I'm delivering them at machine-gun pace. As I look for a hair shirt to don or a whip for some self-flagellation, he holds his hand up like a police officer halting traffic.

'Frenchie, I've no idea what you're talking about, but you might want to stop there before you incriminate yourself.'

His face is a picture of seriousness. I'm still digesting what's he's just said and then he deals the hammer blow. The words come from his mouth with meaning and sincerity, but as crisp and flowing as if he's reading from an Autocue.

'Frenchie, it is my great honour and pleasure to inform you that you have been awarded the Distinguished Flying Cross for your actions in the skies over Afghanistan.'

As soon as he finishes, the seriousness is gone; his mouth widens into a big beaming smile.

I'm poleaxed. Dumbstruck. My chin actually drops, my mouth forming a perfect 'O' – and I thought that only happened in the movies. There's a chair behind me. I literally drop into it as my legs buckle under me. That came completely out of left field. I don't know what to say.

He sits beside me and he's grinning like the proverbial Cheshire cat now. He's delighted and proud because this is the first DFC for 27 Squadron since they reformed with the Chinook. He told me that Group Captain Mason, the Station Commander, would be coming to see me and that although it was his job to tell me of the award, he'd very kindly given that privilege to Dom.

Ten minutes later, Group Captain Mason arrived, congratulated me and told me how delighted he was that the Chinook Force at RAF Odiham had been recognised thanks to the efforts of me and my crew in Afghanistan. Once everything had calmed down and I'd taken it all in, I asked Dom Toriati if there were any others and he told me, 'Yes, there's another one.' I was delighted because I was pretty certain it would be for Morris. It was obvious – if I'd got one for what I'd done, Morris must be odds on to get one too.

Sadly it wasn't the case, and for all that I'd been riding high when I was told of the award, that really brought me down to earth again. I was gutted for him. Obviously you wonder in the run-up to the operational awards whether you'll be in line for anything, and Morris had been geeing me up, telling me that he thought I'd get one and I him; I really believed he would. I'm ashamed to say I avoided him in the immediate aftermath of my finding out. Aside from the fact that I'd been sworn to absolute secrecy for twenty-four hours by the Station Commander and the boss, I just didn't want to have to tell him.

I was truly gutted, but that's the lottery of the whole thing. And it is a lottery. So many people deserve awards, but the way it's done is so political – who gets what, when and why. I was recognised for two of the missions I flew in my 2008 Det – the one in ZD575 when we were shot down, and for Op Oqab Sturga six days later. I feel enormously proud and privileged to have been awarded the DFC for those ops, but I couldn't have done them alone. My crews on the two missions – Alex, Bob, Coops, Andy and Griz – were as much a part of what happened as I was; so to me, the award is for them too.

Fortunately, the crew was acknowledged by the Guild of Air Pilots and Navigators, which awarded Black Cat Two Two its coveted Grand Master's Commendation for 2008/09, at a lavish banquet in London's Guildhall. The Guild had earlier recognised all of us by granting the Grand Master's Commendation for

2007/08 to everyone at the RAF Odiham Chinook Force. The Chinook Force as a whole was also fortunate to receive the award for Best Unit in the inaugural Sun Military Awards in December 2008, beating off stiff competition from 2 Para and HMS *Iron Duke*. The award was presented by the then Prime Minister Gordon Brown, but we didn't let that spoil the occasion.

I think we're all quite proud of what we've achieved as a unit at RAF Odiham and although none of us does it for the credit, it's nice that the work that we do has not gone unrecognised. Since 2001, the Chinook Force's pilots and crews have been awarded two OBEs, two MBEs, nine DFCs, four Air Force Crosses, two QCBAs and ten Mentions in Despatches. One pilot – Wing Commander Jeremy Robinson – has been awarded the DFC three times, a feat unequalled since World War II. I felt my DFC represented well-deserved recognition for 27 Squadron and our involvement in Op Herrick. I know 18 Squadron had been awarded four or five DFCs since the start of ops in Afghanistan, but as far as I'm aware, mine was the first for 27 Squadron since World War II.

The boss said, 'Don't tell anyone, not a soul – at least for twenty-four hours,' and of course, I was all, 'Yes, of course sir. Wouldn't dream of it.' But as soon as I walked out the building, I was on the phone to Alison.

'I don't believe it, I got a DFC!' She was shouting down the phone in the office and I'm saying to her, 'Shhh, you can't say anything, it's supposed to be a secret! What about all the people around you?!'

Eventually she calmed down, but I was so chuffed. I'm not saying we're competitive or anything, but she had an MBE, so at least now we were on a more equal footing, even if, technically, my award trumped hers!

I remember Alison had bought a bottle of Dom Pérignon when we were last in Paris; we were going to open it on my thirtieth birthday but we forgot. Then we said we'd open it for another special occasion. We were going to do it when we were selling our house but that fell through. Then we paid out £10,000 on brain surgery for our dog; we said we'd drink it when she pulled through, but she died. After that there was nothing else, so we kind of forgot about it. When I got home that evening, Alison had already chilled it so we decided to celebrate in style with the Dom Pérignon and a takeaway from our favourite Chinese. Best laid plans of mice and men again – the fucking bottle was corked!

I said to Alison, 'Keep the food hot, I'll be back in five minutes.' I jumped in the TVR and raced to Costco, where I bought another bottle for £67. Got home, put it in the freezer for half an hour and it was perfect. We got there in the end, and what an exquisite way to toast the award – a perfect Champagne.

The official announcement of the latest gallantry awards before the media was at Colchester Barracks, home to 16 Air Assault Brigade, just three days later. I managed to blag the Squadron Range Rover for the trip; it's pretty cool, a black 4.2 Sport with all the toys that we use when we undertake displays around the country. We were sponsored by Range Rover and the car fits nicely in the back of a Chinook; we'd fly in, the ramp would come down and out it would drive, ready to move the crews and the engineers around at our destination. It's a nice way to travel – fly in and drive off to your accommodation or other engagement. I couldn't believe how it worked out – my parents had flown over on the Wednesday for a short visit, a trip that had been in the diary for weeks. It was completely serendipitous – a rare coincidence – but it meant they'd be able to come to the press conference for the official announcement.

I drove us up to Colchester early that morning. With Alison beside me, and Mum and Dad in the back, I felt like a million dollars. When we arrived, there were all these amazing people there, so many brave soldiers who'd won gallantry awards for some incredible things. Society today looks up to some bizarre people – Premier League footballers, models, D-list celebrities famous for taking their clothes off or having been on *Big Brother*, but there's nothing heroic about what they do. I felt really humbled to be in the presence of so many real heroes, men and women who had done things that would make your eyes stand out on stalks. We were all called forward one by one while our citations were read out by Lieutenant General Sir Graeme Lamb. His speech at the start of the press conference was, without question, the most moving and heartfelt I've ever heard. This is what he said:

'Welcome to this day, particularly the families and friends. We in uniform know only too well the silent burden that you carry for those of us who serve this country. Tomorrow Operational Awards List 32 is made public. Today is about those from all three Services who have been recognised for their bravery. It is their stories that are on display here: respect that.

'It is said that true riches cannot be bought – one cannot buy the experience of brave deeds or the friendship of companions to whom one is bound forever by ordeals suffered in common – true friendship itself is an emerald simply beyond price. Those in uniform understand that bond, those here and those they fought alongside recognise simple courage and we, the nation, recognise that these young men and women acted above and beyond the call of duty. "Duty", a word considered rather old-fashioned, seldom heard today, along with integrity, honesty, service, sacrifice, but terms these soldiers, sailors, airmen and marines recognise, live and die by. These quiet and unsung heroes understand only too well what Colonel Paddy Mayne alluded to when he talked of ordeals suffered in common and what held them together.

'These men and women know only too well the burden that is duty. They are no braver nor less courageous than the likes of Col Mayne and his forefathers, no less committed, no less human and they are in every way the match of those who went before them.

'These young people, ladies and gentlemen, are the British Armed Forces.

'I have read ill-judged remarks from casual observers, from armchair critics, that we are an Army that is overwhelmed, humiliated and downtrodden; that we are an Army that struggles to punch above its weight. Challenge those here who spend time – again at world's end – with that claim. They are not consumed by trivial self-interest, barging others aside in order to gain some material advantage for ambition.

'These warriors are the stuff of legend. They know the meaning of life and death, of standing by your friends, of standing up for something which they and we recognise as a mighty force and being counted. They know only too well just how fragile is the gift of life and they know only too well the human cost and will remember those, every bit their equal, who did not make it home. Those who gave their full measure in some foreign field: gone, never forgotten.

'The likes of Sergeant Major O'Donnell, bigger than life, braver than a lion, saviour of others' lives, holder of the George Medal – posthumously awarded to him today a bar to that award. A most gallant gentleman; I only wish I had had the privilege to have met him.

'To those who returned: these young people are splendid company. Tough as nails, they do get knocked on their backsides every so often, but they do not lie there and whine that life is unfair; they get up, dust themselves off and get on with it.

'They are the British Armed Forces; they defend this realm and our way of life, they are made of sterner stuff, and when asked will call out whomever, whenever onto whatever field of battle they choose. Look no further for your twenty-first century role models; these are your real heroes: they live among you, they defend you and your right to freedom and the freedom of those less fortunate than you. There are none better and I would wish to work with none other.

'They are drawn from across this nation and from regiments steeped in history from Scotland, Ireland, England and Wales. Colour or creed matters not, but mark this: they are of the right stuff. If you want to see all that is good, all that is great in this nation of ours and its Armed Forces, look no further than on the pages of the operational awards you are about to print and be humbled. But remember also that what is listed here are those individuals who were seen on the field of battle and their actions recorded – there are quite literally hundreds who were not.

'They make up our ranks, they are no less brave, they have done and continue to do their duty. As Field Marshal Montgomery recalled, "every one an emperor." I salute them and those here, their courage and their sacrifice. I have a soldier's deep respect for the awards they have received, and know only too well that they have been won by iron hearts in wooden ships.'

After the speech and the presentation of the awards, there were lots of generals wandering around, including Air Vice Marshal Greg Bagwell, who came over to me.

'So what next for you then, Frenchie?' he asked.

'I'm a QHI at the moment, sir, but I'm getting a bit tired of the Chinook thing now having done so many years. I think I'd like to finish my tour at the OCF and then go fixed-wing crossover.'

'Well, if the opportunity is there, you should take it. I think you've done more than enough for the Chinook Force.'

He wandered off and started talking to Alison. 'You must be really proud of Alex. I understand he wants to look at a different career.' Alison, having a blonde moment and completely missing the point, said, 'Yes, he was going to leave the RAF, but the recession hit so there were no fixed-wing jobs outside. That's why he's decided to stay.'

AVM Bagwell didn't even break his stride and laughed as he said, 'That's not quite what he said to me but okay, fair enough!' and that was the end of that conversation.

It's like walking a minefield when you bring your family or partner to an event like that and all the generals are there. My father has no shame – he has a brain the size of a small planet and he can talk the hind legs off a donkey. As I was posing for the national press, I could see my father in conversation with General Lamb, Rear Admiral Tony Johnstone-Burt (the commander of Joint Helicopter Command) and AVM Bagwell; two two-star generals, a three-star, and my dad. I was dying inside; the press wanted me to pose, but my attention was on my dad and the likelihood of him saying the wrong thing about me to any one of three generals who all have the power to stall my career before it gets off the ground.

I looked at Alison across the parade ground and mouthed to her, 'For fuck's sake, sort it out!' but she just saw me smiling and waved back. I found out later that my dad had said to Graeme Lamb, 'Loved your speech, can I have it?' which kind of caught the General on the back foot.

In the end, he said, 'Okay, one minute,' and sent his aide-de-camp off to get the speech. I was so embarrassed! What with Alison telling AVM Bagwell that I wanted to leave the Air Force and my dad asking a three-star general for his speech, things couldn't have got much worse!

Interviews over with, we headed back to Odiham where the boss had organised some drinks at the Mess. I know Ali came with me but I can't honestly say I remember much of what happened the rest of that evening!

37

BY ROYAL INVITATION

I was looking forward to visiting Buckingham Palace on July 15th 2009 to receive my award. When they first wrote to me with the invitation, I replied by return asking whether they would permit me three extra tickets so that I could bring Alex, Bob Ruffles and Coops – the whole crew – along. Perhaps unsurprisingly, they wrote back and said sorry but space was really tight. They did however let me have one extra ticket; so, as he was my co-pilot on both missions, I invited Alex, along with Alison and my parents.

I'd arranged for us to stay at the RAF Club in Piccadilly and we came up to London the day before so we could go out for dinner to a fantastic restaurant that had been recommended to us by one of Alison's colleagues. We drove there via the palace, and as we went past I couldn't see the Royal Standard flying and I thought, 'Oh no, the Queen isn't there! I don't want to get my DFC from Prince Charles; I've met him twice already!' I know it might sound stupid, and even a little pompous, but you can't help the thoughts that arrive unbidden in your brain.

On the morning of the investiture, I decided to walk across Green Park to the palace with my dad and Alex, with Alex and me wearing our No.1 uniforms and medals. Of course we hadn't walked more than about fifty metres when the heavens opened, proving that you can never rely on the English summer. Luckily we managed to hail a cab to the palace. As soon as we got out of the car it stopped raining and the sun came out. Just to lift my mood a little further, as I looked up, the Royal Standard was flying, signalling that Her Majesty was in residence.

The main gates saw the usual seething, homogeneous mass of tourists, a crowd two or three deep all craning to get a look inside or a peek at one of the Royal Family. There was a police officer standing there controlling the crowd and, after I showed him my invitation, we waltzed in through the gates. Walking across the main courtyard on the red gravel I had one of those 'this can't be happening' moments, a kind of unbearable lightness of being at the thought that I was actually going into Buckingham Palace to meet the Queen.

It was great having Alison there as, having been before to receive her MBE, she knew the score. She gave me the heads up on where to stand afterwards to get the best backdrop for the pictures. When you're the centre of attention, you don't get a chance to think about all the little things; it just feels like everything is moving at a million miles an hour.

Once inside, it was truly breathtaking. Red carpets, huge tapestries, big works of art, gold – it's quite unbelievable. If you had to design a palace from the ground up, you couldn't do it better. It's a fairy-tale place, the sort of image that little girls must have in their heads when they dream of marrying a prince. A short time later, Ali said to me, 'Okay babe, this is where we part. You go that way and we go this way. We'll see you later.' She gave me a kiss and a hug and with that, I was on my own.

I was escorted into another room by one of the footmen and the works of art literally stopped me in my tracks. Priceless works by Degas, Holbein, Cézanne, Monet and other great masters adorned the walls – I could have spent a day just drinking in the view. But there was no time to stand and admire the paintings; an official placed a hook on my left breast just where the corresponding ribbon would go. The Queen doesn't actually pin the medal on to your uniform – she'd be there all day if that were the case, and she'd never get time to do her 'Queeny' things. She simply places it on the hook that sits on your chest; job done.

I was surprised to bump into Squadron Leader David Morgan, a man I feel privileged to call a friend. David is one of the RAF's most experienced Chinook pilots having flown them during the

Falklands Conflict, and through to the present day. Later, while serving on the Chinook OCF, he gave me my check ride. He was at the palace to receive an MBE. In addition, RAF Odiham's Station Commander, Group Captain Mason, was there to receive an OBE. As it transpired, Dave and I had unknowingly booked adjacent tables at The Ritz for lunch after the ceremony!

We were briefed on what to expect by a retired Lieutenant Colonel, who told me, 'When the person before you is announced, move up by the door and when you hear, "The Distinguished Flying Cross is awarded for operations in Afghanistan to Flight Lieutenant Duncan," walk up, bow your head and take your place before the Queen who will present your award, shake hands and have a chat.'

My palms were a little damp as I walked out to stand in front of our Sovereign – who, as monarch, is Commander-in-Chief of the UK Armed Forces – but I remedied that with a surreptitious wipe on my uniform trousers.

I was really quite in awe as I stood before her. Aside from anything else she might represent, the Queen is a piece of living history who, as I write, has given weekly audiences to twelve British Prime Ministers right the way back to Sir Winston Churchill. I found that difficult to get my head around – the things she must have seen. So many icons through history, and she has had personal relationships with all of them. Notwithstanding that, the Queen is a consummate professional and she put me at ease without my even noticing she'd done so. She starts by asking a benign question to relax you, because she's been doing it long enough now to know that everyone is nervous before her.

She asked me about flying and how things were in Afghanistan and then she said, 'So tell me exactly what happened,' so I told her the story.

'And how is Governor Mangal?'

'Well Ma'am, he's fine now, but he did make me laugh. Even though he'd just survived an assassination attempt, his only concern when I landed at FOB Edinburgh was to find the bed Prince Harry had slept in!' That actually made her grin.

I knew I'd been with her for a while by this stage and I could feel the conversation wrapping up, but just in case you miss the subtle cue, she does this thing where she puts her hand in yours to shake it and you almost sense, rather than feel, the gentlest of pushes. I took a step back, bowed and walked away.

Alison and I now have our own videos of our time with the Queen. Her conversation lasts forty-one seconds, but it's not really important that mine lasted one minute and thirty-two seconds! Ali doesn't find that funny for some reason . . .

After the ceremony, I was approached by Squadron Leader Andrew Calame, the Queen's equerry, who said, 'Ah, you're the chap who took the rocket through the back of your aircraft. The Queen and Prince Philip were laughing at something you said in the report of the incident they were reading at breakfast this morning.'

That is another reason why the military holds the Queen in such affection – she has a genuine interest and goes out of her way to read up on any soldiers, sailors or airmen to whom she is giving awards, and she really drills down into the detail. In any case, it was a nice thought to go away with – that she and Prince Philip had been talking about me at breakfast that morning!

It was only later when I looked at the medal after the ceremony that I noticed the thumb print on its face. It was pristine when the Queen lifted it to pin it on my chest and I noticed that her thumb was on the centre of the cross as she placed it, but didn't think anything of it. I never touched it myself, and then I noticed the slight discoloration where the print was. That's when it dawned on me that it belonged to the Queen.

It's still there, even now.

PART FOUR
THE CRUCIBLE OF FIRE

38

FORTUNE BY NAME, FORTUNE BY NATURE

The year of 2009 turned out to be the bloodiest year of all for British Forces in Helmand Province, with the violence the worst it had been since the Taliban was removed from power in 2001. A total of 108 British soldiers died between January and December.

One of the biggest evolutions to take place that year was the increase in the use of remotely-detonated explosive devices, which were being used to target foreign forces across the country. Around 80% of British deaths in 2009 were as a result of IED explosions, evidencing a change of tactics by the Taliban, who suffered extensive losses in conventional firefights against the better-trained and equipped British and US forces. According to figures from iCasualties.org, ISAF deaths attributed to IEDs rose from 41 in 2006 to 368 in 2010 – an increase of almost 900%.

Predictably perhaps, the knock-on effects were felt by the Chinook Force too, as the tempo of operations increased and the IRT flew more missions than ever. As 2010 rolled around, changes were made to the set-up at Camp Bastion to improve response times; the crews for the IRT cab, the MERT and those Apaches providing the escort, moved to dedicated accommodation just yards from the pan, meaning the aircraft were now just a few steps from the JOC and their tents.

There were other changes, too. US President Barack Obama announced his long-awaited strategy for Afghanistan and deployed a further 30,000 troops to supplement the 70,000 soldiers already in theatre. Britain, already the second largest provider of troops to the region, sent a further 1,200, taking the total number to 9,500 with the vast bulk – 6,200 – in Helmand Province.

At a more local level, JHF (A) integrated into the US 3rd Marine Aviation Wing, part of the 1st Marine Expeditionary Force, a logical and tactical step forward in terms of US and UK helicopters working alongside each other within the new region of RC Southwest. The old RC South was divided along provincial lines: RC Southwest (Helmand Province) and RC Southeast (Kandahar Province).

The pressure on the Chinook Force was alleviated to a degree by an increase in frames; by 2010, we had nine Chinooks in theatre; ten Apaches; four Lynx; four Sea Kings and a total of six Merlins. In addition, the organisation and effectiveness of the IRT was enhanced by the addition of two US Army HH-60 Pedro Black Hawk 'Dust-offs' on call alongside the Chinooks. RAF Fast Air Support was now supplied by Tornado GR-4s which replaced the Harrier GR-7s and GR-9s that had fulfilled that role from the beginning.

While I was busy training the next generation of Chinook crews back in the UK, my colleagues from previous Dets were back out in theatre flying under fire and making the headlines. Flt Lt Ian 'Chomper' Fortune, who flew as JP's co-pilot on Operation Oqab Sturga in 2008, was fortunate to escape with his life in January after coming under heavy, sustained fire on an IRT mission, a sortie for which he was later awarded a well-deserved DFC for some outstanding leadership and inspirational flying under the most testing conditions. His actions also attracted the attention of GAPAN, which awarded him its Grand Master's Commendation for 2009/10, and December 2010's The Sun Military Awards, at which he received the Most Outstanding Airman award. Ian's aircraft came under sustained fire by the Taliban and was hit a total of eight times, resulting in a series of system failures including damage to the flight stabilisation system and forward transmission. Ian was also hit – the first time in the nine-year war that a pilot has been shot while in the air.

The cab that he was flying – ZA718, better known by her squadron code Bravo November (BN) – is interesting in and of itself. One of the original batch of thirty-three Chinook HC2s delivered to the Royal Air Force in early 1982, she's seen action in every major operation involving the RAF in the helicopter's almost thirty-year service life. She was one of four Chinooks that travelled to the Falkland Islands on the *Atlantic Conveyor* which was sunk with the loss of all its cargo. It was struck by two Exocet missiles while waiting to offload at San Carlos Water. By chance, BN was airborne on an engineering test flight at the time of the attack and was diverted to HMS *Hermes*.

As the only helicopter available in the Falkland Islands, she then had to endure a punishing flying programme without spares, tools or appropriate lubricants for several weeks, in appalling weather conditions. On one particular mission, BN ran into a blizzard on her way to San Carlos Water and crashed into the sea at 100 knots. Despite water swamping the cockpit and engines, she still managed to get airborne again due to the bravery of pilot Richard Langworthy, who was awarded the DFC. The cab would go on to see two more of her pilots awarded the Distinguished Flying Cross for actions while in command of BN by 2010; Ian Fortune was the third. Ian and I met up not long after he returned from theatre, when he told me his story:

'We got the shout at around 15:20 and while I confirmed the limited details that were available, Doug Gardner, who was my co-pilot, went with our crewmen – Paul Day and Tony Sutherland – to spin the aircraft up. We were ready to lift within minutes. As well as the MERT and force protection team on board, I also had a camera crew from the Discovery Channel filming for a series called *Frontline Battle Machines*. Information was sketchy, but we knew there were six US and ANA casualties – three T1s and three T2s, all with gunshot wounds – at a grid near Lashkar Gah. They'd been involved in a fierce and protracted firefight which was still going on.

'En route, our Apache escort, Ugly Five Zero, called us and said the LS was too hot, so we held off. To make matters worse, the JTAC – who would normally coordinate the extraction – was one of the critically wounded.

'I flew a holding pattern at height about ten miles out from the emergency LS. We could see events unfolding on the ground and soon another Apache joined our escort – both then engaged the

Taliban, laying down heavy suppressing fire to assist the ground units. Doug worked out we had enough fuel for about forty-five minutes total holding. After about twenty minutes of flying random patterns to avoid predictability, I dropped down to low level to deceive any dickers into thinking we were beginning our run into the LS.

'The ground troops were desperately trying to secure the LS but, even with the two Apaches providing air support, they were struggling. Every time they stepped out of cover, the Taliban targeted them with heavy and effective SAFIRE; we were cleared into the LS at least three times before being told to: "Hold, Hold, Hold!"

'Having already taken casualties, including one KIA, the ground troops were in a very difficult situation. It was obvious that we'd be cleared in at the first sign of any lull in the fighting, but the LS was never going to be fully secure. By this time, we were well aware of how long we'd been holding and we were desperate to get those boys out.

'Eventually, the Apache called us over the radio. "Tricky Seven Three, Ugly Five Zero, enemy are north and north-east of the LS. Route in from the west; the LS will be marked with smoke."

'Around forty minutes after arriving on station, we received positive clearance into the LS with a reminder of the enemy forces' firing points and ingress route. As a result of the radio chat and gauging the general feel of the situation I said, "I think we'll put our visors down on this one chaps," which isn't always practical in the desert, as they can become scratched and dusty, making it harder to retain good references.

'I began the descent from the east at 155kts and explained my intentions to the crew so that everyone would have situational awareness of the Taliban's firing points on the approach. The plan was to route south of the LS and come right until we were going in from the west. Then, as I began the final approach, I'd kick the tail right to bring the starboard M134, which Tony was manning, to bear on the enemy firing points in the 3–5 o'clock position. I saw the white smoke and, with half a mile to run, I began turning the tail through 180° and reversed towards the compounds where the troops had been taking cover. I landed on the smoke with the starboard M134 providing covering arcs.

'Almost as soon as I landed, I saw puffs of dirt as rounds hit the ground in our 1 o'clock, with muzzle flashes in our 4 o'clock. The ground troops were laying down a barrage of covering fire as the stretcher teams worked with the casualties at the rear. Then I noticed dirt being kicked up as rounds tore into the ground in front of the cockpit. The second that ground forces broke cover with the casualties, the Taliban opened up on them. The weight of fire was incredible – the guys in the back could hear the sound of the guns and rounds ricocheting nearby, even over the sound of the blades.

'The rate of fire from the ground troops increased rapidly and I twice saw a line of large impact clouds 100m away in our 3 o'clock, moving parallel with the aircraft axis. I reckoned it was from the Apaches' 30mm cannon. By now, the wounded were coming on board, but even as they were assisted up the ramp, the Taliban had a bead on us and the cab started taking effective fire. I felt a few thuds as rounds impacted the airframe and asked Doug to check the Ts and Ps. Then I heard and felt a round come in somewhere just below me. A few seconds later, I was informed the ramp was up and I got the all clear from Paul. At this stage, the amount of covering fire from the ground forces doubled, but it seemed to me that the rate of enemy fire also increased.

'I pulled full power and stuck the nose down to get the fuck out but, as I transitioned to height, I felt more rounds strike the aircraft. About twenty seconds after lifting, I heard a succession of loud bangs and then my head was forced violently back. When I opened my eyes, there were several large cracks in my visor, which had blood spattered all over it. Then I saw the bullet hole and the spiderweb cracks surrounding it at the base of my windscreen. I smelled burning and cordite, and then my blood ran cold as I realised I'd been shot in the head.

'The bullet came through the windscreen in front of me and struck my visor before gouging a chunk off the front of the NVG rail. That deflected it under the outer skin of my helmet and out the top, where it smashed through the top windscreen into the sky. Talk about lucky – if the round had been fired a fraction of a second earlier, if the gunman had aimed 1mm lower, if the NVG rail hadn't deflected it, its trajectory would have sent it straight through my face and out the back of my head. Now that really got my attention!

'I looked at Doug to make sure he was okay – he was fine and, at that stage, unaware I'd been hit. I could feel blood running down my face and neck and soaking my body armour. I couldn't quite put it all together; I knew I'd been hit in the head, but it didn't make sense – I felt fine. I had good references and, after a cursory glance down myself, I was happy to continue flying.

'"Chaps, I've just been shot in the face but I think I'm okay," I said. "I took a round through the front windscreen which came up and hit me on the head. I've got a bit of a crack and a bleed there."

'"Fuck. You okay mate?" Doug asked, looking shocked.

'"Yeah, bit shaken, but otherwise okay, I think."

He was mindful that if my condition deteriorated he'd have to take control.

' "Ian, we've lost the AFCS and hydraulics, both secured," said Doug as he scanned the CAP. Then, "Mayday! Mayday! Mayday! Tricky Seven Three, nine miles to the south. We've taken rounds through the cockpit; we've also got some transmission problems. Mayday! Tricky Seven Three, contact, nine miles to the south."

'"Thanks Doug, can you keep an extra close eye on the transmission Ts and Ps? I'm going to try and maintain our speed and I think, because of the casualties, I'm going to push towards Bastion. If necessary, we'll land in clear desert, but only if we absolutely have to."

'The aircraft was shaking and handling like a pig without the stabilisation system, but I managed to keep her on track.

'Doug was following me through on the controls in case my injuries were worse than I first thought – at this stage, I didn't know how bad they were. I was covered in blood, but then even the tiniest head wound tends to bleed like a stuck pig. The left side of my face ached like a bitch, but I was still conscious and clear headed. The medics came into the gangway several times to examine me, but due to the fragile state of the cab and the fact I felt fine, I declined assistance. By now, we were clear of the Green Zone and just minutes out from Bastion, so I told them I'd accept treatment on the ground once we'd delivered the casualties.

'I landed the aircraft next to Nightingale HLS at 17:00 to keep the landing site clear and allow access by other call signs. Then I gave clearance for the ramp to be lowered and Paul Day then gave me a running commentary as the casualties were taken off. Aware that I wanted to shut down as soon as possible, both he and Tony assisted with the off-load. They let me know as soon as the ambulances were clear and I shut down. As I climbed out of the cockpit I was immediately supported by the medics who led me off the aircraft and onto an ambulance where I was taken to hospital. I needed twelve stitches in my head, new body armour to replace mine, which was completely soaked in blood, and a new helmet. My shot-up helmet now has pride of place in the Mess.

'The whole crew were brilliant in how they pulled together. In fact, there were several times where Doug, Paul and Tony all went above and beyond the call of duty. Doug's actions were well ahead of what you'd expect from someone on his first tour, working under the constant possibility of having to recover the aircraft alone. Paul and Tony also acted beyond expectations and put themselves in harm's way, assisting the medics and casualties, despite enemy fire landing close to them.

'This is a team I was proud to work with.'

39

ABOVE AND BEYOND THE CALL

Alex Townsend, who had been my co-pilot throughout the missions for which I received the DFC, was back out in theatre in 2010 as an experienced captain, and coming under fire himself. He later received a Queen's Commendation for Bravery (QCBA) and was given the Hugh Gordon-Burge Memorial Award by GAPAN for his actions on a number of sorties that he flew in February.

About three weeks earlier, on January 22nd, his cab took rounds when he was flying the IRT on a mission to pick up Rifleman Peter Aldridge of A Company, 4 Rifles who had been blown up by an IED while on patrol to the north of Sangin. Alex landed next to Peter's colleagues while they were engaged in a firefight, and just as Rifleman Aldridge was loaded, the cab was hit by several 7.62mm rounds, one of which Alex later picked up – it now lives in his room. The Apache providing escort for him was also hit, although none of the rounds hit vital systems or caused injury on either aircraft. Sadly, despite flying the cab at its limits to get back, Peter succumbed to his wounds and became the 250th British soldier to die on operations in Afghanistan.

The missions and events for which Alex received his QCBA occurred on February 13th 2010 – the sort of day where you'd rather have stayed in bed. I'll let Alex explain what happened . . .

'On the day in question, I was captain of the IRT. Waldo was my co-pilot, and in the back I had two very experienced crewmen – Daz Beattie, who had been with me since OCF, and Richie Burke. We were operating in support of Operation Moshtarak, the largest helicopter insert since Gulf War I, and were on five minutes' notice to move.

'We'd already responded to one call out and, shortly after getting back to the tent, were called out again at 10:10 to pick up a T1 and a T3, both with head injuries. They were British soldiers whose vehicle had driven over an IED in the Nadi Ali area, north-west of Lashkar Gah. Just after take-off, I saw a bird in our 12 o'clock that seemed to be doing its level best to commit suicide by helicopter. Whichever way I manoeuvred, it stayed on our nose and, like a rabbit caught in headlights, it stayed there until the inevitable happened; it impacted the windscreen directly in front of Waldo. Result: RAF one, Bird nil.

'Normally, we'd return after a bird strike to have the aircraft checked over properly but with a T1 waiting on us, I elected to carry on. After crossing the Green Zone, I descended to about 50ft and advised the Apache we'd be inbound for the LS in one minute. A few seconds later, we heard a loud explosion and suddenly, the NR decreased and I felt the cab descend. The N1, or compressor speed on the No.1 engine, dropped like a stone, followed by the N2, or turbine speed – both down to zero in under a second, indicating a catastrophic engine failure.

'The aircraft dropped below 40ft and the RadAlt alarm sounded, so I partially flared the cab to arrest the descent. As soon as I established we were in level flight, I turned the residual speed – around 150kts – to minimum power speed, which is about 70kts. This enabled me to turn away from the threat area around Nadi Ali and establish a track towards the Red Desert; if I had to crash-land, that would be the safest option – as far away from the Taliban as possible. Richie had a look at the engine and couldn't see any damage, so I decided its failure probably wasn't down to enemy action.

'Our biggest problem was that we were at ultra-low level, unable to climb, and we still had to cross the Green Zone, which is a very high-threat area. With an engine failure, there's usually no way you'd be able to maintain level flight in Afghanistan due to the heat and the altitude, but we were exceptionally lucky the engine failed earlier in the day when it was cooler. As air is denser when it's cool, you need less power. The worst thing was leaving the guys we'd been scrambled to pick up – that was truly gut-wrenching, probably the worst feeling I've had in Afghanistan. They were badly injured and relying on us but we had to abandon them, flying away to save the cab, and our own asses.

'First things first; I shut the engine down. Then I tried to radio ahead to Bastion – firstly, to let them know what had happened, and also so that Air Traffic could clear the area for our approach. Because we were so low, we couldn't establish comms with them. I didn't put out a Mayday call because I knew we could maintain level flight, so I broadcast a "Pan Pan Pan" distress call instead. I got a response from another aircraft in our vicinity and he relayed everything back to Bastion for me. The cab was really struggling because I was flying constantly between emergency power and maximum torque, so the remaining good engine was right on the limit of what it could do. I knew it was going to be a struggle to get above the wadi and across the Green Zone but I was confident we could do it – and we did.

'I landed on at Bastion with a running landing and taxied over to the engineers, where I shut down and signed the frame over to them. I then ordered them to strip the cab of the medical kit and I signed for a replacement cab. Then we went across the runway to the spare, lifted off and went to one of only two spare refuelling spots. Helicopters were two deep in some places, because of Op Moshtarak. It was while we were refuelling that we all noticed a strong smell of hydraulic fluid; it's got a pretty distinctive smell and Daz, to his credit, searched tirelessly for its source. He eventually found it in a control closet, just as we finished fuelling – one of the control actuators was leaking.

'That's serious enough that, on any other day, we'd immediately shut down in situ for the engineers to fix the leak – flying with it like that meant a high risk of fire. This, though, wasn't any other day. Because Op Moshtarak was going on, we'd effectively be leaving Bastion with only one refuelling point available, so I pulled power and flew at a low hover back to where I'd picked the cab up from. While the guys moved their kit and themselves off, I ran across the runway to sign the second cab back in and sign out a third cab, then ran back and we all got in that aircraft. We lifted to the refuelling spot and filled up and on this one, we experienced no problems. So having fuelled, I landed on near the engineers so we could get the MERT on board with all their kit.

'That took the best part of an hour and it was painfully frustrating, knowing there were casualties out there; although, thankfully, the US Pedro call signs had been scrambled to pick up our casualties from near Nadi Ali. We later learned the T1 survived, which was a massive relief.

'The engineers told us that the reason we lost the No.1 engine on the first cab was due to mechanical failure in its accessory gearbox. That is quite literally unheard of – something that, as far as we are aware, has never happened before. The accessory gearbox measures the power going into the engine – N1 – and the power coming out of it – N2. Something that simple and it could have caused us to go down. Had it happened an hour or two later in the day, we would probably have lost the aircraft, possibly the whole crew as well. That was a really sobering thought. We didn't have time to dwell though, and things were about to hot up for us when we responded to another call out at 12:47.

'We'd been called out for a T1, a British soldier who'd been shot in the neck between Nadi Ali and Marjah – a real No Man's Land. He was part of a recce team to the south of the Helmand River that was still engaged in an intense firefight with Taliban forces to the north, so our Apache escort told us to hold. I banked away and flew a holding pattern about five miles out, over the desert, so the Taliban wouldn't hear us and know we were coming.

'Looking at the map, I saw that our planned route in would take us directly over the enemy firing point to the north. That was an obvious no-no, so I decided to fly the long way round to our casualty, routing due south. I bugged the RadAlt at 10ft and, flying fast and low, used as many trees and compounds as I could find for cover – never the easiest thing to do in a Chinook!

'With the weight of fire the ground troops were taking, we were never going to have a completely secure LS. My thoughts were confirmed when the Apache pilot eventually said, "Look guys, it's really bad out there but it's only going to get worse so we're going to get you in now. You're clear in."

'That was pretty much a guarantee that we'd take fire on the way in, but there was nothing we could do. I flew directly over the point where Chomper was shot in the head two weeks earlier, so I told Richie to man the port Minigun because we'd be coming in with the enemy on that side. I flew in hard and fast, sticking the aircraft on its nose and booting the tail left and right to scrub off speed at the last second. I came in south of the ground troops with the ramp facing them and touched down as close as I dared to the casualty.

'The guys were off and on again with the casualty in quick order, but even while they were doing so the ground troops to my right were laying down a ferocious weight of fire to keep the Taliban's heads down. Despite this, they were still returning fire and Daz, who was on the starboard Minigun, said he had a clear firing solution. I said, "You're clear to engage," and he opened up and let them have it with a few long bursts from the Crowd Pleaser. I was flying from the right seat, right in the line of fire, so I told Waldo to follow me through on the controls in case I was hit, and as soon as the ramp came up, I pulled power and lifted.

'I transitioned away at 10ft as quick and as dirty as I could, with Daz laying down fire on the Minigun and Richie firing from the M60 on the ramp. That was no mean feat, because I was flying evasive manoeuvres and throwing the aircraft all over the sky, but it's testament to the professionalism of the guys and their training that they were able to keep firing on the targets. They both ranged in on the Taliban firing points and took them out, which was extraordinarily brilliant shooting by them both. I then flew away as fast and as low as I dared. As I departed the area, our Apache loosed off a couple of Hellfire AGM-114N enhanced-blast missiles at the compound where the remaining firing was coming from and it all went quiet, leaving the troops free to tab out a klick or so into a safe area. Thankfully, I got us back to Bastion and our T1 survived, which lifted everyone. It had been a tough mission, the codicil to a day from hell, but it was a mission with a positive outcome all round.'

40

AS IT HAPPENS

I had a great time working as an instructor on the OCF, but there was no ignoring the feeling that I was somehow missing out by being away from the cut and thrust of operational flying. Despite the satisfaction of regular flying and more civilised hours that I got from training the next intake of Chinook pilots, I missed being a part of 27 Squadron and all my friends on 'C' Flight.

By June 2010, I'd made my decision and set in train the events that led me back to the world I'd left after my 2008 Det. Nothing had changed – same friends, same faces and the same boss – but instead of being there as a training captain, I was now a QHI, meaning I could train, evaluate and sign-off other members of the Flight as training captains. I hit the ground running and went straight into the work-up for 'C' Flight's next tour of duty in Afghanistan. That's how I found myself on a TriStar bound for Helmand Province once again, when the Flight deployed there at the beginning of October 2010. What follows are extracts from the diaries I kept during that deployment . . .

OCTOBER 21ST, 2010

What a hard couple of days this has been. Can't say too much about the job that follows, but it had already been postponed once due to bad weather. Ended up launching a day later than planned. Saw a tornado in the middle of the desert on the way to this US marine base. Absolutely amazing! Anyway, landed in this base at

16:00. We'd spent the whole of the previous two weeks leading up to this mission, a major assault with British troops involving five Chinooks – one formation of two and a formation of three. I ended up as formation leader of the three cabs.

This operation involved more than 800 people in support. There was a US marine battalion of light armoured reconnaissance vehicles on the ground – basically 150 small tanks. Above us there were two Apaches, two Sea Kings with sensors, two A-10 Warthogs, two F-18s, one Compass Call Electronic Warfare Hercules, one Spectre, two Predators and two B-1B bombers; all that to support us. We inserted more than 130 troops.

Took off at 19:00 on one of the darkest nights I've ever flown in. Couldn't even see the ground from low level initially. That was tough, especially as we had to fly low in the Southern Afghan mountains.

We attacked a village next to the Pakistan border. The B-1 bomber dropped six tonnes of bombs on various targets around our landing sites ten minutes before we arrived. We saw the flashes and the massive explosions as 2,000lb bombs hit the ground. Then the A-10s, which have got the biggest air-to-surface gun ever built, strafed our LS three minutes before we landed to explode any IEDs that might have been planted. That was followed one minute later by the Apaches putting missiles in numerous buildings.

Needless to say, we didn't see even a hint of the enemy during the assault, thank fuck! We disappeared as quickly and stealthily as we arrived. Soon as we cleared the vicinity, the JTAC unleashed hell onto the target area and for thirty minutes jets, helicopters and bombers did his bidding and destroyed the target. Should emphasise that the grid had been observed for weeks and there were no women or children within a country mile. The only people there were all fighting-age males in what was identified as the Taliban's equivalent of Sandhurst. Great result: thirty-six KIA, loads of drugs destroyed and ten tonnes of explosives captured – enough to make 2,000 IEDs. Two senior Taliban were killed.

We extracted the troops tonight without any problems and flew back to KAF where it's now 05:00, so I feel fucked.

NOVEMBER 2ND, 2010

Passed my 2,000hrs on the Chinook yesterday. Not in the way I'd have liked though. Was on IRT for 24hrs. Relieved Gez Wyatt and his crew at 08:00, a process that entails us turning up at the back of the aircraft with all our kit at the same time the outgoing IRT crew gets all their kit on its ramp. Once we're all ready we quickly swap over in case we get a shout just as we're doing it. We then prepare the aircraft so it's ready to start at the press of a few buttons.

First shout was at 08:45. Received a radio call from the Watchkeeper: 'Do you know you have a shout?' We run the 400m to the aircraft, get dressed in body armour, panting and sweating. When the cab's turning and burning and the secure radio is online I call Ops requesting details.

Their response? 'Why are you up? There's no shout.'

Turns out someone got their wires crossed and called one of the many agencies for some details on something: 'No panic, there's no shout.' This person heard 'shout' and called everyone on line . . . wankers!

Next call was to pick up a British soldier suffering from appendicitis from a grid just south of Sangin. At that point I needed fifty minutes flying to achieve my 2,000hrs. We landed after forty minutes. I then had a total of 1,999 hrs and fifty minutes.

Next shout occurred at 13:00; airborne at 13:09. Told to go to Marjah, a nasty shithole. An American soldier had been shot and had a sucking chest wound. He was choking on blood and breathing with difficulty. I was in the left seat; Nobby was flying from the right. I was encouraging him to go as fast as he could with some colourful expressions:

'Whip that bitch!'

'Thrash the bastard!'

I wanted to get there yesterday. The cab was giving all she could but it wasn't as much as I wanted.

We had to wait for the Apache to establish comms. The Americans on the ground were struggling to answer our call. We were holding four miles west of Marjah. Had been waiting for ten minutes when called in. Again I encouraged Nobby to fly hard and make us a difficult target. Called for smoke and saw it.

Nobby slowed down for descent but it was too shy an approach so I took control to reduce our slow airtime by five seconds. Fuck, it was dusty! Gave the aircraft back to Nobby and off we went. She was giving all she had – thrashed her like a jockey does his horse. People commented on our speed of arrival at Bastion. Sadly, the young US soldier died before we reached Nightingale. That was me at 2,000hrs and twenty minutes. A milestone achieved in the worst way possible. One I won't forget.

Trained Pete Amstutz today; he had a tough day on IRT. Taliban attacked a school with grenades earlier. It only opened a few days ago. He had to medevac ten children aged between two and four. Six were critical, one dead. None of us could believe that human beings, especially ones claiming superiority to the West, could do such a thing. Evil, inhuman fuckers.

NOVEMBER 8TH, 2010

Tired today. Started work 20:00 yesterday, finished 10:00 this a.m. Had to lead another op that went superbly. Planned it so there were no radio calls between the cabs involved, everything was done on timing, which I'd worked out to the last second. It was literally military precision in action. Unbeknownst to me, full colonel in charge of aviation was watching our progress on the Predator feed. We hit the target dead on time, right down to the second. As he walked away he said, 'Well done guys, that was very slick!' I love it when a plan comes together like that. The boss was delighted.

Had some other good news. Looks like my report has made

the cut for the promotion board. I'll be one of 150 Flight Lieutenants scrutinised for potential promotion, one of two from 27 Squadron. The OC said there's a chance that even if I fail to make this year's, I'd be in good stead for next year. Am currently riding an 'A-', provided I don't fuck up. It means appearing twice on the board, but with those marks, plus my DFC, it should help towards promotion. We'll see; Strategic Defence Review ahead so nothing certain.

NOVEMBER 11TH, 2010

We get up at 06:50 to make morning brief at 07:30. Today we're on the IRT out of Bastion. Brief consists of Met for the day, summary of last 24hrs of ops and various contacts with enemy. Also an intelligence brief (which, to be fair, isn't!).

After, we drive to Safety Equipment Section to collect our aircrew flying gear (jacket with armour plates, emergency radios, survival bag). From there, drive to the armoury to draw our personal rifles and pistols. Then make our way to the aircraft where the previous IRT crew awaits eagerly to swap duties. They had busy 24hrs with three shouts. After aircraft handover we position all our flying gear and 'cock' the aircraft, so a minimum of button presses to start whenever we're scrambled.

Make our way back to IRT tent, which is kitted out to be as relaxing as possible between each very intense period of work. Put on *Gavin and Stacey* DVD, chill out, laughing out loud for two episodes. Halfway through the third episode, phone rings – we leap into action.

I grab the phone to get the details – a badly injured civilian in Lashkar Gah – while the rest of the crew run outside. I have to catch up over a 400m run across dirt tracks, between hangars and onto the pan to get to the back of the aircraft. Do quick walk-around, flicking two aerials at front as per my superstitious habit, while crew rush in and get ready. Meanwhile MERT and ground force protection arrive.

I jump in behind them and make my way to front. Fit my anti-fragment vest followed by armour-plated jacket, remove clip from my pistol to check, then reseat it and holster weapon on my chest. Slip my helmet on and jump in the left-hand seat; co-pilot is already in the right-hand seat, starting the engines. Once start-up's complete, we've all the details of the casualty along with his status and the grid. This one doesn't sound very good. From experience, I know there's little chance we'll get to him in time. Nonetheless we're ready in seven minutes and taxi out.

Area of Operation is busy today so our Apache escort's already overhead, engaging enemy. We route on our own, at height initially, to cross the most dangerous part out of reach of enemy small arms. Eventually descend to low level for final run into HLS. Land with no problems, but after a couple of minutes on the ground we're told the casualty was returned to the hospital as he's too unstable to travel by air. We read into this that he was on his last breaths; we've all seen it too often before. Depart Lash and return to Bastion without incident.

Once we shed our kit and re-cock the aircraft it's back to the tent. Pick up with *Gavin and Stacey* again. 14:39 and phone rings; airborne by 14:46. This time shout's for two casualties in Green Zone north of Nadi Ali. Both are children who walked on an IED laid by Taliban.

Pick-up area is crawling with enemy forces so I give crewmen orders regarding response to enemy fire – if they see a threat they've my authority to engage. Apache meets us overhead and comes down closely on our wing, bringing his formidable array of weapons to bear on anyone who might dare engage us. It works, as we don't take any fire. The landing is a difficult one in a tiny site with a lot of dust. Once it clears, stretcher-bearers approach from the front. The second has a blanket covering someone very small. Our hearts sink; we hate to pick up children. We're sent to a hospital thirty minutes south that is ready to receive both children for surgery.

We thrash the aircraft to get there as fast as possible. Struggle to get radio communication with destination airfield so I have to make a tough decision: make an unauthorised approach to an American airfield, or hold. Holding not an option due to condition of children, so continue approach parallel to a cargo plane on finals to the runway. Wonder what they thought of the British Chinook flying in formation with them. Finally US controller comes on frequency asking our intentions and he's quickly told. Doctor passes a piece of paper forward to me with casualty status to pass to hospital. I read and gulp: one seriously wounded eight-year-old male and a dead four-year-old girl. Land on hospital LS and unload casualties, waiting for the doctors to do their handover to the surgical team. Once everybody's onboard, we start a long and silent thirty-minute journey back to Bastion.

Back at the tent, we pick up with *Gavin and Stacey* but we're a lot more subdued. Laughter doesn't come so readily. 18:30 passes with no shouts so make our way to evening brief. Same as this morning's, except it's in the evening! That complete, make our way to dinner with the medics. Halfway through meal our radio crackles alerting us of another shout. We jump up, run through the canteen, climb in our wagons and drive like lunatics to the cab. This time it's a different ball game as it's night. Not night at home, with reflected light from 100,000 street lights, cultural lighting, light pollution. Night is night here, and even our NVGs, some of the most advanced military technology in existence, struggle to perform. Sometimes, the best science can offer isn't enough.

Again, we're airborne very quickly. I get initial casualty report over air. One eight-year-old involved in IED strike. No pulse, not breathing. On the way, informed artillery is firing in vicinity of our destination, so I negotiate around it and initiate descent through the darkness into black hole that is the low-level environment. We know the ground's there, but can't see it. Eventually mortar illumination shells are fired from destination enabling us to finally see some ground texture 100ft below us. On run in we get another radio call. There's a second casualty; the child's father. Once on the ground, only one casualty is brought to us. I radio ground call sign asking about second casualty already knowing the answer. The eight-year-old doesn't need evacuating as he passed away. We lift and rush back to Bastion. Once again an aircraft with twelve UK military personnel on board is deathly quiet on its return journey.

Once on the ground, we debrief some of the issues as a crew, I sign the aircraft which served us beautifully throughout the day and night back in, and we make our way to our beds praying for a quiet night. It happens. A relatively good night's sleep the only saving grace after another difficult day in Helmand.

41

DESTINY'S CHILD

Remember what Woodsy said to me in the immediate aftermath of my return to Bastion, following the attack on Black Cat Two Two? Meeting me off the cab with JP, he'd said, 'Don't worry Frenchie, lightning never strikes twice.' Yeah, right . . .

December 15th 2010 was never going to fill me with excitement. Offer most of us a choice of IRT or taskings, and nine times out of ten we'll take the IRT, thanks. On IRT, there's never a dull moment, and you feel like you're making a difference. It's dynamic and unpredictable – but there's always the prospect of riding your luck and avoiding fire. Taskings – sure, they're vital and important, but they just feel routine. And nothing ever happens on a tasking, does it?

It's 07:00 at Bastion. I've slept reasonably well for here (nobody ever sleeps well in theatre) and having showered, I dress in my uniform and walk out of the tent that's been my home for the past few weeks. I'm not overly excited about today's planned tasking, but there's a definite spring in my step as I think of home and our impending departure from theatre in just a couple of days' time. The harsh sunlight is blindingly bright after the darkness of the tent, and I squint as I turn left and walk the short distance along the Rola-Trac walkway towards the crew tent. Ah yes, the crew tent. I'm showing my age in Det terms – it's what used to be the IRT tent, but now serves as a rest area for aircrew before and after sorties. The widescreen TV is still there, along with a selection of newspapers, a console, games etc. And the coffee machine.

'Morning Waldo,' I say as I walk in. As per usual, Flt Lt Andrew 'Waldo' Waldron is early and already has the coffee machine on.

'Morning Frenchie! It's just brewed and ready to take out,' he replies, as he pours and hands me a cup. 'Cheers pal. Shall we?'

There's nothing better than walking across to the JOC to plan the day's formation, with a nice strong coffee. The JOC tent complex is a few steps across the dusty road that runs just outside the crew tent. We walk across to it, shortly followed by Master Aircrewman Mick 'Fryster' Fry and Flight Sergeant Dave Wray. The four of us are operating on task line one as formation lead for today's tasking. Our wingmen, Flt Lt Pete Amstutz and Flt Lt Doug 'Snoop Dog' Gardner, both appear a short time after.

Waldo has been my co-pilot on this Det for a few weeks now. I've had him doing most of the flying so that he can develop his flying skills in theatre and come out on our next Det as a Captain. It's what Nichol did with me on my first Det in 2006, and it's the best way to gain experience. Waldo's a very conscientious pilot, straight down the line, and he has a brilliant sense of humour. It's a pleasure being crewed with him.

I look at the tasking, which has not changed from the previous night; some kind of plan is already in my head. The J2/J3 (Intelligence/Current Ops) briefs confirm my ideas are viable.

There are two things that make our mission different. Whereas on all previous Dets, we've flown all but the most vital of our sorties by night, we're flying by day this time. Secondly, and perhaps most controversially, the threat assessment for all HLSs has been downgraded by the powers that be due to 'lack of enemy activity'. To my mind, this lack of activity reflects the quality of the tactics that we in the Chinook Force employ, rather than a lack of capability in the enemy's operation. The fact that we have previously flown to the most dangerous landing sites in the wee small hours of the morning to accomplish our taskings was largely down to the simple fact that there was less enemy activity then because Terry Taliban was sound asleep.

The effect of this downgrading means that sites that were previously designated as safe at night only are now allowed by day. We are told to mitigate the risk so that we don't fly after 08:30, as the enemy might be up then. Ah yes, that'll be because Terry Taliban uses an alarm clock that's set for 08:00. Personally, I'd bet that he gets up when the sun comes up, but what do I know? All we do is cross the wire and face the dangers on a daily basis, whereas the people who come up with these great ideas fly desks instead of cabs and rarely leave their tents.

The changes have had one other major effect: on some sites, where previously we could only fly with an Apache escort, we can now fly as a pair with two Chinooks providing mutual support for one another. The threat isn't deemed high enough to warrant wasting Apache hours on escorts. Some said that was fair enough, an opinion that events would soon prove wrong, warranting a U-turn of policy.

The plan for the day will see both us and our wingman taking underslung loads (USLs) to FOB Kalaang on the southern patrol base line in Nadi Ali South. Following that, there's a troop move from Bastion to PB3 and PB2 for a single cab, which Pete and Snoop will undertake while we provide mutual support. Then we'll fly to a grid 3km south-east of PB3, where we will drop off a USL of helium gas bottles. From there we'll recover to Bastion, where we'll pick up a whole lot of our colleagues and fly them to KAF, their last stop before flying home. These guys are surplus and need to be out of the way as space is limited at Bastion. This is the end of our tour and 27 'A' Flight have started to replace us.

FOB Kalaang is a site that, had we been flying yesterday, we'd have visited by night only. PB2 and PB3 are both locations that we've previously only flown to under escort by the Apache, and the grid we are to deliver the helium bottles to is right in the middle of the Green Zone – again, not a place we'd normally fly to at midday. Still, we can only play with the hand we're dealt; it's time to brief the crew. . .

'Right Pete, for Kalaang we'll approach from the west with a small split, where we'll drop each load one after the other so that we don't expose ourselves too long in the area. For PB2 and PB3, I'll remain in the overhead at FL60 2km to the west; you'll run in from the NW to PB3 and then direct north to PB2. You then go back to Bastion, I'll complete this other job with the Lynx and we'll meet up at Bastion to transit back to KAF with our engineers and aircrew. Happy?'

It's all good, so I carry on with the rest of the brief, covering admin points for the formation, Rules of Engagement, emergencies, frequencies etc. Everyone happy, we walk out to the cabs, spin up and hover-taxi to the load park where we collect our USLs.

'Bastion Tower, Ultimate Two One Flight, formation consisting of Ultimate Two One and Ultimate Two Two. Four POB on each, ready for departure from load park through HALS 19, no southern cross required.'

'Ultimate Two One Flight, Bastion Tower, clear for take-off load park, wind is two-two-zero at seven knots.'

'Ultimate Two One Flight clear for take-off load park,' I call.

Waldo already has us in the hover, our four-and-a-half-tonne load of food and ammo destined for Kalaang hanging like a pendulum from the centre hook on the cab's belly. He gently transitions forward as I scan the engine instruments and monitor the increase in temperature caused by the additional power required to accommodate the weight of the load; it's vital we stay within limits. Everything looks good, so he accelerates smoothly from the load park, turns right and flies down the HALS heading south.

Our Apache escort for the first run is already ahead of us, where he has established comms with the unit receiving our load at Kalaang.

'Ugly Five One, Ultimate Two One Flight, inbound Kalaang in figures ten, request HLS brief.'

'Ultimate Two One Flight, HLS is clear and secure. Route west to west initially with a right-hand turn to the south on short finals.'

It goes like a dream; we're in and out with no problems. It's on the way back to Bastion that my ears suddenly prick up as I hear the Apache talking to a JTAC on the ground saying, 'Yeah, Widow Six Three, Ugly Five One, can you confirm the grid for the small arms fire at the Chinook?'

I look at Waldo. 'Fucking great. So much for their "08:30 will be safe" bollocks.'

'Ugly Five One, Widow Six Three, both call signs were engaged on the way in and out by bursts of SAFIRE, we think 2km north-west our location.'

'Widow Six Three, that's copied. We'll investigate now.'

'Don't you just love taking fire first thing in the morning?' asks Mick.

We land on at Bastion for a suck of gas and pick up our three-tonne load of helium bottles in a USL net, while Pete and Doug collect their pax from the passenger handling facility. In a replay of our earlier lift, Waldo transitions away from Bastion to the south, this time turning south-east and heading towards PB3.

We climb and I establish comms with the JTAC controlling PB3 to get his HLS brief and instructions, while Pete and Doug maintain low level and take a longer route. This is to ensure their arrival coincides with the end of my call to the JTAC, so I can relay the details to Pete before he immerses himself in the 'low-level, dirty dash, initial point to target run.' As he starts his run in, we follow at height to ensure his safety.

It's paramount that responsibility for providing cover to Pete's cab is passed from Mick to Dave and back again whenever each one reaches the limit of his lookout and arc of fire. Pete's aircraft will remain in sight at all times and it's technically a very difficult exercise in CRM; however, not for this crew. We've been together in theatre for almost two months by now, so it's all well rehearsed.

Suddenly my radio crackles.

'Ultimate Two One, Widow Six Five, your wingman Ultimate Two Two is taking SAFIRE north-west of our location. Multiple firing points.'

I relay the message but Pete has already heard and taken evasive action. He makes it into PB3 without getting hit, where he unloads one lot of pax and collects another for the sortie to PB2.

I wonder how we're going to get out of this. Pete has two options – he can carry on to PB2 or cancel the serial, but even if he does that, he still has to fly through the contact zone to get out.

I have an idea. I know that Apaches are regularly in the area providing air support for ground units so I throw it open . . .

'Any Ugly call sign, this is Ultimate Two One.' I wait for a few seconds and I'm rewarded with a response.

'Ultimate Two One, Ugly Five Three, pass message.' Result!

'Ugly Five Three, Ultimate Two One formation, flight of two consisting of Ultimate Two One currently in the overhead at PB3 and Ultimate Two Two at PB3. Two Two was contacted between PB2 and PB3. Request assistance and escort from PB3 to PB2 if you have the fuel to ensure his protection.'

'Ugly Five Three, that's no problem. Your location in figures five.'

I call Pete to give him a heads up, 'Ultimate Two Two from Two One, I have Ugly Five Three inbound in five minutes to provide you with escort for the next serial if you are happy to continue.' Of course, Pete's more than happy. Sorted!

Ugly Five Three arrives on station just as Pete's ready to lift and bizarrely that's when the contact stops. Cheeky fuckers are happy to take us on when we're by ourselves but they're not so brave when the extra muscle turns up. Pete flies on to PB2 without trouble and completes his mission, although I'm not happy – that all-too-familiar feeling returns, as the hairs on the back of my neck stand up and I sense that we're not out of the woods yet. That's twice we've been under enemy fire now in the space of just an hour and a half.

I push the sense of impending trouble to the back of my mind – there's nothing I can do and we still have to deliver our USL. Waldo flies us across the Green Zone at 3,000ft and we position to the east of the Helmand River to start our run in to target.

'Frenchie, do you fancy flying this one?' asks Waldo. 'I've flown it all day yesterday and today.'

'Are you sure?' I ask, trying my level best not to push him too much the other way in case he changes his mind. I want to get some stick time; I've missed handling.

'Sure, take it. You have control.'

'I have control, thanks Bud. Right, next pre-landers and hook checks please.'

Waldo runs through the pre-landing checks to prepare the cab for the drop-off while we're still at height, meaning we won't need to do it in the more dangerous environment at low level where we'll likely need all our concentration.

I gently manoeuvre the aircraft down from 3,000ft approximately two miles east of the Helmand Desert, giving us approximately five miles to run in at low level.

Waldo talks me on to target, giving me the headings I need, pointing out features on the ground and counting down to the HLS. Meanwhile, Dave Wray has his head in the hatch looking at the load while giving me regular updates on its behaviour, which is different at speed and in the higher-density air at low level. Mick Fry stands sentinel on the starboard Crowd Pleaser. All the crew are working in unison, each of us engaged in a different task, all of which are vital to the success of the mission. Remove just one of us and it all goes tits up.

'Three miles to run,' calls Waldo as I descend over the wadi on the eastern bank of the Helmand River.

'How can somewhere so pretty be so shit?' I ask myself.

We cross the river. 'Two miles to go, 12 o'clock, you should be visual with the grid on the nose.' Good, I'm on target. My spine is tingling for some reason. I remember this feeling . . .

'One and a half miles to go,' calls Waldo, as we start to cross the Green Zone with its abundant crops, trees and compounds – all of which provide boundless cover for Taliban forces.

Straight ahead, I see a motorbike. It's stationary and I see two fighting-age males dressed all in black looking at us; no sign of weapons though. The tingling sensation increases; all my senses are on overdrive. I put my thumb over the USL release switch on the cyclic just in case. We fly over the motorbike.

BANG! BANG! BANG! BANG!

'Fucking hell,' shouts Waldo.

'What the fuck was that?' asks Mick, sticking his head in the cockpit.

BANG!

Almost simultaneously, there's a huge explosion just outside the port door, which caves in under the force of some kind of blast, shards of paint and metal hitting Waldo and Mick in the face. The aircraft lurches to the right.

'Fuck! Fuck! Fuck!' I think. 'Not again.'

I throw the cyclic hard left and hit the USL release button; immediately, the load pings away and becomes a dumb bomb, falling to earth and who gives a fuck where it lands. My only priority is the cab and my crew; I need lightness and manoeuvrability.

I hear Waldo on the radio: 'CONTACT, CONTACT, Ultimate Two One, small arms hit 3km south-east of PB3. Turning east. Wait out.' Good lad, I didn't even have to prompt him. In fact, I couldn't have done it myself – I have problems of my own to deal with.

'Shit, we've lost an engine!' I say as I watch the N2 drop like a stone. I look at the torque. 'What the fuck? Shit, we've lost both . . .' This all happens in a millisecond. 'Hang on, we're still flying, we still have power. Fuck it, turning left,' I say, manoeuvring out of the engagement zone and shrinking in my seat to make myself as small a target as possible. The lead's flying and I don't want to get hit.

We take another round in the engine.

I get the aircraft to the eastern edge of the Helmand River and we're still flying. I pull power to get further away from the enemy. Height is safety. 'Right, time to assess what's going on,' I say to myself.

I'm struggling. Nothing makes sense. We've taken rounds, that much I know; an RPG has exploded outside the port door; we have no torque on either engine, which indicates how hard the engine transmission is working. I scan the engine instruments checking the Ts and Ps. We've got an N1 reading for both engines, meaning there's power going in, but the N2, which measures power coming out, reads zero for the No.1 engine, meaning its turbine isn't turning. What the fuck? It doesn't make sense.

All the pressures on the five gearboxes are showing zero PSI, but the caution advisory panel is clear; there are no warnings for low pressure in any of the gearboxes. The fuel gauge is showing

9,900 – the needle's spinning like my bedroom after a night on the lash. Bollocks! I can't even tell if we have a fuel leak. The list goes on . . .

I need to get a grip; first things first. 'Guys, check yourselves. Are we all ok?' They all check in with no injuries reported. 'Okay, let's have a look outside to ensure we're not pissing fuel.' Both Mick and Dave look and confirm we're not. I explain what we've got at the front. Everyone is baffled, but we all concur that some of the malfunctions must be gauges or sensors affected by whatever hit us.

'All the forward hatches have been blown open by something,' says Mick.

'There's an increase in vibration in the back,' Dave reports.

I make a decision. 'Okay guys, I'm going to fly us north so we pass FOB Price and if the aircraft's still flying nicely, we'll push on to Bastion. I'm loath to land at Price because the logistics for repairing the cab are going to be a nightmare. If it comes to it, the area between Price and Bastion is benign enough for us to land on. Happy?' They are.

We're still flying level so I decide against calling 'Mayday!' I make the next call: 'Pan Pan, Pan Pan, Pan Pan, Bastion Tower, Ultimate Two One, Pan Pan.'

'Ultimate Two One, Bastion Tower, Pan acknowledged, pass your message.'

'Pan, Ultimate Two One, CH47 with four POB eight miles east. We have taken multiple hits with multiple system failures. She seems to fly okay but many of our instruments have been knocked out. Request HALS 19 and Runway 19 if we can't make it to the HALS. Request emergency services.'

'Ultimate Two One, Bastion Tower, all copied. Let us know if we can be of further assistance.' How nice to deal with somebody who understands not to ask too many questions; someone who isn't trying to get in our cockpit, who knows implicitly we are running at maximum capacity.

'Ultimate Two One, Bastion Tower. All air traffic held; you have priority on the approach. Good luck.'

Despite the vibration, the lack of functioning instruments and the damage and destruction caused in the attack, ZH891 holds out and responds to my every input as I fly us to the HALS, performing a precautionary running landing. As in any Hollywood airport disaster movie, fire engines follow us until we come to a halt. I taxi the aircraft to the nearest parking slot and stop.

'Ultimate Two One, Bastion Tower. For your information, there is a suspected IED at the PHF, request you move further up.'

I look to my left and see a line of Hesco blast walls, another Chinook, another blast wall and then the PHF.

'Bastion Tower, Ultimate Two One. Passed the point of caring, shutting down. Thanks for your help.'

And we shut down. We are flying in the same area again tomorrow – at night! I can hardly contain my enthusiasm.

EPILOGUE

We were supposed to be flying home on the 17th, but the weather in the UK that saw Heathrow, Gatwick and countless other airports buried under a mountain of snow, and the coldest December for 300 years, also affected those of us stuck in the sandbox. The TriStar that was supposed to fly out from Brize Norton to pick us up stayed where it was, with the knock-on effect that we also stayed where we were. The homecoming curse that had somehow managed to blight every single one of my previous Dets returned with a vengeance!

Eventually, the greatest minds in the MoD and RAF conferred and a way was found for them to snatch defeat from the jaws of victory – instead of arriving back in England on the 18th, we got back to a wintery white RAF Odiham late in the afternoon of the 22nd – just in time for Christmas, but minus our luggage. I don't think I've ever been so pleased to see Ali and the kids.

Not long after Christmas, I called into work and found a report on my desk detailing the conclusions from the inspection of ZH891. Among its findings, I learned that we'd taken a 7.62mm round through the nose of the aircraft, which narrowly missed Waldo's leg and lodged itself in the instrument panel. On its way, it severed thirty-six wires leading from various instruments, hence the bizarre and inexplicable readings we received.

The round that missed Waldo's leg was to prove lucky for us all; although it severed the wires leading to the engine instruments and others, they proved its undoing, as the loom stopped the round in its tracks. When the trajectory was worked out, it was discovered that had it carried on travelling, the round would have lodged itself in the control closet where all the aircraft controls are situated. I prefer not to think about the implications of that particular scenario.

Another round hit the area where Dave Wray should have been sitting, had he not been busy looking at the USL. And as I manoeuvred away, another one went through the engine mount from behind, embedding itself in the mouth of the engine. I've no idea how, but – miraculously – it wasn't ingested into the engine itself. Had it been, it would more than likely have resulted in a fire. Ordinarily, that wouldn't necessarily prove particularly troubling, except for the fact that among the thirty-six wires severed by the round hitting the wiring loom were those controlling the fire extinguisher and fuel shut-off valve.

Several other rounds hit the cab, but none of them caused anything more than holes in the fuselage.

Luck seemed to be with all of us that day, but none more so than Mick Fry. The RPG that detonated next to the aircraft caused the port door to cave in, burn marks to the side of the aircraft and shrapnel that tore through the root of one of the blades on the aft head. It exploded at the precise moment Mick stuck his head into the cockpit. Had he stayed where he was, he'd have taken the full impact of the explosion and would almost certainly have died.

The aphorism 'lightning never strikes twice' isn't meant to be interpreted literally and I guess I'm living proof of the phrase's fallibility. For me, lightning did strike twice. Am I charmed? I don't know. I have my superstitions, but I'm smart enough to be a pilot, so I know at a fundamental level that they make no difference. Is life trying to tell me something? Or have I simply been in the wrong place at the wrong time too many times now? Whatever the reasons, I feel like the luckiest man on earth because, against the odds, I'm still alive. I'm still able to be a husband to Alison, and a loving dad to Guy and Max, our two gorgeous sons. I'm still able to walk my two dogs. And I'm still here to tell my story, which has hopefully shone a light on the valuable work done by the Support Helicopter Force.

I know that everyone reading this book will have their own opinions on the war in Afghanistan, but whether you're for it, against it, or you simply don't know, never doubt that every serving member of the Forces engaged in the war is putting their life on the line every day and you've no idea how proud I am to say that I'm one of them.

All of us who serve in theatre have our own reasons for doing so, and while some people might regard what those of us in the Chinook Force do as dangerous, it pales into insignificance compared with what the guys and girls living in the FOBs and PBs face every minute of every day. For me, and for all my fellow pilots at RAF Odiham, however much we enjoy flying and feel privileged to do what we do, those on the front line are the reason we take risks.

On my last deployment, there was one two-week period where eleven British troops survived who, given their injuries, should be dead. The fact they survived is down to two things – the existence of the MERT and the ability of front line medics. It's thought that in total, we've rescued well over 1,500 casualties in Afghanistan. The fact we're prepared to fly in under fire to get the wounded out, and the fact that the MERT's surgeons, paramedics and nurses take the risks they do, means all those soldiers we've recovered are still able to be dads to their kids, husbands to their wives, and sons to their mothers and fathers. What more reason do we need?

None of us knows what the future holds, but as long as I have the ability to do so, I'll be flying and living my dream. Sadly, I've learned the hard way not to look too far ahead, because we never know what tomorrow brings. My philosophy now is just to get on with today and let tomorrow take care of itself.

Finally, this is from all of us in the Chinook Force to the guys and girls on the ground in one of the most hostile environments on this planet. In your hour of need, however desperate you may be, fear not because we will come and get you.

POSTSCRIPT

When I wrote the original edition of this book in 2011, I selected from my logbook only those sorties and missions that I thought best illustrated a typical tour. Now, for this edition, I'm able to talk in detail about something that happened on the deployment that I describe in the epilogue. Senior officers have now decided that what we did on that fateful night is worthy of official recognition. That recognition saw the first ever award of an Air Force Cross to an Army Air Corps pilot on operations in Afghanistan – Captain Steve Jones – who flew our 2nd Apache escort. I was also awarded an Air Force Cross for the actions I detail in the diary entry that follows . . .

CAMP BASTION, DECEMBER 4TH, 2010

The weather took a turn for the worse today. The wind is routing all the way round Helmand and as it travels it gathers dust, creating brownouts that obscure and mask everything. The dust storms are the worst I've ever experienced here and visibility is down to just 500 metres. I'm on IRT, which is the only type of mission allowed in such low visibility; all other taskings have been cancelled as the weather is deemed too risky for any flights that aren't about saving lives.

At 12:30 we get a shout. We depart towards a grid about fifteen miles east-south-east of Bastion. The casualty is a six-year-old boy who has been shot in the abdomen.

With the sun behind us, visibility is about 1000 metres; with it ahead of us, it's down to as low as 500 metres. I manoeuvre so that my run-in places the sun behind us. I haven't got a clue where I am or where I'm going; I can only see as far as three fields ahead. Suddenly, out of the gloom appear the two masts of Patrol Base 2. They pass by on the starboard side, way too close for comfort. I have to manoeuvre the aircraft harshly to avoid two compounds as the HLS is surrounded by woods and the wind is coming from behind. I slam the aircraft on the deck bang in the middle of what would be considered a confined area in the UK, thus requiring at least two orbits to get in. That makes me smile.

The JTAC informs us that fighting is going on one hundred metres south of our position; that wipes the smile from my face. The little boy is loaded and we're off back to Bastion. The aircraft gives 160 knots, its max allowable speed; if I could fly faster I would but I'm using all available power. When we get to the airfield it's difficult to see the runway or the tower until we are on top of them. Some of 1310Flt are on the ground as I fly through the base like a hooligan to get the kid to the hospital asap. They later tell me it looked good!

According to the nurse in the MERT, the kid will be okay. He was nicely sedated and the wound was clean but still, a six-year-old should never be involved in this shit. We head back to the tent and chill out by watching a movie. I pray we won't get scrambled tonight as the visibility is going to fall even further – there's no moon and no cultural lighting so it'll be red illume. With no ambient light to amplify, NVGs are useless in these conditions.

I speak to Neil, the pilot of Ugly Five Zero, our Apache escort for this shift, and we discuss tactics should we be called out after dark. The solution is crazy but it's the only way – flying in close formation so that I can hang on to the AH's tail lights while he flies using his cab's FLIR (Forward Looking Infrared). The Apache's 36-times magnification FLIR camera can see over 2000 metres through the dust; it's not perfect but it's better than my Mk.1 Human Eyeball, which sees nothing in these conditions. My prayers go unanswered; we're called out to Sangin at 19:20 to an

ISAF soldier who's been shot in the stomach. As we lift all I can see are the AH's position lights, but even that's hit and miss and, when I'm flying just 30 metres from Neil's aircraft, I lose sight of it. I get him to switch from infrared lighting to normal position lights on. I can see him again. I can't see the ground, I can't see the horizon, all I can do is try to keep the Apache's lights in the same position in my windscreen. Later, the engineers tell me that when we lifted, they lost sight of our cab just 50 metres from their hangar – that with the cab lit up like a Christmas tree.

We transit at 400 feet above ground but it's so dark I can't even tell how close we are to the Apache. I ask Neil to advise me of the range between my aircraft and his using the AH's radar and when he tells me, I'm shocked. I think I'm close but I'm 500 metres away; I think I'm way back but I'm 30 metres aft. Not ideal when our wings are rotating at 400mph on each aircraft; the idea of what would happen if we touched each others' wings is unthinkable. My brain can't handle the lack of detail – it invents things instead, and I get all sorts of visual illusions. I think he's slowing down when he's moving away, so I end up flying very slowly, which is dangerous and makes control of the aircraft more difficult.

It only takes 30 minutes to approach Sangin but it feels like 30 hours. Neil has arranged for infrared mortar rounds to be fired from the PB to give us some illumination; it should provide enough light for our NVGs to perceive, but it's so dark that even with this mortar illume we can't see the ground. It's so desperate that I request that the camp turns all vehicle lights on. I start the descent following Neil on the way down. Through 400ft, no sign of the ground. 350, 300, 250, 200, 175 . . . I can see some faint light ahead, but there's still no sign of the ground. As we pass through 150ft I am just able to see some water reflection in the light from the IR mortar.

I manage to control the aircraft in a slow hover-taxi even though the disorientation is total and I can't see how fast we're moving across the ground. I continue low and slow and, eventually, I find the camp, skip over the fence and land on. We wait for the casualty to be loaded. 'Phew!' Mick Fry, my No.1 crewman, says. 'You know, Frenchie, I'll always back you but I think this time we found the edge of the envelope!'

Even as the casualty is loaded the radio alerts us to another. An ISAF soldier has been wounded by an IED at a grid atop a hill about two miles west of the wadi; he's taken shrapnel to his face and is in danger of losing his eyesight. I ask the boys if they're happy for us to have a go and they agree. Neil talks to the JTAC to try to organise an infrared fire mission to help guide us in, but five minutes later we're still waiting. Time's ticking on and I'm aware of the impact on our current casualty. I tell Neil to give the JTAC one more minute to sort it, and then one way or the other we'll have to leave. The minute elapses, plus another 45 seconds . . . no news. I lift and advise that we're departing to Bastion.

As I key the mike, the IR mortar arches across the sky and lights up the wadi. I tell Waldo, my co-pilot, to amend the GPS to the new target. The visual cues are terrible, utterly disorientating even with the mortar illumination. The ground is getting steeper ahead. The RadAlt is bugged to 180ft so I have some margin. We're 0.7 miles off the target and right at the edge of the illumination – I can't see anything past 100 metres.

Suddenly the RadAlt shows us rapidly descending; we go through 80ft, the alarm sounds and I see the ground coming up fast. We go through 70ft: Waldo's screaming 'Pull up!' but even as he says it, I've already yanked the collective and I'm applying 120% of power available, well into the engines' limit. The aircraft lurches up and we get away with it.

I'm not doing this again; the visibility is far too low. The normal limit for flying is a significant amount north of 1500 metres and we are flying through 150 metres. I abort the pick-up and climb to 1000ft, routing directly to Bastion. I call ahead to arrange an ambulance to be waiting on the main runway in case we can't make it to Nightingale and have to use the runway lights to land on – the NVGs can see light through dust or cloud from over 2000 metres.

Even so, it's a difficult landing as it's very dark in the middle of the lit area, with no ground texture visible. It gives the impression that we're descending into a black hole so I have no idea what the wheels are going to land on. Somehow, we get down and with the casualty off, I reposition to the helicopter ramp to refuel. While we're doing this, I listen to a radio conversation between base and Neil in the Apache; they want us to fly to another FOB for another casualty. The Lieutenant Colonel commanding JHF (A) comes on the radio and asks me for my thoughts. I take a deep breath and tell him to 'Wait, out.' I need to talk to the crew.

We are all in shock after our last sortie. I'm shaking, adrenaline coursing through my veins. I need to find something for the crew to hang on to, something that would make the return different from earlier, make it safer. I know FOB Edinburgh can fire 155mm shells that provide sunlight-like illumination. If they do that, I think we should be able to get in. I advise the CO over the net; he says he'll look into it and let me know. I taxi back and hold, turning and burning so we're ready when the launch release is given. While parked I talk to Neil to refine the technique for getting into the site.

Ten minutes later, we're told to shut down; the Brigadier has decided that the casualty should be moved to Sangin. Someone obviously thinks that as we've proven we can get in there, it'll be safer to make the pick-up from there. It's all relative though – it's still going to be a nightmare sortie to fly. I preferred the previous idea of FOB Edinburgh firing 155mm shells. Still, this way, at least we have time to get some dinner.

After we eat, I stop by the Apache crew tent. Neil's gone off shift, so I want to brief the new crew on what tactics we're going to use. Turns out that the new crew includes Captain Steve Jones, a guy I've enjoyed working with throughout this Det – we have some good banter going, which helps to boost the crew's confidence.

When we set off again, conditions have deteriorated and the visibility is even worse. However, I've a frame of reference now so I have some idea of what to expect – and I'm more than aware of all the disorientating tricks my mind might play on me. The transit is easy enough and we get to our initial point, NW of Sangin, to start the run in to the PB over the low wadi.

I know it's there but I just can't see it. Steve calls that he is turning on heading 130, and I accelerate the aircraft as I'm on the outside of the turn. I need to remain within two to three spans of his Apache just to stay visual with him – any further and I'll lose him. It's difficult enough at two wingspans – all I have to refer to are two very dim lights on his cab but if I lose him, that's it. We're on our own and will somehow have to avoid hitting him in the dark. It works, though – I make the turn, and stay with him. Steve calls from the mortar illumination at that moment to provide us with the required illumination for the approach.

He calls to say he's descending; we are five miles out, still at 80 knots. This is the difficult bit – I must not let the rate of descent increase too much, as we are close to the ground. I mustn't be too slow; he would disappear in the darkness below me. Still no mortar illumination. It is very dark, the ground is close and I am getting tense. Suddenly I hear Steve calling 'We've overshot.' I'm still not visual with the camp, even as he makes the call. I just can't conceive of how the visibility could be so bad that the camp's lights wouldn't be shining through, but this time we are operating without the artificial infrared light that we so badly need. I trust Steve and his cab's FLIR to keep us high enough that we don't hit the ground but it's tough when you can't see it.

I look right and notice that Steve's Apache is really close to us, so I turn left by twenty degrees to increase the separation. When I look again, though, he is closer still. This induces something in me called 'the leans', which can occur when you have no visual reference for the horizon; without it, the balance organs in my ear tell me that I'm turning right, even though I know I'm turning left. I feel as if I'm falling out of my seat, so I concentrate on the head-up display in my NVG monocle and my visual reference to the artificial horizon clears the problem.

I look right again and despite my turn to the left, Steve is closer still – there can't be more than one span between us! I call him over the radio: 'Check your heading mate!' and he corrects. It turns out that when he saw some lights pass under his aircraft, he thought they had overshot Sangin, got disorientated, looked down at them and up again, and he got the leans too, which caused him to turn to the left because it felt straight and level to him.

While all this is going on I see some faint lights ahead. We pass through 200ft and we're still not visual with the ground, so I move ahead of Steve's Apache and call visual with what appears to be the camp, intending to make the approach. At 100ft, I finally get eyes on the ground and that's when I realise that the lights aren't those of the landing site! I notice a flag painted on the wall ahead bearing the symbol of the Afghan National Police. We are hovering just outside the door of Sangin's Police Station!

I check the GPS and realise that we're east of where we should be and instead of being over the PB at Sangin, we're just south of a place called Wombat Wood, which was a favourite firing point for the Taliban. There we are in the hover just 20 feet over one of the most dangerous places in Helmand Province! Realising this, I quickly get my bearings, crosscheck with the GPS and hover-taxi the last half mile to the camp, where I once again hop us over the fence and on to the LS where the casualty is promptly loaded on board.

That done, the return flight to Bastion was uneventful, except for us not seeing the runway lights on approach until even later than on our previous sortie because the visibility had deteriorated so much; in fact, as we landed we heard an ISAF crew take off and then request an immediate recovery as conditions were just too bad for them to fly in.

The events of that night proved a salutary lesson for all of us in the crew – that out here, you don't always have to face the enemy to find yourself confronting fear. The weather we faced was sufficiently bad that it saw all other flights grounded, so I suppose the obvious question is: was it worth the risk in us being deployed? So far as we were all concerned, the answer has to be yes. Us fighting our way through the gloom meant that a six-year-old child was treated quickly, and survived; the ISAF soldier we picked up would have died had we not got to him when we did, and the other ISAF soldier we hooked up kept his eyesight. Against that backdrop, it was worth it all and more.

I found out about the award of my AFC on September 29th, 2011, while on another deployment to Afghanistan. It came when I had sixty days of flying behind me, with just nine left until the end of a tour that would see me having spent a total of fourteen months of my life on high-intensity combat ops in Helmand Province. That was a pretty high-tempo deployment – the previous twelve days had seen me flying back-to-back sorties.

There were several standout incidents on that tour, which began with us taking rounds again on a sortie in our first week in theatre; a round passed through the rear cabin and just missed a passenger's head, embedding itself right in the edge of the ballistic protection panel. She didn't even wake up. Then soon after, one of my mates was shot down when his Chinook was hit by several rounds of 7.62mm – some went through the AFCS and engine, which lost all of its oil, and one of the force protection guys in the back took a round through his shoulder, so they put down about six miles short of Bastion. We were coming off duty and I'd just signed my aircraft back in as this was unfolding so I heard it all over the radio. I shouted to my crew to grab their kit and get back on board and one of my crewmen grabbed his rifle so quickly that it hit him in the face, cutting him. We were airborne within four minutes and I hadn't even signed the aircraft out. I landed next to the stricken Chinook just after a Merlin had lifted some of the passengers, so I hooked up those still remaining, together with the crew, and brought them all back to Bastion. The aircraft was later recovered by engineers and repaired, but I digress . . .

I was woken unexpectedly at 22:30 on the evening of September 29th by Sergeant Stuart Thorlby-Coy, who'd been one of my crewmen on that sortie of December 4th, 2010. He told me that the OC JHFA wanted to see me. As I swam up through the folds of the sort of deep sleep you only experience in theatre after a busy day of flying, my mind was racing ahead; what on earth could the OC want with me?

The only thing I could think of had occurred the previous day when I'd been flying the IRT. We'd been scrambled to pick up an ISAF solider near Gereshk, a T2 who was the only surviving member of a four-man team that had been hit in a mine strike. He was concussed and suffering some minor shrapnel wounds, but other than that had escaped unscathed. Icom chatter indicated that there was a good chance we'd be engaged on departure, and as I lifted with the casualty on board, one of my loadies opened up with the Minigun and fired at the areas where the enemy were located. The two firers rushed their shot and loosed off an RPG that missed us by a whisker, passing by the right-hand side of the cab.

That incident aside, I honestly couldn't think of any other reason why I'd been woken and summoned to see the OC of JHFA, so it was with a heavy heart that I made my way to the JOC. I was soon put right though; as soon as he saw me, he smiled and said, without any preamble, 'Frenchie, congratulations, you've been awarded the AFC for your actions on 4 December 2010.'

I have to say, it was the absolute last thing I expected and it took my breath away. Getting the DFC in 2009 had been the biggest thing in my career so far, but now an AFC? I was in a state of disbelief; I just couldn't take it all in. My response isn't likely to go down in squadron history as memorable though – the only words to escape my lips were a rather unoriginal 'Fuck, sir!'

He told me that I'd have to keep it quiet, at least until the official announcement the following day, when the operational honours would be announced by the MoD to the media. There was one person I had to tell though: I called Ali to give her the news. She was as speechless as I had been. I saw Stuart T-C as I headed back to my tent, so I told him too – he was dead chuffed.

The news came out the following day and I was very moved by some of the comments made by friends and colleagues. Mick Fry was in the UK and wrote a message to me on Facebook. He said,

Only four people know the magnitude of what went on that evening, and I am sure they will agree with what I have written below . . .

For having vision, but no visibility,
For knowing the difference between utility and futility,
For saying yes when others said no,
For saying no when others said yes,
For exploring the envelope, but staying within it,

For all these things, your AFC is very much deserved and I salute you.

For not hitting the ridgeline that evening, I thank you.

Well done mate, I will raise a glass this evening. Not long to push, I'll see you all when you get home.

October 12th, 2011 saw me on a flight home to England. As my flight gained altitude and Helmand fell further and further away, I reflected on the deployment I'd just completed. I'd flown over 170 hours in two months – that's pretty much a year's flying back here in the UK – and had only one thought in my head: I know it's not my decision to make, but I have no desire to see Afghanistan again.

To me, its legacy is simply pain – physical pain – from the stress on my spine of flying so much while wearing body armour, helmet and all the assorted kit; and mental pain – like jumping out of my skin every time I hear a loud noise that reminds me of the sound of a bullet cracking through the cockpit. All those near misses, taking rounds, almost being shot down twice, rescuing my mate who'd had to put his aircraft down after bullets took out vital systems, seeing so many of my colleagues in danger – it all has an effect. The intensity of ops in theatre may be showing signs of abating, but obviously the more we fly the more we come under fire. The courage of the crews isn't in doubt – two more of my colleagues at RAF Odiham received DFCs for bravery in the same honours list that announced my AFC.

My AFC was formally presented to me when I attended Buckingham Palace for the second time on 14 Feb 2012. I was accompanied by Alison, my son Guy, my parents Ian and Nicole, and my whole crew; Andrew Waldron (Waldo), Stuart Thorlby-Coy (T–C) and Mick Fry (Fryster). It was a wonderful day, one of the highlights of which was when His Royal Highness the Prince of Wales presented me with the Air Force Cross. It was an immense honour and privilege for me to walk once again into the Ballroom for the medal ceremony. I could not stop myself beaming with pride when Prince Charles expressed his surprise at my award by saying 'But you already have the other one?' [The DFC]. After the ceremony, I made sure that every member of the crew was photographed holding the AFC. I firmly believe that while the medal was awarded to me as the aircraft captain on that fateful night, it truly would not have happened without the bravery and commitment of my crew. I feel it is their award as much as it is mine.

I've no idea what the future holds for me. All I know is that I value my life with Alison, Guy and Max too much to put myself back in the firing line again. Maybe it's just an aspect of getting older; maybe it's a combination of that, and everything that has happened to me in Afghanistan, but I truly appreciate the full extent of what I have and what I stand to lose. After some thought, I made the decision to leave front line ops and return to where I began – as an instructor on the Chinook OCF. In some respects, it was a hard decision to make and one I made with a heavy heart, but I know deep inside me that it is the right choice.

I feel I have given 110% to combat ops in the Afghanistan Campaign but I know that I am not indispensable – there are plenty of younger, more talented pilots ready to take on the role and fly into the face of the enemy. By day or by night, in good weather and bad, they will take the war to the Taliban and perhaps more importantly, risk all to pick up any ISAF soldier needing assistance. To the crews, *that* is the most important part of the Chinook mission and as long as British and ISAF soldiers remain on the ground, the Chinook force will be ready to respond whenever and wherever they need us.

GLOSSARY OF TERMS

2i/c: Second in command.

50 Cal: British L1A1 Heavy Machine Gun, .50 inch (12.7mm) calibre. Usually vehicle-mounted to provide top cover.

Apache AH1: British Army Apache Attack Helicopter fitted with Longbow Radar.

Bingo: Nominated fuel amount sufficent to make it back and land with the minimum fuel allowance.

Bowman: The latest generation tactical communications system used by the British Armed Forces.

CAS: Chief of the Air Staff or Close Air Support, depending on context.

CDS: Chief of the Defence Staff.

CGS: Chief of the General Staff – the head of the Army.

Carbine: Short barrelled SA80 5.56mm used by Chinook and Apache pilots.

Casevac: Casualty Evacuation.

CRM: Crew or Cockpit Resource Management focuses on interpersonal communication, leadership, and decision making in the cockpit. Simply put, it's a management system that ensures optimum use of all available resources, whether procedures, equipment or people, to enhance the safety and efficiency of operations.

D&V: Diarrhoea and Vomiting is a perennial problem on deployment and no matter where you go in any base, you're never standing far away from a bottle of disinfectant hand gel or a sign drumming into you how serious and debilitating a bout of D&V is. It spreads like wildfire with predictably debilitating results for operations.

Danger Close: Proximity to a weapon's effect considered to be the minimum safe point when wearing body armour and combat helmet. The term is used by Forward Air Controllers to indicate that friendly forces are within close proximity of the target. The close proximity distance is determined by the weapon and munitions fired.

DC: District Centre. Commercial/military/political centre of a particular area.

Decompression: Project launched by the MoD in 2006 to act as a buffer between fighting on the front line and being at home. Front line personnel deployed to Afghanistan for four months or longer fly from theatre to Cyprus, where they spend two weeks 'getting things out of their system'.

Det: Detachment.

DFC: Distinguished Flying Cross, awarded in recognition of exemplary gallantry while flying during active operations against enemy forces.

Dicking: A term coined by British soldiers in Northern Ireland during the 1970s referring to terrorist surveillance of location and movements of military forces or assets.

Dushka: Nickname of the DShK, a Soviet heavy anti-aircraft machine-gun firing .50 cal (12.7mm) rounds. Nickname 'Dushka' (lit. 'sweetie', 'dear'), from the abbreviation.

Fast Air: Offensive military jet aircraft such as the Harrier GR-7/9, Tornado GR-4 or F-16.

Flechette: Eighty five-inch tungsten darts fired from a rocket travelling above Mach 3.

FOB: Forward Operating Base.

Force protection: Military term given to a range of measures designed to preserve and protect the combat power of our own forces.

GAPAN: Guild of Air Pilots and Navigators, established in 1929, and a Livery Company of the City of London. The Guild advises the Government on air safety and aeronautics. The Guild presents trophies and other awards for outstanding performance in aviation by individuals or organisations.

Green Zone: Lush habitation of irrigated fields, hedgerows, trees and small woods on either side of the Helmand River, bordered by arid desert. Most of Helmand's population lives here and the natural cover means a high concentration of Taliban forces.

HALS: Hardened Aircraft Landing-Strip. Small runway.

HEAT: High Explosive Anti-Tank. An explosive-shaped charge that on impact creates a very high-velocity jet of metal in a state of superplasticity that can punch through solid armour.

HEDP rounds: High Explosive Dual Purpose 30mm cannon rounds.

Hellfire AGM-114N: Enhanced blast version of Hellfire air-to-surface missiles carried by Apache AH-1.

Hesco Bastion: Square wire mesh cubes lined with hessian. Filled with sand and/or rubble and used as defensive ramparts to protect bases from fire.

HLS: Helicopter Landing Site.

HRF: Helmand Reaction Force.

ICOM: Radio scanner used by Coalition and Taliban forces to monitor one another's radio transmissions.

ICOM chatter: Intelligence Communication. Term for intercepts of Taliban radio chatter.

IED: Improvised Explosive Device.

Illume: Term given to light conditions for night flying in theatre. Green illume signifies good vision using NVGs; red illume signifies no vision, even with NVGs.

Intel: Intelligence.

IR: Infrared.

IRT: Incident Response Team consisting of aircrew, medical team, EOD (bomb disposal) team and fire rescue team. The medical team is made up of a surgeon/anaesthetist, paramedics and emergency-care specialist nurses. Protected on the ground by Quick Reaction Force.

ISAF: International Security Assistance Force. NATO multinational military force in Afghanistan.

ISTAR: Intelligence, Surveillance, Target Acquisition and Reconnaissance – a practice that links several battlefield functions together to assist a combat force in employing its sensors and managing the information they gather.

JDAM: Joint Direct Attack Munition. Guidance system bolted on to 500lb or 2,000lb bomb to make it an accurate, all-weather weapon.

JHC: Joint Helicopter Command. UK-based command for all British military helicopters in the UK and overseas.

JHF (A): Joint Helicopter Force (Afghanistan). Main at KAF, 'Forward' at Bastion. Afghanistan helicopter HQ operating under authority of JHC.

JOC: Joint Operations Centre. The control centre of operations in Helmand Province.

JTAC: Joint Terminal Attack Controller, also known as **FAC**, or Forward Air Controller. A soldier responsible for the delivery of air ordnance on to a target by combat aircraft. Call sign normally 'Widow'.

KAF: Kandahar Airfield.

KIA: Killed in Action.

Klick: Military slang for kilometres.

LAW: Light Anti-Tank Weapon. A portable one-shot, disposable 66mm unguided anti-tank rocket launcher; pre-loaded w/HEAT rocket.

LCJ: Load Carrying Jacket.

Lockheed AC-130 Spectre: A heavily-armed ground-attack aircraft based on the Hercules C-130 airframe.

M60D: 7.62mm automatic, gas-operated machine-gun mounted on the Chinook's rear ramp. Rate of fire of up to 550 rounds per minute.

M134 Minigun: 7.62 mm, multi-barrel machine-gun with a high rate of fire (up to 4,000 rounds per minute), employing Gatling-style rotating barrels, either battery- or externally-powered. Fitted to forward side doors of RAF CH47 Chinooks.

Max Chat: A euphemism for full power or top speed, the term originates from World War II when most aircraft were piston engined. It stands for Maximum Cylinder Head Air Temperature.

MERT: Medical Emergency Response Team or Combat Air Ambulance based at Camp Bastion.

Military Cross: Third-level decoration awarded in recognition of gallantry during active operations.

NVG: Night-Vision Goggles. Optical instrument that magnifies available light by 50,000 times.

OC: Officer Commanding – Wing Commander in charge of a Squadron.

Operation Herrick: British codename for all military operations in Afghanistan.

Operation Telic: British codename for all military operations in Iraq.

PHF: Passenger Handling Facility at Bastion.

Paradigm: Prime contractor for the Skynet 5 contract with the MoD. It enables military personnel deployed on two to six-month tours to make thirty minutes of Government-funded phone calls to any location in the world each week.

Pinzgauer: High Mobility All-Terrain 4x4 and 6x6 military utility vehicles with open backs, covered by a canvas roof. Used alongside or in place of the Land Rover Defender as a patrol vehicle.

QRF: Quick Reaction Force. Members of RAF Regiment or Army used to provide force protection on IRT missions.

R&R: Rest and Recuperation; a fourteen-day break from deployment given to everyone in theatre on a six-month tour.

RadAlt: Radar Altimeter, cockpit instrument that measures altitude above the terrain beneath an aircraft.

RAF Regiment: The RAF's own military corps responsible for force protection, airfield defence, forward air control and parachute capability.

RIP: Relief in Place – one aircraft replacing another over the battlefield.

RoC: Rehearsal of Concept.

GLOSSARY OF TERMS

Rock Ape: Colloquial term used within the RAF for members of the RAF Regiment.

RoE: Rules of Engagement. Laws set by a country's Government laying down rules for the use and proportionality of arms and military force.

RPG: Rocket-Propelled Grenade. Soviet-designed, shoulder-launched rocket with a powerful grenade warhead.

SAFIRE: Small arms fire.

Tracer: Bullets coated with phosphorous paint that burns with a red, orange or green glow. Usually loaded every fourth round to check trajectory and accuracy of fire.

USL: Underslung load.

Wingman: The other aircraft in a pair.

Yaw: Side-to-side movement of the nose of an aircraft. Defines the aircraft's heading.

An invitation from the publisher

Join us at www.hodder.co.uk, or follow us on
Twitter@hodderbooks to be a part of our community of
people who love the very best in books and reading.

Whether you want to discover more about a book or an
author, watch trailers and interviews, have the chance to
win early limited editions, or simply browse our expert readers'
selection of the very best books, we think you'll find what
you're looking for.

www.hodder.co.uk